Portfolio, Programme and Project Offices

London: TSO

information & publishing solutions

Published by TSO (The Stationery Office) and available from:

Online
www.tsoshop.co.uk

Mail, Telephone, Fax & E-mail
TSO
PO Box 29, Norwich, NR3 1GN
Telephone orders/General enquiries: 0870 600 5522
Fax orders: 0870 600 5533
E-mail: customer.services@tso.co.uk
Textphone 0870 240 3701

TSO Shops
16 Arthur Street, Belfast BT1 4GD
028 9023 8451 Fax 028 9023 5401
71 Lothian Road, Edinburgh EH3 9AZ
0870 606 5566 Fax 0870 606 5588

TSO@Blackwell and other Accredited Agents

First published 2008

ISBN 9780113311248

Printed in the United Kingdom for The Stationery Office

N5896218 c10 10/08

Contents

List of figures

List of tables

Foreword

In today's fast-paced and ever-evolving commercial and business environments, it is vital to maintain a high level of assurance and stability in the delivery of programmes and projects. Organizations are exposed daily to unnecessary risks and inefficiencies because they have failed to apply the simple principle of establishing, developing and maintaining appropriate business-support structures. It is shocking that this exists, when the remedy to remove or minimize these risks and inefficiencies could be so simple.

This new Portfolio, Programme and Project Offices (P3O) guidance is aimed at helping organizations to overcome many of the challenges they face in portfolio, programme and project management. It adds to the growing suite of key methodologies created by the Office of Government Commerce, including PRINCE2, Managing Successful Programmes (MSP) and Management of Risk (M_o_R).

P3O provides universally applicable guidance that will enable individuals and organizations to establish, develop and maintain appropriate business-support structures. It will be particularly vital in the delivery of the huge portfolio of public sector projects and programmes, and looks to contribute to providing value for money. This is an important consideration ordinarily, and even more so when operating in uncertain economic climates.

The guidance brings together a set of principles, processes and techniques to facilitate effective portfolio, programme and project management by proposing proven support structures, roles and responsibilities. These structures also bridge the gap between the process of developing the organization's strategy and that of its delivery.

P3O draws on real-life experiences from both public and private sector organizations to produce guidance that will help senior management make informed decisions on strategic alignment, prioritization, risk management and optimization of resources to deliver business objectives successfully. This rigorous yet flexible approach will help organizations to obtain the best possible value for money from their investment.

Nigel Smith
Chief Executive (Chair)
Office of Government Commerce

Acknowledgements

PRINCIPAL CONTRIBUTORS

Lead author — Sue Vowler, Project Angels Ltd

Lead reviewer/mentor — Craig Kilford, Project Angels Ltd

Authoring team member — Anthony Close, SMS Management & Technology

FURTHER CONTRIBUTIONS

In order to ensure that P3O was a true reflection of current best practice in this emerging field, and to produce guidance of lasting value, OGC consulted widely among key stakeholders and experts at every stage in the process. OGC would like to thank the individuals and their organisations set out below for their contributions to this new guidance.

P3O concept viability workshop

Colin Bentley, PRINCE2 Chief Examiner (1998–2008); Sarah Branwhite, Docklands Light Railway; Anne-Marie Byrne, OGC; Chris Churchouse, Mindshift Ltd; Neil Glover, OGC; Andrew Godfrey, 1st Milestone Ltd (Primavera Systems authorised representative), representing Best Practice User Group Ltd; Chris Hobson, CITI Holdings Ltd; Dominic Joyce, CLM Delivery Partner Limited (London 2012 Olympics); Catherine Locke; Richard Pharro, APM Group Ltd; Chris van der Hoven, Cranfield University; Sue Vowler, Project Angels Limited

P3O guidance pilot group

British Geological Survey (NERC); NHS National Programme Office; NHS South Central Strategic Health Authority; Programme Office, Workforce Directorate, Department of Health; Scottish Borders Council; Tameside Metropolitan Borough Council

Reviewers

Colin Bentley, PRINCE2 Chief Examiner (1998–2008); Sarah Branwhite, Docklands Light Railway; Anne-Marie Byrne, A-M Byrne Consulting; Chris Churchouse, Mindshift Ltd; David Crawford, Think-Link Ltd; Steve Daniels, Siemens plc; Alan Ferguson, AFA Project Management; Melanie Franklin, Maven Training Ltd; Chris Hobson, CITI Holdings Ltd; Nick Johns, Research Councils UK; Dominic Joyce, CLM Delivery Partner Limited (London 2012 Olympics); Don Kavanagh, Griffiths Waite; Daniel Keller, Swiss Federal Strategy Unit for Information Technology (FSUIT), Swiss Federal Administration; Dr Piotr Kotelnicki, Centrum RozwiÐzaÐ MenedÐerskich S.A.; Stuart Ladds, OGC; Duncan Leeks, Sellafield Ltd; Geof Leigh, Goaldart Ltd; Laurence Lemmee, Clarion Consulting (UK) Ltd; Catherine Locke, Land Registry; Martin McCann, Tameside Metropolitan Borough Council; Michael Mooney, Civil Nuclear Constabulary; Wendy Mills, NFU Mutual; Cezary Paprocki, Centrum RozwiÐzaÐ MenedÐerskich S.A.; Michael Pears, Department for Children, Schools and Families; Stefan Plocki, BBC; Tim Reeks, HM Revenue & Customs; Ian Rimington, Vodafone UK; Michelle Rowland, A&J Project Management Ltd; Steve Salvini, Heriot-Watt University; Ian Santry, Home Office; Claudia Schulte, PA Consulting; Andrew Schuster, Department of Health; David I. Shepherd, Consultant; Jonathan Simcock, OGC; Gary A. Smith, Cancer Research UK; Rod Sowden, Aspire Europe Ltd; Jennifer Stapleton, Outperform UK Ltd; Liz Underhill, Government Olympic Executive; Peter Weaver, The Programme Support Office Limited; Glenn Webb, P&PM Group, Fujitsu Services Ltd; Mike Weston-Burt, KPMG; Gerald Williams, Project Labs Ltd; Sébastien Wingerter, NGR Consulting

Introduction 1

1 Introduction

1.1 PURPOSE OF THIS GUIDE

The purpose of the Portfolio, Programme and Project Offices (P3O) guidance is to provide universally applicable guidance, including principles, process and techniques, that will enable individuals and organizations to successfully establish, develop and maintain (or in some cases re-energize) appropriate support structures that will facilitate:

■ Informing senior management's decision-making on prioritization, risk management, and deployment of resources across the organization to successfully deliver their business objectives (portfolio management)

■ Identification and realization of outcomes and benefits via programmes and projects

■ Delivery of programmes and projects within time, cost, quality and other organizational constraints.

The P3O model will provide a focal point for defining a balanced portfolio of change and ensuring consistent delivery of programmes and projects across an organization or department. It could successfully take many forms, all of which are explored in this guidance – from a single all-encompassing physical office to a virtual office made up of a permanent Portfolio Office supported by permanent hubs or temporary Programme/Project Offices.

In summary, the guidance seeks to answer the questions:

■ Why have any form of P3O?

■ What is P3O?

■ What services/functions should be offered?

■ How to set up and operate a P3O model?

1.2 BEST-PRACTICE APPROACH

This guidance was developed using the principles of PRINCE2 through the establishment of a project governed by a Project Board. Following the Office of Government Commerce (OGC) principles of consultation and fitness for purpose, an international review group was established to provide advice on both scope and direction, and quality assurance.

The review group members were selected for their expertise in P3O across both public and private sectors in the UK and globally to ensure the guidance provides a balanced view and that the latest innovative approaches are captured and incorporated. The reviewers were also recruited from a mix of directors, managers and 'doers' to cover the full range of audiences for such a publication.

1.3 HOW TO USE THIS GUIDE

This guide has been written to answer the variety of questions often asked about P3Os. Different roles within an organization may have a different interest and perspective. The whole publication should be read to understand all these different perspectives; however, Table 1.1 may be used as a navigation aid to quickly locate the answers to specific questions the reader may have.

Table 1.1 Publication navigation guide

Audience/role	Questions asked	Where to look – chapters/appendices
Corporate/portfolio/senior management	■ Why have any form of P3O? ■ What value does it add to our bottom line or overall organizational performance? ■ How will a P3O model enhance and improve the effectiveness of programme and project delivery? ■ What is the best model for us? ■ Where is the plan to create the right P3O model for our level of P3RM maturity?	■ Chapter 2 ■ Chapter 3 ■ Appendix B ■ Appendix E

SROs/programme directors/programme Managers	■ What P3O models exist?
	■ How can I use existing services within permanent P3O units to best advantage?
	■ Do I need to set up a temporary office to serve my programme/project? If so:
	  ● What should it look like?
	  ● How will it add value?
	  ● How do I set it up?
	  ● How big should it be?
	  ● What roles do I need?
		■ Chapter 3
		■ Chapter 4
		■ Appendix A
		■ Appendix C

Portfolio/Programme/Project Office manager	■ What P3O model should we create? ■ How will organizational maturity in P3RM influence our choices? ■ What functions/services should we be offering? ■ What roles should I have in my P3O unit and how big should it be? ■ How do I set the office up? ■ How do I improve the current P3O or add value?	■ Chapter 2 ■ Chapter 3 ■ Chapter 4 ■ Chapter 5 ■ Appendix A ■ Appendix B ■ Appendix C ■ Appendix E ■ Appendix F
P3O staff/roles within P3O Programme and project managers	■ What is my role profile? ■ What do we offer as functions/services? ■ Where do I go to learn more about the standards we use? ■ What tools and techniques will help me do my job?	■ Chapter 3 ■ Chapter 5 ■ Appendix A ■ Appendix D ■ Appendix F

1.4 RECOMMENDED COMPETENCIES/ KNOWLEDGE PREREQUISITES

It is recommended that readers of this guidance have a basic understanding of portfolio, programme and project management principles. The guidance doesn't set out to replace existing guidance on portfolio, programme and project management; it has been developed to enhance and build on the challenge, enablement and support structures referred to in existing OGC guidance.

1.5 ORGANIZATIONAL CONTEXT OF PORTFOLIO, PROGRAMME AND PROJECT MANAGEMENT

Many organizations operate in a complex environment, with many programmes and projects being launched to deliver change at any one time. A portfolio can formally be defined as follows:

> A portfolio is the totality of an organization's investment (or segment thereof) in the changes required to achieve its strategic objectives.

1.5.1 What is Portfolio management?

Portfolio management is a coordinated collection of strategic processes and decisions that together enable the most effective balance of organizational change and Business as Usual.

Portfolio management achieves this by ensuring that:

■ Changes to Business as Usual are agreed at the appropriate management level and contribute to at least one strategic objective

■ Strategic decisions are made based on a clear understanding of cost, risk, impact on Business as Usual and the strategic benefits to be realized

■ Resources and changes are prioritized in line with the current environment, existing changes, resource capacity and capability

■ All changes are reviewed frequently in terms of progress, cost, risk, priority, benefits and strategic alignment.

Portfolio management involves the collection in one place of relevant information about the organization's investment initiatives, including programmes and projects, and aligning their delivery with strategic objectives, business requirements and the organization's capability, capacity (to deliver change and adopt change) and maturity.

Portfolio management should not just consider those programme and project commitments comprising the organization's change agenda, in terms of resources (i.e. money, people, infrastructure and other facilities), but should also consider the wider business picture taking account of Business as Usual). Only by understanding and appreciating the organization's full suite of commitments, i.e. corporate, programme, project and operational (Business as Usual), can a fully balanced business portfolio be achieved.

> In this context Business as Usual is defined as the things done to keep the business operating day to day. By understanding the demands on Business as Usual, its lifecycles and key events, the delivery of change through programmes and projects can be timed and managed to ensure least disruption.

The process of developing a portfolio to deliver an organization's or department's strategy will need to take into account operational priorities as well as strategic priorities. In defining the portfolio, existing operational programmes or projects that are not aligned to the strategy may have to be realigned or terminated. Operational programmes or projects may also be put on hold while higher-priority projects supporting the strategy are delivered. There will only be a finite amount of resource available to deliver both strategic and operational change so there will need to be a balance to ensure scarce resources are deployed to best effect.

In practice portfolio management is carried out at many different levels in an organization, at the corporate level, at directorate or divisional level and within business units.

1.5.2 What is programme management?

OGC's related guidance, Managing Successful Programmes (MSP) defines programme management as the action of carrying out the coordinated organization, direction and implementation of a dossier of projects and transformation activities (i.e. the programme) to achieve outcomes and realize benefits that are of strategic importance to the business.

> A programme is defined as a temporary, flexible organization created to coordinate, direct and oversee the implementation of a set of related projects and activities in order to deliver outcomes and benefits related to the organization's strategic objectives.

MSP should be referred to for detailed guidance on the management of programmes.

1.5.3 What is project management?

> A project is also a temporary organization, usually existing for a much shorter duration, which will deliver one or more outputs in accordance with a specific Business Case.

A particular project may or may not be part of a programme. OGC's related guidance, PRINCE2, should be referred to for the management of projects.

1.5.4 Relationship between Business as Usual, change and P3RM

The relationship between Portfolio, Programme, Project and Risk Management (P3RM) and Business as Usual is represented in a simple concept – 'Run the Business, Change the Business'. Figure 1.1 describes the model highlighting how P3RM and Business as Usual are integrated and collaboratively realize strategic objectives.

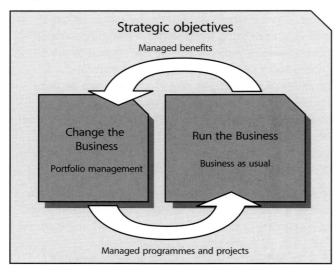

Figure 1.1 'Run the Business, Change the Business'

Portfolios, programmes and projects are undertaken to deliver change into an organization's business operations/delivery environment and the correct level of engagement with the wider business (i.e. corporate and operational levels) is vital for success. The engagement may be through ensuring the change delivers what business operations needs and wants (strategy, business planning and scoping) and at a pace and to a timescale (planning) that ensures least disruption to Business as Usual. Any function such as P3O that provides support to change portfolios, programmes and projects must therefore engage with business operations as effectively as it engages with the P3RM community. Two key stakeholder groups are senior managers within an organization and the operational delivery teams who will run the changed organization during the change, through transition

and after transition. The latter group includes Service Management teams, who are often forgotten in many change initiatives until the latter stages of delivery; these may include IT, HR or Finance.

If a proposed change does not directly contribute to, or underpin, the delivery of any of the organization's strategic objectives, or enable another change to benefit such, it should not be started or allowed to continue. Equally, if any existing change does not align to the strategic objectives, it should be stopped. The exceptions to this rule are 'must do' changes, such as regulatory and statutory changes, or programmes and projects that are necessary to ensure that Business as Usual can continue to operate – i.e. the replacement of obsolete IT or other business systems or infrastructure. In these cases the objectives may need to be changed and priorities reviewed.

Whilst change and Business as Usual may be regarded as separate activities, they cannot survive without each other; also, the transition from one state to the other must be actively managed. Therefore, any decisions relating to either need to be made collaboratively by the appropriate people at the correct decision-making level of the organization.

One of the key benefits of using a P3O model is that it provides the mechanism to ensure decisions are made at the correct level in the context of Business as Usual and that the right mix of portfolio(s), programmes and projects are delivered.

1.6 WHAT IS P3O?

P3O provides a decision-enabling/delivery-support model for all business change within an organization. This may be provided through a single permanent office, which may exist under several different names, e.g. Portfolio Office (strategy/organization or business unit focused), Strategy or Business Planning Unit, Centre of Excellence, Enterprise or Corporate Programme Office, or be provided through a linked set of offices (Portfolio Office, Programme Offices, Project Offices), both permanent and temporary, providing a mix of central and localized services.

There is no 'one size fits all' approach – the model to be deployed in an organization will depend on:

- The vision and goals of both the organization and the P3O Sponsor (see Appendix A for a role description)
- The business needs
- The portfolio, programme, project and risk management (P3RM) maturity of the organization

- The size of the resource pool
- The numbers of programmes and projects being undertaken
- The wider organizational, political and cultural environment
- The business divisional/departmental structure and the geographical location of staff
- The maturity of matrix management structures.

The size and complexity of the P3O model will vary greatly between organizations. In a large government department or large corporate the model outlined in

Figure 1.2 may be the ideal, but in a small organization the P3O model may simply be a single individual acting as a multitasking P3O officer. This is explored further in Chapter 3.

The key terms used throughout this publication are defined in Table 1.2.

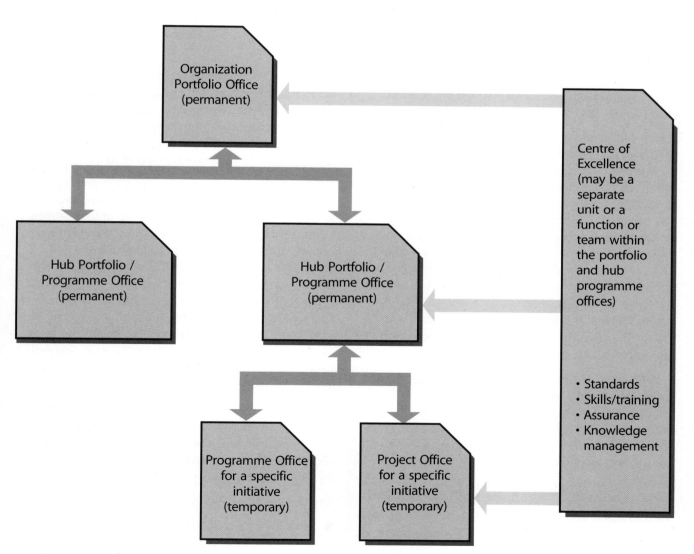

Figure 1.2   High-level outline P3O model

Table 1.2 P3O definitions within model

Model	Definition
P3O model	The total structure put in place to deliver functions and services across an organization or enterprise through a single or multiple offices
Organization Portfolio Office	Permanent office set up to support the definition and delivery of a portfolio of change across the entire organization or enterprise.
Hub Portfolio/Programme Office	Permanent office set up to support the definition and delivery of a portfolio of programmes and projects within a department, division, geographical region or business unit.
Programme Office	Temporary office set up to support delivery of a specific change initiative being delivered as a programme
Project Office	Temporary office set up to support delivery of a specific change initiative being delivered as a project
Centre of Excellence (COE)	A portfolio, programme and project management standards unit, which defines standards (processes, templates and tools), skills and training, manages knowledge and may provide independent assurance. The COE may be part of a Portfolio Office or exist as a separate independent unit

Note: throughout this guidance, P3O refers to the P3O model and its constituent offices across the organization.

Simply implementing a P3O model will not provide effective change governance support. It is the P3O maturity that makes the difference, leading to improved organization success rates (getting better at delivering strategy through change). A mature P3O may have been in existence for many years, with mature processes, trained experienced staff and senior management commitment. Organizations with mature P3Os are characterized by more effective sponsorship, accountability, competent and motivated staff, quality of leadership and demonstrated value. A key attribute of a mature P3O model is higher morale among staff, both staff in P3O roles and those in programme and project management roles.

However, even organizations with low maturity in P3RM stand to gain much from a good P3O model, in particular establishing an effective Portfolio Office to ensure the right things are done. More information on the concept of maturity in portfolio, programme and project management can be found in Appendix E.

1.6.1 Portfolio, Programme or Project Office?

The P3O model will operate through Portfolio, Programme and Project Offices, all of which may add value at different stages of the portfolio, programme or project lifecycles (see Figure 1.3).

A Portfolio Office will provide the decision support behind successful portfolio management.

Its key role is to answer the questions – 'Are the right things being done?' If not, 'What should be added, removed or changed?' 'Can the time-to-decision cycle be speeded up?' In some organizations the key question to ask may be 'How can we stop doing so many of the wrong things?'

The Portfolio Office will be responsible for advising senior management on the composition of the portfolio, its progress against plans and any conflicting priorities (including impacts on business operations), risks and issues. The Senior Management Board may have to make hard choices about programmes, projects and resources in the light of changing priorities. It therefore requires the Portfolio Office to provide the challenge and scrutiny of portfolio information and recommend options/decisions to support those choices. A Portfolio Office can add real value by focusing decisions on the things that matter most to the organization or departmental board.

It is important that the Portfolio Office reports directly to a main board director or it will have insufficient influence over investment decisions. If there is no commitment or ongoing consistent support from senior management then the Portfolio Office will not be effective.

A typical Portfolio Office provides the means to:

- Establish a structure for selecting the right programmes and projects for the organization
- Ensure ongoing alignment of programmes and projects with strategic objectives and targets
- Assess whether new requirements can be accommodated within existing organizational capability, capacity and maturity

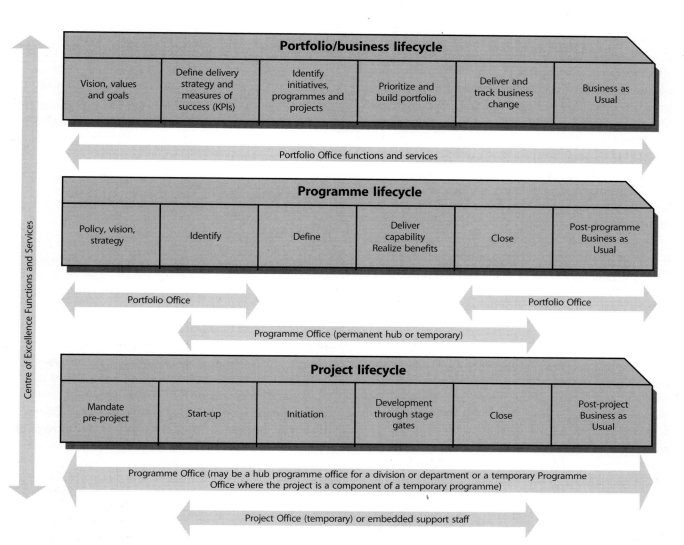

Figure 1.3   P3O model aligned to portfolio, programme and project lifecycles

- Allocate the right resources to the right programmes and projects
- Ensure scrutiny and challenge
- Identify and manage dependencies between programmes and projects
- Resolve conflicts and contentions for scarce and costly resources (these could be technical or business resources as well as change resources)
- Assist with identification of threats and opportunities and evaluate the true implications of the aggregate level of programme and project risk
- Monitor progress of programmes and projects against key objectives
- Ensure ongoing successful delivery of programmes and projects

- Adopt value management – active management of the portfolio to optimize value, realize benefits and feed back learning into the investment selection and portfolio prioritization process
- Achieve value-for-money savings and efficiency gains from programme and project rationalization
- Ensure the organization has a balanced portfolio, with consideration given to the ability of the organization to absorb change with least disruption to Business as Usual
- Link change benefits to the Performance Management structure
- Ensure investment in Research and Development activities for the long-term survival of the organization.

Whereas the key role of a Portfolio Office is identified as ensuring the 'right' things are delivered, there is also a requirement to ensure that change is delivered consistently and well, through standard processes and trained competent staff. This consistency of delivery is often provided by a Centre of Excellence (COE), which provides standards, consistency of methods and processes, knowledge management, assurance and training across the full portfolio of change. This may be a team or function within the Organization Portfolio Office or may be set up as a separate office. When a new programme or project is set up, the COE is the first place to go to get methods, tools, training, or advice and to seek guidance on any lessons learned on previous similar changes. Throughout the programme or project, and at the end of it, this is also the team you go back to with your lessons learned that can be used for future teams. In this way, the organization carries on up the maturity curve for programmes and projects.

When a specific change initiative is launched as a programme or project, it may require its own temporary Programme or Project Office. This may be resourced from an organization-wide permanent Portfolio Office, or a local Hub Portfolio/Programme Office (based on business units, divisions, departments or geographic regions) that provides resources and standards for the life of the programme or project. The temporary Project or Programme Office may support the project or programme manager and relevant board with planning, risk management, issue resolution and change control, or act as information librarian. On small projects the support may simply be provided by a multitasking project support officer.

In some organizations the P3O model will exist as a virtual model. This can occur at both ends of the maturity spectrum. In immature organizations individuals may have been appointed to act in a Programme or Project Office role but they are not allied to a single line manager and do not work to consistent standards. In mature organizations where matrix management is well established, individual roles/pockets of excellence may exist under business line management with virtual links to an organization P3O network.

Portfolio Offices differ from Programme and Project Offices in that:

- They are primarily concerned with doing the right changes, whereas programme and project management office are primarily concerned with doing the change right

- They define the right changes as those changes that align best to the strategic objectives and, at that particular time, attract acceptable levels of risk, complexity, cost and impact on Business as Usual
- They are usually permanent and align with corporate financial governance structures and decisions. Ideally they should have direct contact with the Senior Management Board

A Portfolio Offices is not simply a bigger Programme or Project Office.

1.7 P3O HISTORY

Project (and Programme) Offices have been in existence in some form (and under many different names) since the introduction of project management as a disciplined approach to managing change. Initially this began in construction and engineering projects; however, the biggest growth in programme and project support came through the development of project management in IT and technology departments. With the advent of PRINCE2 in 1996 and the shift of emphasis to business-based change programmes and projects, Project Offices expanded their remit from the disciplines of planning, risk, issue and change support and administration to include more focus on a standards and assurance role. Business units also saw the value in using Programme or Project Offices to assist in the prioritization of limited spend and using resources more effectively.

In the 2000s the shift to Portfolio Offices has been driven by organization-level offices asking 'Are we doing the right things?' and 'Are we getting the benefits from our investment?' During the same period the P3RM tool and methods markets have matured, as have organizational Performance Management tools, allowing the aggregation of programme and project performance data to allow strategic and business-level analysis to be undertaken.

Both PRINCE2 and MSP have contributed to increasing numbers of both Centre of Excellence offices, providing consistency of approach through standards, and temporary Programme and Project Offices, established to support a specific change initiative.

1.8 P3O EVOLUTION AND MATURITY

When a new P3O model is established, its vision and scope are often unclear and the offices are resourced with a mix of individuals (more often under-resourced or resourced with the incorrect skill sets). In many cases the office is led by a 'champion' with a personal vision of what the office needs to achieve, who then has to find resources to help deliver that vision. Individuals brought into the P3O are often selected simply because they are available, not necessarily because they have been trained for the role.

This is not a criticism; it is a fact of life for many P3Os that they do not reach or deliver their full potential because they find themselves endlessly having to justify their existence, rather than being allowed to contribute to the delivery of organizational objectives. What many senior managers fail to appreciate is that a mature and effective P3O model adds real value by helping management to reduce risk, effect control and also support the delivery of change.

A mature P3O model costs less to operate as a percentage of overall portfolio spend, and adds value both to staff and to its customers.

P3Os evolve over many months and years, and the best have been planned to lead the evolution in P3RM maturity across an organization (or department) and similarly evolve their own individual competencies, functions and services.

In an immature or new P3O, the services and functions offered are limited to data gathering, reflecting the lack of competency of individuals, whereas in a mature P3O, individuals will possess the competencies to offer a wider range of functions/services, challenging and using the data gathered. Functions and services are tailored to individual programmes and projects with an underlying performance culture. See section 3.6 for more on desired skills and competencies.

Mature P3O models provide:

- **Governance** – supporting governance (including structures and accountabilities) through scrutiny and challenge, ensuring return on investment through effective management of delivery and risk
- **Transparency** – relevant, accurate and timely information (single source) to support decision-making
- **Delivery support** – ensuring programme, project managers and operational business managers do things right (competency and skills) and do them well (assurance), reducing bureaucracy and encouraging consistency
- **Reusability** – embedding industry and sector best practice and sharing lessons learned
- **Traceability** – history and documentation.

The best P3Os are led by a senior P3RM or strategic/business planning professional (dependent on the focus of the P3O unit) with the influence, experience and credibility to gain commitment from all levels in the

organization. The whole tone and approach is set by the person at the top.

These concepts are explored further in Chapter 3.

1.9 GOVERNANCE AND CONTROL

The P3O model underpins organizational governance and control that runs through all change programmes and projects within an organization and the transition of change into business operations. Formal decision enablement rules – who makes what decisions, when and what information do they require – should be developed, and the P3O model is responsible for ensuring information is escalated and cascaded appropriately through the different levels of the portfolio, programme and project management environment. This should drive appropriate decisions to main board level.

Where a single P3O unit exists, this may be easier to implement. Where multiple offices exist in an overall P3O model, both permanent and temporary, then rules should be established regarding levels of plans; dependency tracking; examination and escalation of risks, issues and changes; and roll-up of progress information.

Overall the intention is to ensure the right decision is taken by the right person or group, based on the right level of supporting information. There should be a single source for any piece of data, which is then amalgamated appropriately through the layers of governance and decision-making.

The same rigour should be applied to restraining decisions, ensuring stage gates are not passed through without the appropriate authority and sign-off, ensuring Management Boards are equipped with progress reports, exception reports and options.

P3Os should provide a comprehensive set of data to enable governance decisions and be resourced with individuals with the right level of expertise and competence to advise management boards appropriately.

Where a Centre of Excellence (COE) exists it should define the standards to be applied to information management and provide appropriate tools to allow for ease of roll-up of information. The COE should also define standard methods of working (such as tailored uses of MSP, PRINCE2 and M_o_R) and assure their use across the portfolio.

An example of enabling consistency of decision-making is to have a single approach to the setting of traffic-light alerts across the portfolio of change, based on agreed tolerances.

1.10 BEST-PRACTICE GUIDANCE

P3O is part of a suite of guidance (see Figure 1.4) developed by OGC, aimed at helping organizations and individuals manage their projects, programmes and services. Where appropriate, this guidance is supported by a qualification scheme and accredited training and consultancy services.

Although this guidance has been written to align to OGC standards, P3Os will exist in organizations where other bodies of knowledge, standards and methods are deployed. This guidance can readily be adapted to suit any organization regardless of P3RM language or standards in use.

For details of other sources of P3RM reference material, please see the Further Information section.

1.10.1 Portfolio Management Guide (PfM)

This guidance has been developed by OGC to provide a strategic understanding of PfM, including the key principles and practices, aligned to other OGC guidance.

1.10.2 Managing Successful Programmes (MSP)

MSP is a proven programme management good practice in successfully delivering transformational change, drawn from the experiences of both public and private sector organizations. Setting up and developing a P3O model involves transformational change at all levels in an organization, and MSP should be used to define and manage the change. P3Os also exist to support MSP programmes.

1.10.3 Managing Successful Projects with PRINCE2

PRINCE2 is a structured method to help effective project management. Adopting a structured project approach is necessary in successfully managing a P3O model. Using PRINCE2 to support standard approaches across projects will significantly improve chances of success.

1.10.4 Management of Risk: Guidance for Practitioners (M_o_R)

Portfolios, programmes and projects exist in a fundamentally uncertain world and, as such, effective management of risk is crucial to managing the delivery of the strategy, outcomes, benefits and outputs. Management of the portfolio's risk exposure and promoting good risk-management practices for programmes and projects are key functions of the P3O, and M_o_R puts the management of risk into the context of the wider business environment.

1.10.5 OGC Gateway™ Review Process

OGC Gateway™ is a well established Programme and Project Assurance review process that is mandated for all UK government IT, construction or procurement-enabled programmes and projects. OGC Gateway delivers a 'peer

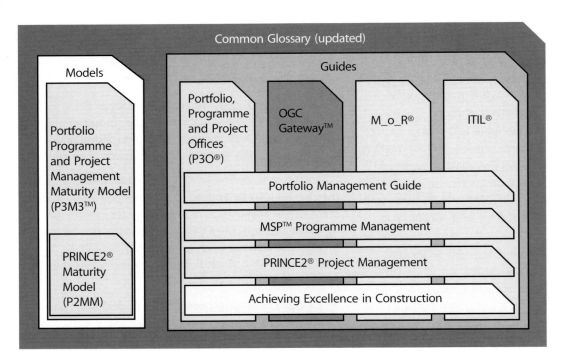

Figure 1.4 OGC best-practice guidance

review', in which accredited independent practitioners from outside the individual programme/project use their experience and expertise to examine progress and assess the likelihood of successful delivery of the programme or project. They are used to provide a valuable additional perspective on the issues facing the internal team, and an external challenge to the robustness of plans and processes.

Gateways give a measure of assurance based on the professional assessment of the reviewers on the ability of the programme or project to deliver its aims and objective to time, cost, quality and requirements as in the Business Case (Delivery Confidence Assessments).

This service is based on good practice and there are many similar examples across all business sectors of this type of peer review, designed to provide assurance to the owner of the programme or project.

P3O units often provide the coordination service and assurance support to a Gateway Review and may be organizing and coordinating multiple Gateway Reviews at any point in time. Full details of the OGC Gateway Review Process are available from the OGC website.

1.10.6 Service management – ITIL (the IT Infrastructure Library)

A well-managed transition of business change outcomes into Business as Usual is a crucial part of the P3O approach, and sits comfortably alongside ITIL's service management practice, both for managing this transition and for the future realization of the benefits in the long term via ongoing service management.

1.10.7 Portfolio, Programme, Project Management Maturity Model – P3M3

The P3M3 maturity model has been created to enable organizations to measure themselves against a set of standard processes and to create performance improvement plans to enable focused continuous improvement. P3O enables improved maturity within an organization through its standardization of processes, consistency of approach and knowledge management approach. How an organization scores against the P3M3 model can be a good indicator of its ability to adopt advanced P3O functions.

The P3M3 maturity model is made up of:

- Overview
- PjM3 – Project Management Maturity Model
- PgM3 – Programme Management Maturity Model
- PfM3 – Portfolio Management Maturity Model.

P2MM is a project management maturity model focused on PRINCE2 processes and language. It is fully embedded within PjM3.

1.10.8 Achieving Excellence in Construction

Through the Achieving Excellence in Construction initiative, central government departments and public sector organizations commit to maximize, by continuous improvement, the efficiency, effectiveness and value for money of their procurement of new works, maintenance and refurbishment.

Why have a P3O?

2

2 Why have a P3O?

2.1 PURPOSE OF THIS CHAPTER

This chapter seeks to answer the questions: 'How do I convince senior management of the value that a "best-in-class" P3O model can add to our organization?' and 'How do I start the process of change?'

Chapter 1 gave a brief history of P3O and touched on its evolution and maturity. Many P3O models that exist in organizations have developed bottom up from a need to establish and assure consistency in methods across programmes and projects. However, recent best practice has looked at where P3O models can add value to all levels of an organization, in particular to senior management, enabling timely decision-making.

Programme and project management disciplines have matured and so have the senior managers' attitudes to change. Senior managers now take an active interest in their sponsoring role and are beginning to demand P3O models that meet their needs as well as those of the programme and project delivery teams.

The need to deliver business strategy whilst ensuring value for money with reducing resources has focused attention on ensuring the 'right programmes and projects are delivered' and that investment is spent on things that matter to an organization. As decision-making cycles have contracted, so the need for better-quality information to drive those decisions has increased. In this climate of change, a fully functioning P3O model can no longer be an optional element of an organization's business model.

As a minimum, an effective P3O model provides operational efficiencies in the successful delivery of business change initiatives. At its best, a P3O model is an integral part of ensuring that:

■ The strategies and performance requirements of an organization are realized via projects, programmes and operational business units
■ A joined-up set of outcomes and benefits is measured, managed, monitored and refined to ensure that optimal investment and strategic goals are achieved.

Without the involvement of a P3O model in strategic change management these goals may still be reached, but in a fragmented or unstructured way that generates significant threats to the best use of scarce resources and achievement of required outcomes.

A P3O model can significantly increase an organization's chances of successfully delivering its strategy, reducing benefits loss and delivering programmes and projects more cost effectively.

It can do this in a number of ways:

■ Maintaining a 'big picture' understanding of the business change portfolio
■ Providing decision support to ensure the right programmes and projects are launched
■ Providing standards and processes to ensure consistency of delivery
■ Providing independent oversight, scrutiny and challenge to ensure things are done well (and right first time more of the time)
■ Providing assurance, coaching and mentoring to build a competent workforce capable of first-class programme and project delivery
■ Providing a 'single source of truth' reporting function with Management Dashboards to focus decisions and management interventions
■ Reducing the likelihood and impact of events that would have a negative consequence; and (conversely) increasing the likelihood and impact of events that would have a positive consequence
■ Improving organizational accountability, decision-making, transparency and visibility
■ Identifying, understanding and managing multiple and cross-cutting risks and issues
■ Protecting revenue and spend, and enhancing value for money
■ Executing change more effectively and efficiently and improving organizational programme and project delivery
■ Protecting reputation and stakeholder confidence.

Developing a P3O model that delivers value from all of the above requires full senior management support; an investment of both time and money by senior managers to design and build the most effective, suitable and affordable model for the organization; and an investment in the skills required to ensure it is successful.

Senior managers' time is required to understand the challenges an organization faces, what its priorities are and which programmes and projects will help them deliver the strategy. They need to invest time in attending workshops and meetings with their peers and P3O professionals to understand what model is right for them and agree a P3O vision for the future.

Getting value out of a P3O model will not happen overnight; it takes time, effort, investment and belief from all stakeholders. So why do it?

2.2 HOW DOES A P3O MODEL ADD VALUE?

The phrases 'doing the right programmes and projects' and 'doing programmes and projects right' are often used to describe the role and focus of an individual office within the P3O model.

- Doing the right programmes and projects – describes the need to ensure business investment is spent on the things that matter and that the focus is on delivering programmes and projects that enable achievement of the corporate strategy.
- Doing programmes and projects right – describes the need to deliver programmes and projects consistently and well.

This can be expanded as in Figure 2.1. Any P3O model should be capable of meeting all these requirements, but the way in which they are supported or enabled will vary between organizations.

Case study

A government agency set up a Portfolio Office to fulfil the aim of 'doing the right programmes and projects'. It aims to provide 'proactive, reactive, knowledgeable, integrated and intelligent strategic decision support'. The key questions it asks and provides answers to are:

- Are we making the right investments and continuing with the best value programmes and projects?
- Are we serving our stakeholders in the right way?
- How much money will we spend collectively and for what return?
- What programmes and projects under our control are delivering the best value?
- What resources are available to us and what are our options?
- If we have to alter priorities immediately, because of policy or strategy changes, where can we get funding out of our existing portfolio? Which programmes and projects should we stop, and what are the consequences?
- Are we making the best use of our resources, spending our finances correctly and making the right decisions based on the facts?
- Can we respond effectively to external information requests quickly, efficiently and factually?

Throughout OGC guidance there are principles (see Table 2.1) for extracting more value from programme and project investments – all of which rely on an effective P3O model to ensure 'programmes and projects are done right' and 'the right programmes and projects are done'.

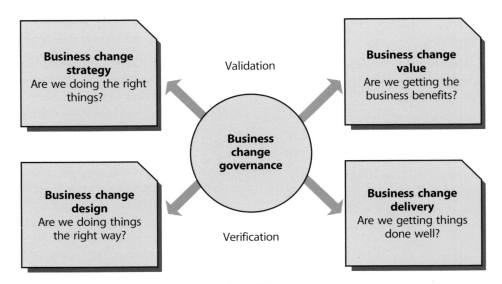

Figure 2.1 Business change governance support and enablement

Table 2.1   OGC principles for extracting value from programme and project investment

Principle	Description	How P3O model can help
Govern effectively	■ Governance – concept of having SRO for portfolio and programme management, Project Executive for projects and associated boards ■ Hierarchy based to achieve scalability with a focus on single points of accountability ■ Governance provided by delegated limits of authority (tolerances) with escalation routes and rules for issues, risks and changes ■ Gated Reviews – strategy, business justification, etc. through to benefits review	■ Provide support to SROs and senior management ■ Support governance – ensure the issues, risks and changes are escalated to right decision-making authority. Assist in consistency of approach through the levels of governance ■ Provide independent Gated Review coordination and assurance ■ Ensure complete, timely and accurate data is collected at source so that analysis and amalgamation enable quality decision-making
Hold people to account	■ Accountability of Senior Managers for overall portfolio investment decisions ■ Clear accountability of SRO or Project Executive for programme or project outcomes and benefits ■ Clear accountability of business managers for change transition and benefits realization ■ Clarity of roles and responsibilities in programme and projects teams and the P3O	■ Provide Senior Managers with decision support– analysing options and consequences ■ Ensure the right decisions are escalated to the right people with relevant information to support the decision-making process ■ Provide support, coaching and training to all levels of role ■ Provide standard role descriptions and terms of reference for boards
Prioritize investment, align and adjust to business strategy	■ Prioritize all business change, ensuring a balanced portfolio of programmes and projects aligned to strategy ■ Ensure all regulatory, statutory and 'must do' (obsolescence/replacement) programmes and projects are balanced with strategic change ■ Aim to ensure all initiatives are clearly aligned to business strategy; and, where appropriate, adjust to maintain alignment (or reinvest funds elsewhere) ■ Programme and project start-up should ensure alignment with organizational or department strategy	■ Provide Senior Managers with decision support – analysing options and consequences ■ Maintain a register of all programmes and projects in the portfolio, including ideas in the pipeline ■ Facilitate and support pre-programme and project scoping workshops ■ Facilitate and support risk identification workshops across the portfolio of programmes and projects ■ Provide a fast-track mobilization service to programmes and projects, ensuring alignment of scope and plans to strategy and Business as Usual priorities ■ Scan the business horizon for upcoming changes to strategy, business issues or delays in decision-making and analyse the probability and impact of risks on the portfolio of programmes and projects ■ Support feedback from programmes and projects to strategy
Safeguard value	■ Ensure all investments have a Business Case and investment funds are awarded on the basis of realizable benefits ■ Through a gated decision process, periodically re-evaluate the ongoing viability of the Business Case and ensure benefits continue to be tracked and realized at the planned levels	■ Support the Business Case process ■ Provide a benefits tracking service to business owners ■ Ensure benefits aren't double counted and that the measurement process is robust and usable ■ Help get more value via benefits from investment across programmes and projects ■ Help identify potential opportunities to be realized, exploited or enhanced as part of risk analysis

(continued)

Table 2.1 OGC principles for extracting value from programme and project investment (continued)

Invest in people and process	■ Recognize portfolio, programme and project disciplines; acknowledge the link between strategy and programme and project execution ■ Use standard approaches, e.g. MSP, PRINCE2, M_o_R, ITIL ■ Develop capability, capacity and risk models to suit the organizational maturity and culture ■ Consider using OGC's P3RM skills model	■ Develop tailored approaches based on OGC approaches and ensure they are made available to all people in the P3RM environment through accessible means ■ Develop training, coaching, mentoring approaches for all roles with P3RM environment ■ Advise on Skills and Capability Assessments and training plans using OGC P3RM skills model
Track progress through highlight and exception-based reporting	■ Use exception-based management to execute programmes and projects ■ Ensure management time is engaged appropriately, based on risk factors and exception-based reporting	■ Provide reporting and exception management service from project to portfolio level ■ Develop Management Dashboards to engage senior managers on the key risks and issues that affect delivery of the portfolio ■ Make sure the data collection process operates correctly

2.3 CONSEQUENCES OF NOT INVESTING APPROPRIATELY IN THE RIGHT P3O MODEL

An appropriately designed and resourced P3O model, working effectively across all levels of an organization, interfacing with decision-making bodies and aligning its services with other service providers such as finance, procurement, audit, legal, etc. adds real value to senior management decision-making and governance capability.

Unfortunately, many P3O offices are restructured or are closed down within a short space of time before they start to deliver measurable benefits. This is often because they do not exist within a coherent P3O model; there may be elements of the ideal P3O model in place but they do not work effectively together.

Here are some typical scenarios that do not add value to an organization.

Scenario 1 – Perceived overhead

Some organizations do not see the value in providing support to individual programmes or projects either at start-up or during their lifetime. This means the programme or project manager takes on support tasks that could be more efficiently and cost effectively delivered by a programme or project support officer or through a Hub Portfolio/Programme Office. This may lead to a slower pace of change, exhaustion of the programme or project manager, or delay in the realization of planned outcomes and benefits.

Scenario 2 – Reinvention or outsourcing

At the other end of the scale, every new programme and project may seek approval for a new Programme or Project Office set-up within its Business Case. Each new office may generate its own frameworks, approaches and tools and develop skills independently of other such offices. Equally, as programmes and projects complete their lifecycle and new ones form over time, established P3O offices and practices are reinvented because staff are not aware of their existence, creating significant duplication of investment and effort. This often occurs where external staff are brought in to run temporary programmes and projects, each new person bringing with them their own standards and templates. These are then tailored to the organization, with little or no learning being transferred across programmes and projects.

Scenario 3 – Disparate, not joined up

Different business units deliver initiatives and activities that deliver improved P3RM capability, sometimes independently of each other. For example, the IT area may invest in establishing an Enterprise Project Management (EPM) tool or timesheet capability, while the Human Resources area is identifying and implementing training in programme and project management methods. Both of these initiatives are operating with no knowledge of (or input from) organization governance policies, organizational risk standards or Performance Management and reporting. This may lead to significant process inefficiencies or different principles across these disparate business change initiatives. In this scenario a key factor is not having an Organization Portfolio Office taking a wider view across the whole business.

Case study

An organization in the energy industry had an unstructured P3O model, which meant that a project manager had to record project-related information into five different IT systems so that individual departments were able to amalgamate and report on different requirements:

■ Project registration, planned benefits identification, benefits measurement and benefits reporting were provided for the Strategy business unit via a customized database

■ Financial management was required for the Finance business unit via the organization's Enterprise Resource Management system

■ Risk management information for the Enterprise Risk Management business unit was entered via spreadsheets

■ IT resource requirements and tracking to the IT business unit were done via an IT resource management system

■ Schedule progress and status reporting for Project Boards was developed using scheduling software and a word processor.

This led to project managers producing a lot of duplicate information and reformatting it for different requirements. This had a severe impact on the time available to project managers to focus on delivery, and increased the cost of delivering projects because of the excessive reporting overhead.

2.4 THE P3O CHALLENGE – GETTING THE INVESTMENT

By putting in place an appropriate P3O model, organizations can improve delivery of business change and optimize investment to a far greater extent than they could by implementing disciplines within individual programmes and projects on their own.

Senior managers need to understand what they are getting for their money. If they invest in a joined-up, coherent P3O model that works effectively within a matrix management organization, what benefits will they get and how much will it cost in terms of whole-of-life cost investment to deliver more successful change?

The key challenge is to deliver a Mandate for the design of a P3O model, based on delivering an agreed value to the organization and approved by the owners of the key business processes it will support or contribute to.

The P3O model should be capable of operating and delivering services within the organization's matrix structure, ensuring temporary structures such as programmes and projects can coexist with and enhance permanent functions and departments that support Business as Usual.

Before developing or enhancing a P3O model, the organization's requirements for such a model need to be examined. Any model should answer the questions 'What value will it add to the organization?' and 'How will it work across organizational and business division boundaries?'

All P3O models have to link into a wider organizational business model, so understanding, documenting and agreeing the P3O vision, business operating model and transition plan to achieve it, with all impacted senior managers, is critical to sustained success. Equally, the functions and focus of these interrelated business units will change over time, so careful monitoring is required to maintain value after it has been established.

One way of implementing an organization-wide P3O model is to run it as part of a business change programme, where the establishment of the P3O enables the achievement of the required P3RM culture, improves the skills of programme and project managers, or revises business process to ensure joined-up delivery of strategy. The outcome of the business change programme will be an overall improvement in P3RM maturity across the organization, which will ultimately ensure that the right programmes and projects are delivered to meet the strategy and are delivered consistently and well.

2.5 APPROACH TO 'GETTING THE BEST FROM THE INVESTMENT IN P3O'

As in all change programmes, the key to success is in understanding the problems that need to be fixed or opportunities that need to be responded to, getting commitment to the need for change and consensus on how the change will be delivered. A Vision Statement of the future P3O provision then needs to be generated and agreed, culminating in building a Business Case to justify the investment in the P3O model.

Introducing a P3O model can be a major culture change, and it may be necessary to implement it in several steps. Each step must deliver real benefits, ideally at all levels of management – first to gain commitment, then later to sustain it.

Therefore, it is recommended that the implementation of the P3O is run as at least a project or preferably as a programme with appropriate governance, that a P3O Sponsor is in place to act as Project Executive or Senior Responsible Owner, and that an appropriate lifecycle and processes are followed. The P3O will bring widespread change affecting multiple stakeholder groups, requiring changes to business processes and relationships and also requiring a shift in mindset and behaviours. For these reasons we recommend the change is run as a programme using MSP principles, processes and products, and both this chapter and Chapter 4 (lifecycle – section 4.2) reflect that approach.

However, in some organizations programme management may not yet have been adopted or the change may in the first instance be limited to a simple office set-up, in which case the P3O design and implementation may be managed as a project. In small organizations where the P3O is simply one or two individuals, the P3O implementation may simply be managed as a series of small business changes, being delivered as part of Business as Usual.

Whatever the approach taken, it is important to have a good understanding of the problems you are intending to solve or the opportunities you want to maximize, supported by a vision of the future P3O provision and a time-phased plan to achieve that vision. It is also important to engage effectively with stakeholders, communicate well and keep a focused eye on benefits. So even if the P3O is being implemented as a project or Business as Usual change, some elements of MSP are well worth incorporating in the approach to be taken, including the Vision Statement, Blueprint, Benefits Realization Management, and Leadership and Stakeholder Engagement.

In the context of the P3O implementation lifecycle, the remainder of this chapter discusses understanding the problems to be solved or opportunities to be maximized and how to engage senior management's attention in supporting a new or re-energized P3O. It sets the scene for Chapter 4 by defining the first part of the P3O lifecycle (see Figure 4.1) – Identify the P3O – considering the Business Case, Vision Statement and outline Blueprint for the future P3O provision. Chapter 4 describes the remainder of the P3O lifecycle, once the outline Business Case has been approved, from the detailed design of the Blueprint through delivery and on to closure and evaluation.

Scaling hints and tips

Even if you are a small organization with a P3O unit of one or two people, it is still worth taking time out to assess what you do, who values you, what you offer, what you could offer, and assessing the business value that you could improve. Building a Business Case and examining your costs and whether further investment in your team would add exponential value and benefits to the organization is a worthwhile exercise and could lead to the expansion in people and competencies you need in order to make a bigger impact on successful delivery of programmes and projects. Improvements may simply take the form of adding additional skills through training or taking time out to focus on what you do in terms of senior management support, which may have been neglected in the past. These could raise your credibility or profile and lead to further funded changes. Consider the concepts raised in this chapter and Chapter 4 and think how they could be scaled and applied to fit your circumstances.

2.5.1 Identify the P3O – assess the current state of P3O provision and identify the key stakeholders

It does not matter where the idea or Mandate comes from to develop, enhance or re-energize a P3O model: what is critical is that senior managers who will benefit from the change are identified and engaged. Once they understand, and buy in to, the benefits they will receive, they can use their influence and leadership to champion the change.

Senior managers responsible for providing investment for the P3O model will want to see some personal success as an incentive for supporting the change. They need to see that the P3O model will provide clear information, enabling them to make effective decisions. They also need to feel comfortable that the planned changes and investment they are agreeing to will address their key concerns, both now and in the future, or they will not support the investment.

Senior managers need to be asked which issues and problems they rate as critical, so that these can be defined. Consensus needs to be gained across a group of senior managers, preferably the main board. This ensures that the P3O team understands what success looks like across the organization from differing viewpoints and allows them to gain consensus on a common P3O vision.

Gathering these views and gaining consensus may take the form of a series of structured interviews or workshops focusing on recent issues or reviews, such as:

- We recently undertook a portfolio review and 48% of projects are currently at red light status in the corporate Risk Register
- We are currently investing in training, tools and methods; however, our programme outcomes are not where we want them to be. Should we consider a more structured approach to P3O investment?
- Investment in an Enterprise P3RM tool is being planned. What Enterprise Business Model will need to be in place to integrate with this tool to ensure that we achieve the business value out of the investment?
- The current P3O model is no longer meeting our needs and we need to re-energize it to add value
- A P3M3 Capability Assessment was undertaken and our next key competency is to achieve an organizational focus. How might this be applied in our organization?
- We have recently aligned our existing portfolio of projects and programmes to the strategic objectives of our organization and initial findings are that 27% of our current proposed changes do not support the strategic objectives.

Very few 'best-in-class' P3O models appear overnight in a greenfield site; an organization often has existing Programme or Project Offices carrying out some, if not all, of the services required by the ideal model. Therefore, in order to create a vision of what the P3O model should be providing, we need to understand what is offered now and how effective it is. Typical questions to ask during data gathering are:

- Are the existing P3Os doing the right things?
- What is the current perception from stakeholders – is it favourable, and why?
- Are they doing what they do well?
- Do we have the right people and skills with the correct level of seniority and authority to get things done?
- What should the P3O stop doing?
- What should the P3O start doing?

By debating the issues in an open session, core problems can be identified, defined and the P3O model designed to resolve or limit them through the services provided.

A simple tool to assist senior managers in determining their core problems and agreeing the value and scope of the P3O model is the P3O Value Matrix (Figure 2.2). The matrix considers the three levels of change management – portfolio, programme and project – and describes the role of a P3O model in providing support or assurance services or both across the three levels. It is intended to generate discussion and should be considered as part of a well-planned and facilitated workshop or interview.

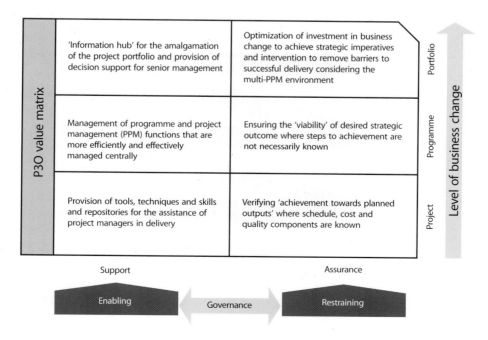

Figure 2.2   P3O Value Matrix

One of the key benefits of the P3O Value Matrix is to demonstrate to senior managers the nature of the change that needs to be effected, and that it will not happen overnight.

Another aspect of this matrix is that a P3O model will generally provide both enabling and restraining governance in parallel. This has to be carefully managed to minimize the potential for conflicts of interest. For example, a key change that needs to be managed very carefully is project start-up. In the past a project may just have started with local management authority; with the discipline a P3O model will bring, business managers will now need to develop an outline Business Case, and get it reviewed and agreed by the relevant governance board.

One of the debates that this matrix can provide is a discussion and validation of who the key stakeholders (customers or business owners) are in the process areas that are affected by the scope of the P3O model and who will get the benefits from any P3O model that is implemented. It is important to understand what value the different users of the P3O services will get. Users with differing requirements are:

- Programme and project managers who need practical hands-on help, start-up support, consistent standards and language, and delivery resources available when they need them
- Senior managers with responsibilities for prudent investment and strategy realization at the portfolio level who are looking for timely and concise information to enable them to make appropriate investment decisions
- Other support business units with whom information flows may be necessary
- The customer/user community that change is being delivered to, which needs to be reassured that change will happen with least disruption to Business as Usual and that any delivered capability will generate the benefits they require, e.g. they need to understand how operational plans may have to be adjusted to meet the additional demands of business change activities

- Suppliers that contribute to the business changes required. The P3O can provide a central point of contact for the management of the supplier relationship, especially where the supplier is providing a service across multiple programmes and projects. The P3O can manage the forward view of requirements to ensure timely provision of external staff and services.

In order to get the full benefits from a P3O model, a stepped improvement plan needs to be developed that moves the organization from support at the project level through to assurance and decision support at the portfolio level, building the value over time. Concentrate effort on solving the key concerns and issues up front, followed by a planned series of improvements. The key concern might be that the organization needs to improve its programme and project prioritization to focus on delivery; therefore the improvement plan may initially concentrate on establishing portfolio disciplines (e.g. strategic alignment), rather than improving individual project delivery.

2.5.2 Identify the P3O – create a P3O model Vision Statement and outline Blueprint

Once it has been agreed what problems the organization is trying to solve and how a P3O could help, the next step is to develop the P3O model Vision Statement. This should be a clear vision of the required changes to the organization's business model and how success will be measured, with a clear link to the business strategy showing how these changes will contribute to the organization's key objectives.

The Vision Statement will be supported by a Blueprint, defining what the new or revised P3O model will look like in terms of organization and services (a picture of the desired future state).

The Senior Responsible Owner (SRO) for the programme to develop the P3O model should be identified at the appropriate level in the organization to give it the time, attention and level of authority it deserves and needs. To increase the chance of success, the SRO should be at or above a peer level to other parts of the business being impacted. For example, if you are establishing a portfolio-level P3O model (i.e. the organization's entire portfolio of programmes and projects is in scope), then the SRO should be the CEO. If you are establishing a P3O model at the business unit or divisional level, then the director or senior manager for that division or business unit should be the SRO.

Scaling hints and tips

If you are a small organization with a P3O of one or two people, consider developing a services document that defines your purpose (vision), who your customers are and how you serve them, highlighting recent successes. Often people are not aware of the services you can or could provide and the skills you can bring to their success, so by writing this down and publicizing what you do, you improve your profile. As demand for your services grows, you can take the opportunity to design a future-proofed P3O with a Vision Statement and mini-Blueprint.

Example P3O model Vision Statement

P3O vision

A fully integrated P3O will be operating within the organization to provide oversight, scrutiny and challenge, enabling full traceability between agreed strategic plans and the investment in delivering new capabilities and the realization of benefits.

Supporting statements

The key value for this investment (and the driver behind functions and services) will be through reducing the barriers to successful delivery programmes and projects and optimizing investment in strategically aligned programmes and projects.

In order to achieve this we need to work closely with the following impacted stakeholders: xxx and yyy.

Success will be measured by:

- All programmes and projects within the approved portfolio representing within six months the optimal investment to achieve the agreed strategies when assessed quarterly
- Achievement of a capability maturity of 3 against the P3M3 Capability Maturity Model within two years
- A reduction in costs associated with issue resolution of 10% each year for the next three years

- The conversion of benefits planned to benefits realized increasing by 15% each year for the next three years
- The level of defective products delivered by projects being maintained at less than 2%
- Stakeholder satisfaction surveys undertaken consistently showing satisfaction with programme outcomes of greater than 90%
- The time to market of new products or services reducing to less than three months from concept stage.

Case study

A UK government agency is revising its Hub Programme Office to develop a challenge and scrutiny role with embedded Centre of Excellence, which will work in partnership, within a virtual unit, with its government department.

Hub Programme Office vision

- The agency Hub Programme Office provides professional programme and project management support services to all divisions, project teams and the department.
- We help projects to:
  - Utilize skills in the most effective way and repeatedly deliver projects on time, within budget and to a standard that both ourselves and the public can be proud of.
- We can provide this service because:
  - We are skilled professionals
  - We view all divisions as one team
  - We believe that our programme management standards, experience and skills are key to our success.

Figure 2.3 shows the supporting high-level example P3O model Blueprint organization structure that may be used in developing a suitable model for the organization. Both these examples use the MSP Vision Statement and Blueprint product outlines from MSP as their base, but in this chapter they have been adapted and expanded beyond MSP's requirements to illustrate how to use them effectively to gain commitment from senior management.

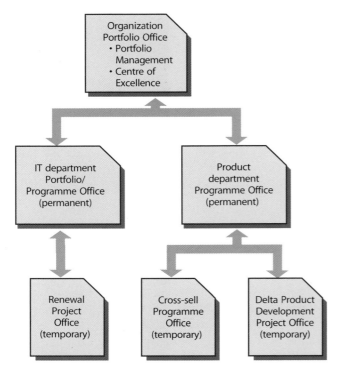

Figure 2.3   Example P3O model organization structure

The following example Blueprint is not yet fully formed and is developed further in Chapter 4.

- **Portfolio level:**
  - There is managed progress towards the achievement of strategic outcomes by maintaining an Organization Portfolio Office to facilitate the translation of strategy into the programmes required
  - An appropriate level of standardization of programme and project planning and controls exists to enable meaningful amalgamated reporting
  - Monitoring and tracking is in place for the enterprise-level portfolio to identify and resolve resource and financial constraints and ensure ongoing optimization of investment to agreed strategies
  - All investment is subject to Gated Reviews to support successful delivery
  - A register of potential initiatives is maintained to provide input into the development of baseline approved portfolios
  - Dependencies are identified, risks are aggregated and understood against the portfolio and external factors are periodically assessed (e.g. competitors, political, environmental or operational impact) to enhance the potential for successful delivery

- The forward planning of resource and capability requirements is proactively managed to balance the supply and demand constraints for programme and project delivery
- Training and the development of skills and competencies are centrally managed for portfolio, programme and project management across the organization

- **Programme level:**
  - There is a strong focus on the achievement of outcomes and benefits through the use of the MSP methodology, supporting processes and systems, skills management, the provision of advisory services and facilitating Gated Reviews at appropriate points in programme lifecycles
  - The Programme Office acts as the Information Hub through tracking and reporting, information management, financial accounting, risk and issue identification and tracking, quality control and change control at a programme level to support good governance, and Performance Management towards required outcomes
  - Strategic governance and senior stakeholder engagement is supported through management reporting at a highlight level or by exception (where required) and Gated Reviews
  - Excellent leadership and management standards are in place, supporting people at times of change.

- **Project level:**
  - Highly effective project delivery is supported through the use of PRINCE2 project management methodology, with supporting processes and systems, risk identification and management and skills management; advisory services are provided through a Centre of Excellence function; and appropriate accountability for large and complex projects is in place
  - The quality of project management outputs is assured through a flexible governance structure to monitor all significant projects, project health checks, Gated Reviews and ad hoc assurance of key project management deliverables.
  - The transition of new capabilities to Business as Usual is assured through full integration with Service Management functions and gating of readiness for service.

2.5.3 What performance improvement can be expected?

A P3O model must measure and promote its value to the organization it serves.

Failure to do so is the greatest possible barrier to P3O continuity, regardless of how much value is actually being generated by the P3O model.

Minimum principles for measuring the P3O model's success should include the following:

- Overall programme and project success rates in relation to capital cost, duration, operating cost and benefits realization for each portfolio
- Improved portfolio balance – in terms of overall risk, programme and project lifecycle stages, strategic alignment and investment type
- Enhanced contribution to strategic objectives.

Improving the portfolio balance will not only involve developing the right mix of programmes and projects but avoiding the scenario where multiple programmes and projects are in the start-up process at the same time or are intending to deliver key outputs into a business function simultaneously. Another performance improvement outcome of balancing the portfolio is that not all programmes and projects will be planning to use limited resources at the same time. This helps to ensure that internal resources are used more effectively with less reliance on external contractors.

Typical Key Performance Indicators (KPIs) to assist in the measurement of these principles are included in Table 2.2. KPIs will depend on what the P3O model was set up to achieve; however, all measures of success for the P3O model should be aligned to overall portfolio, programme and project success and meeting targeted benefits.

Table 2.2   Sample P3O KPIs across P3O models

Reduction in benefits loss, % increase in actual benefits delivered by the portfolio (rather than planned benefits)
Reduction in programmes and projects started for the wrong reasons – number of projects stopped
Organizational P3RM Maturity level of 3 (or more) by target date
Predictability of delivery – % increase in number of programmes and projects delivering to time and scope
Predictability of cost – % decrease in cost overruns on programmes and projects
Reduction in overall resource costs to deliver the portfolio
Reduced staff turnover and subsequent reduction in recruitment and training costs
Happy scale – increased customer satisfaction scores
Reduced number of programmes and projects scoring amber or red on Gated Reviews
Increased overall P3RM skills score of programme and project management community

Case study

A large private sector organization implemented an Organization Portfolio Office to support the delivery of a £60 million portfolio of change to deliver the new business strategy. The portfolio was governed by a portfolio review group, who met monthly to consider additions to the portfolio; prioritize existing programmes and projects against new initiatives; review progress of approved programmes and projects; and track delivery of benefits. The things that mattered to the senior management team were getting its products to market within an acceptable time window to compete effectively, and improving predictability of delivery timescales for new projects to ensure the operational teams could plan their Business as Usual. The combination of the portfolio review group, an effective portfolio process and timely and concise progress reporting (under control of the Portfolio Office) led to a significant increase in predictability of project delivery timescales and decrease in time to market for new product launches. Project delivery to time and cost as predicted in the Project Initiation Document improved from 24% success rate to more than 80% in one year. There was a similar decrease in the time it took to take a product to market, from 13 months to between 3 and 6 months.

2.6 IDENTIFY THE P3O – DEVELOP THE BUSINESS CASE

Like any investment decision, the programme or project to deliver the P3O model should have a formal agreed Business Case outlining the reasons for change, the costs, benefits, constraints and risks.

The Business Case is the justification for the proposed investment and should be reviewed throughout the introduction of P3O.

There is no 'one size fits all' solution, as the Business Case may be required to set up a full P3O model within an organization, an individual office within the P3O model, e.g. a Portfolio Office or departmental Hub Programme Office, or it may be used to re-energize or refresh an existing P3O model or office.

Appendix B defines the key elements typically found within a Business Case, which can be adapted and scaled to meet the challenge the organization may face.

The purpose of the Business Case is to identify clearly the plan, benefits and risks involved with the implementation of the P3O model. As with every Business Case, it should answer the questions often asked by senior management: 'Why have any form of P3O?' and 'What value does it add to our investment portfolio?'

The Business Case should be aimed at senior management, and if a Business Case approval process exists, it should be agreed via this.

If the Business Case does not highlight benefits that are important to the organization's leadership, and how it will facilitate their goals, it will not lead to sustained improvement and value and may be seen as an 'overhead' and be a target for future cost cutting.

It should be developed using a collaborative approach, using workshops involving senior management. The key questions to be answered at these workshops are:

- What problems are we looking to solve?
- What will be the scope of the office or model?
- Who will be its customers?
- What outcomes/added value are we expecting?
- How will we measure its success?
- What are the key services?

Having answered the above, the Business Case including options, costs, benefits, constraints, risks and success criteria will follow.

2.6.1 Benefits and constraints

In constructing the Business Case and gaining commitment from senior managers, there is a requirement to understand what benefits are achievable and what elements of P3O capability will need to be in place to realize those benefits. Table 2.3 shows examples of expected benefits, linked to elements of P3O capability.

There will also be organizational constraints, which may restrain the new P3O capability being achieved and therefore limit the ability to realize the benefits in full:

- **Pace of change:** One key constraint will be the organizational expectations of the pace of change for the P3O implementation and the organization's actual ability to adapt to change. The full benefits of a P3O model will not be realized overnight and the P3O transition plan needs to be aligned with the expectations of senior managers and take into account any other change initiatives under way. There is little point in creating a Vision Statement that seeks to achieve level-5 maturity (as defined in P3M3) within a two-year period, underpinned by a P3O model, if the organization needs to build level-3 capability (as defined in P3M3) to support an acquisition within eight months or senior managers expect to see demonstrable improvements within three months.

- **Culture:** The culture of the organization will either facilitate or inhibit its ability to adopt a P3O approach. If the leadership of the organization is not supportive of such a move, then it is unlikely that any P3O model established will succeed – top management support should be seen as critical for success. If the people within the organization are not ready for change or are not appropriately skilled, then it may well be that the pace of change may need to be slowed, and stakeholder engagement and communications increased to secure wider commitment. Anyone seeking to develop a new P3O model or enhance an existing one should not underestimate how difficult it may be to change the culture (behaviours and mindsets); it can slow the desired pace of change by months or even years.

Table 2.3   P3O capability and linked benefits

P3O capability	Benefits
An established structure for enabling the selection of the right programmes and projects	■ Reduced risk, quicker starts, quicker to market, increased confidence in investment ■ Pet or rogue projects stopped at the initial investment stage gate ■ Business strategy proved or disproved as quickly and cheaply as possible before major investment is committed
Enable optimization of organizational investment	■ Money spent on the right programmes and projects, focus on strategic returns and regulatory or 'must do' programmes and projects ■ Balanced portfolio, to ensure growth as well as keeping Business as Usual happy and able to function effectively
Enable maximization of returns from investment	■ Looking at the overall investment, looking to the future and ensuring the portfolio returns the right mix of strategically aligned benefits ■ An individual project may predict benefits within two years and demonstrate a good Business Case, but if the organizational strategy is due to change within the two-year period, the benefits may not be realized
Enable the allocation of the right resources to the right programmes and projects	■ Cost savings through correct resource requirements, reducing the likelihood of failure by assigning resource to prioritized programmes and projects
Ongoing alignment of programmes and projects with strategic objectives and targets	■ Increased clarity of strategic objectives being met ■ Improved decision-making ■ Recommendations for programmes and projects to be stopped if they no longer align with changed strategic objectives ■ Informs senior management if changes to the business strategy are required to be successful
Able to resolve conflicts and contentions for scarce and costly resources	■ Reduction of management overhead dealing with prioritization conflicts for resources ■ Able to plan the programmes and projects to make the best use of scarce resources, ensuring money is not wasted on expensive 'just in time' external resources
Able to identify and manage interdependencies between programmes and projects to reduce the risk of failure or delay	■ Reduction in delays to delivery, saving money on resources and ensuring predictability of delivery ■ Prioritization of critical path activities to optimize effort
Able to evaluate the true implications of the aggregate level of programme and project risk	■ When the true aggregated impact of risks is known, some programmes or projects may not be started, or their scope may be altered to reduce overall risk exposure of the organization's objectives
Able to monitor progress on programmes and projects against key outcomes	■ Able to ensure ongoing successful delivery of programmes and projects
Ensuring there is no duplication of scope or double counting of benefits or that the outputs of one programme or project will negate the outcomes of another	■ Achievement of value-for-money savings and efficiency gains from programme and project rationalization
Able to coordinate the change control process across multiple projects, programmes and business operations	■ Ensures that the right Requests for Change (RFCs) are passed to the correct service organization ■ Identifies opportunities to bundle multiple related RFCs into a project or programme

- **Capability and capacity:** Depending on funding available, the new or revised P3O model may have to be delivered using existing organizational capability and capacity. An assessment will need to be made as to whether requirements can be accommodated within existing organizational capability and capacity. If it cannot, then a different plan and Business Case may need to be developed or consultants brought in from outside the organization to fast-track some quick wins to finance future expansion of the P3O role. If consultants are brought in to design the P3O model and get it off the ground quickly, then an early deliverable should be the recruitment of a permanent Head of P3O, who can be involved from the beginning, influence the development and benefit from an early skills transfer from the external consultants.

- Budget restrictions: Is the budget sufficient to deliver the full value from a P3O model, or is it limited to a single division or strategic change only?

Case study

The CIO of an international logistics and transport organization was keen to establish a P3O model in a short period of time to support the timely integration of strategic acquisitions. An assessment of the IT staff determined a significantly high level of resistance to change of this nature, resulting from multiple failed attempts at implementing fragmented parts of an unstructured P3O model, such as methods, tools and Project Offices. When interviewed as to whether a corporate project management methodology existed, the respondent, a career project manager with the organization replied, 'Oh yes, we have at least five gathering dust on the network.'

Accordingly, the approach was altered and external consultants/contractors were engaged to develop and operate an effective P3O model, achieve the rapid pace of change required by the CIO and allow for the longer-term transition to existing staff.

Figure 2.4 provides a senior management summary of key P3O tools and techniques and the benefits that could be realized once they are in place and operating effectively. This could be used to supplement the Vision Statement to sell the concept of the P3O model and to develop the building blocks of the Business Case.

Appendix B gives an example Business Case for a typical P3O change programme.

Scaling hints and tips

For a small P3O, the formality of a Business Case may seem a daunting prospect, but by developing one you are simply practising what you preach to programmes and projects. By systematically challenging your costs and benefits, you may be able to focus your scarce resource in more effective ways or attract increased funding to extend the services you offer or improve on those you already deliver.

2.6.2 P3O funding, including running costs

The Business Case should cover both set-up and ongoing costs. Any P3O model has to justify its value to the organization. The P3O functions or services will incur both operational and enhancement costs and an early decision will need to be made regarding funding policies to appropriately reflect P3O costs to their users.

In many organizations P3O units are now moving away from being simple Cost Centres and are now charging business units for their services. Also, P3O models are now increasingly seen as a key corporate Performance Management and governance function, and are therefore funded from central budgets. In others the basic services are centrally funded but the P3O unit will have to recoup some delivery costs through a cross-charging regime.

Key types of funding model available for a P3O model are:

- **Temporary offices:** The costs of the P3O support functions for a project or programme are rolled into the cost of the project or programme itself and funded accordingly. It is critical to ensure that these are categorized separately due to the potentially varying treatment of these expenses from an accounting perspective

Senior Management Board		
Services cost elements		**Value benefits**
Portfolio build and prioritization		Reduction in programmes and projects started for wrong reasons
Information Hub		Predictability of delivery More programmes and projects delivering to time
Single source of truth reporting Management Dashboards		Predictability of costs – fewer cost overruns
Planning and dependency management	P3O model	Reduced resource costs
Capacity planning Resource management Flexible resource pools		Reduced staff turnover and subsequent reduction on training and induction costs
Monitoring and tracking		Happy customers Increased customer satisfaction scores Increased business
Fast-track start-up of programmes and projects		More programmes and projects delivered right first time – less costly rework
Standard programme and project approaches PRINCE2, MSP, M_o_R		Reduced delays in decision-making, faster delivery and lower costs
Training, coaching and mentoring Embedded skills and capability		Reduction in mobilization timescales and therefore programme or project resource costs
Assurance Health checks Advice and guidance Gated Reviews		Reduced costs of tools P3O operates on behalf of programmes/projects
Aggregation of risk		
Centralized tools		

Figure 2.4   Senior management summary of P3O tools and techniques leading to realized benefits

■ **Permanent offices:**

- Absorbed costs – in some organizations the P3O model is considered a key corporate function and as such is funded entirely from the central budget

- Cost allocation – metrics are developed and agreed to understand usage levels and then used to determine the proportion of the P3O's costs that will be allocated back to each of the business units that undertake projects or programmes. Metrics to periodically assess usage of the P3O functions and services by P3O user group may include:

  - The financial value
  - The number of projects
  - Resource numbers used in the delivery of projects
  - Weighting against historic business benefits achieved.

  The relevant metric should be selected to most closely align to determining the relative usage of the P3O functions or services and be assessed frequently enough to reflect the changing nature of the portfolio.

- **Charging (part):** The basic services are centrally funded but the P3O unit(s) will have to recoup some delivery costs through a cross-charging regime. An example of this is that the P3O unit may be centrally funded for the development of standards/methods and the provision of standardized toolsets, but it may charge for the provision of resource to programmes and projects through a flexible resource model or for the facilitation of workshops (start up, risk, planning, lessons learned, etc.) by internal P3O consultants. An understanding is required of which functions/services will require central funding and which functions/services will be chargeable. This is generally achieved by assessing which function or service is undertaken by users of the P3O unit on a 'per use' basis, and it can easily be corralled with clear entry and exit points. A clear understanding of the level of usage and some stability in the number of projects is desirable to ensure that supply and demand for the function or service are matched.

Case study

A large services organization developed a Portfolio Office that was composed of two teams: the Centre of Excellence team responsible for standards, methods, best practice, facilitated workshops and health checks; and a delivery-focused Project Coordinator team providing delivery support to individual programmes and projects through planning, risk, issue and change control, quality review support and acting as configuration librarian.

The Head of Portfolio Office and the Centre of Excellence team were centrally funded along with the accommodation for both teams, but each project coordinator's time was cross-charged to the individual project budget. This meant the Project Coordinator team could flex in size to meet demand from projects without affecting headcount restrictions.

Over time the demand on the small Centre of Excellence team expanded through requests for workshop facilitation, and a charge was introduced to manage demand. Unfortunately this led to a drop in demand from the areas of the organization that had not really embraced good project management, thereby discouraging best practice in the areas that needed it most.

To reverse this trend, in the following financial planning year a decision was taken to scrap charging for workshops and increase headcount for the Centre of Excellence team through the centrally funded pot.

- **Charging (full or part):** The P3O unit operates as a Zero-based Cost Centre and develops charging models against each of the functions and services to fully offset its cost of operations. This model is the most advanced (and can be the most complex) and should only be considered when the functions or services of the P3O are embedded at the 'defined' level of capability maturity (P3M3 level 3 or higher).

Case study

The P3O for a large banking and finance organization was a centralized Portfolio Office and was assessed at greater than level-3 capability maturity. The P3O had two key areas of value:

■ A **Centre of Excellence** with P3O staff providing standards, methods, toolsets, knowledge management, communities of practice, resource competency and Capacity Management, continuous improvement, portfolio and strategy translation services

■ A **project delivery** area with P3O staff providing project investigations, project initiation, the provision of a centralized resource pool for project management and business analysis, project accommodation and Project Assurance services

The staffing for this P3O across both of these value areas numbered more than 120.

From the feedback it received, the P3O found out that Senior Responsible Owners (SROs) and Project Executives across the business were concerned that project costs were highly variable depending on whether a permanent staff member of the P3O or an externally engaged consultant or contractor was used as the project manager for a project. The cost differential between these two options could vary by as much as 375% and whether an internal or external resource was used would sometimes determine whether or not a project's Business Case would meet the required return on investment hurdle rates.

The P3O relied on external organizations to supplement its own staff to more effectively match supply and demand to the normal peaks and troughs of resource forward planning and thus provide a lower overall cost to serve. Unfortunately, the existing funding model of cost allocation for the Centre of Excellence and the direct allocation of project delivery costs into the projects was creating this problem.

A secondary issue was that, in some cases, the SROs and Project Executives were then utilizing their own business operations staff (against corporate policy) to undertake project management, without understanding the need to match competencies to the complexity of the project, and the level of successful delivery was being negatively impacted.

With significant analysis, the P3O moved to a full charging model where a blended rate was developed for project delivery services: each project was charged the same rate for project delivery staff, regardless of whether they were sourced from the internal pool or externally contracted. This blended rate was determined by the average cost of project delivery staff across the portfolio and included the underlying overhead of Centre of Excellence staff to create a Zero-based Cost Centre.

With a carefully managed stakeholder and implementation plan, the outcome of this change in funding approach was that the overall savings achieved by having a centrally managed internal resource pool supplemented by external resources when necessary (against the alternative of each project providing its own project manager and project support staff) was better reflected back to the P3O user groups.

Projects were charged rates for project delivery that were always better than if they were to engage externally contracted project resources by themselves (reflecting value back to the SROs and Project Executives). The P3O was able to continue its remit to operate a centrally managed project delivery service and set the number of permanent project management resources against the inherent level of demand, and was therefore more cost effective across the organization. Additionally, the cost of developing and maintaining Centre of Excellence services (which was previously seen by senior management as an overhead) was offset against the savings that were always in place but not previously understood by the business because of the constraints of the previous funding model.

2.7 OVERCOMING COMMON BARRIERS

2.7.1 Lack of focus on the full P3O model

Often there is no appetite among senior managers in the business to consider the full requirements of establishing an effective P3O model in the organization. There can be a reluctance to look beyond a single component (such as training, PPM tool implementation or framework development). This can result in partial delivery of P3O functionality, which ultimately leads to great restrictions on the usefulness of the P3O to the business and failure to deliver the benefits. If it is not possible to achieve consensus at this level, then it is critical that the Head of P3O maintains the vision, intermediate Blueprints and plans and attempts to gain acceptance of the components of the P3O model through tranches of delivery.

In many organizations there are two problems that inhibit gaining the consensus of senior executives:

- Many executive just do not understand how change management should work; they do not see that it is any different from any other form of management
- Executives who do have some understanding of change management do not understand what is in it for them.

Case study

In the early 2000s a major bank addressed this problem of lack of consensus, led from the top (chairman of the group), first by better education, and second by ensuring that a significant part of each executive's remuneration was dependent on them personally realizing operational improvement through the successful implementation of strategy via programmes and projects.

2.7.2 Funding the P3O model

Another significant barrier when building consensus at the senior management level is the perception of the overhead associated with P3O operation. Some stakeholders may think that the current situation is satisfactory where programmes and projects are completed without structured P3O models. Others may simply be reluctant to fund the overhead, so expect resistance.

The key goal in developing the Vision Statement and the Business Case is that focus is applied to the value provided by the P3O services, not simply looking at the cost. Tangible success measures that demonstrate achievement of the planned vision and value should be documented and agreed.

Once the P3O model is operational, then reporting on achievements towards these success measures against the cost of the P3O business unit(s) is an effective way to maintain focus on 'added value' and balance the threat/opportunity equation.

2.7.3 Challenging current culture or approaches

The proposed P3O model may challenge the current culture or 'ways we do things around here' and there are threats that the P3O model will not deliver the benefits it is designed to do, because of a lack of commitment at best or sabotage at worst. If the embedded culture is at senior management level, then the potential for failure is higher.

In these circumstances it is valuable to carry out a stakeholder analysis and develop a Communications Plan, aimed at addressing the required changes to the culture, in order to break down this barrier.

2.7.4 Perceived overhead of the P3O model's processes and standards

A common barrier when building consensus at the senior management level is the perceived overhead associated with compliance to repeatable processes and governance arrangements for the delivery of business change. In addition to noting the requirement for minimalist processes, an early deliverable should be the development of tailoring guidelines to allow standards and templates to be flexed to meet the requirements of the programme or project.

Wherever possible, keep processes simple and align any new processes to existing processes and activities that are already seen to add value. Also consider a stepped approach by concentrating on those processes that give instant visibility to senior managers, e.g. building a Portfolio Register of programmes or projects to illustrate the breadth and value of the portfolio or strengthening formal sign-off of Business Cases and implementing a gated sign-off approach to stop rogue projects at inception or at the earliest sign of non-viability of the Business Case.

Most of the services described in the P3O model have to be carried out anyway if programmes and projects are to be successful. The question to pose to senior management is not whether P3O services are needed, but where is the most cost-effective place for them to be managed.

2.7.5 Other barriers

Other common barriers include:

- Lack of authority for the P3O model to provide the governance and control arrangements
- Inadequate use of P3O units or lack of integration with other functions of the wider organization
- Lack of clarity in role(s), responsibilities and accountabilities of P3O staff
- Lack of clarity in the scope of P3O units
- Lack of senior management sponsorship/commitment to the P3O concept.

Case study

A senior manager in the financial sector identified the need for stronger discipline leading to more successful delivery in business change through a programme to establish an Organization Portfolio Office and repeatable approaches at the programme and project levels. The key area of concern, in terms of the cultural aspects of the programme, was the minimalist approaches used in the organization.

In designing the P3O model, governance arrangements were developed that minimized additional effort, but refocused decision-making on the basis of more targeted information. For example, the senior manager held fortnightly direct-reports meetings; the agenda associated with these was modified to included portfolio monitoring, tracking and requests for changes to the approved portfolio, and the business planning cycle was modified to shape the outputs of the process to become the input to the portfolio identification process. This did not add any overhead to the management effort of the senior manager, but brought the portfolio management and decision-making into a controlled state to enable more proactive decision support and improved delivery rates.

The timescale will also be driven by the senior management's ability and appetite for making decisions on the way forward.

Hints and tips

When designing a transition plan, the outcomes of the P3M3 Capability Assessment are an excellent way of prioritizing the specific order of capability development and implementation and ensuring early value is delivered.

2.8   TIMESCALES

The timescales required for a programme to develop a P3O model and implement it will differ depending on the level of value to be achieved and the level of activity to be undertaken.

Expect an 18-month to 2-year business change programme to move an organization from an 'awareness' level of capability maturity (level 1 P3M3) to a 'defined' level of capability maturity (level 3 P3M3).

This may be varied with different levels of investment (such as investing more in external consultants to shorten the time frame) or slowing down the throughput of programmes and projects while the P3O implementation programme is running (to enable more P3RM community involvement in the P3O programme).

The key requirement here is to allow for a stepped approach to change, where the introduced capabilities are allowed to fully embed and become natural ways of working.

What is a P3O model? 3

3 What is a P3O model?

3.1 PURPOSE OF THIS CHAPTER

This chapter explains the different ways that organizations may seek to implement Portfolio, Programme and Project Offices concepts and support processes through physical offices and typical roles and responsibilities. Some organizations may implement a P3O model through a single office supporting both the needs of the senior management at the portfolio level and those of individual programmes and projects.

Other organizations may seek to distribute support across the organization so it is physically located with the teams it supports, or aligned with business functions or departments. There are many different ways of doing this and there is no 'one size fits all'. This chapter outlines some of the more commonly used models and lists the advantages and disadvantages of each one, and also seeks to give the reader an understanding of typical roles and their responsibilities and the different ways these may be applied to real job descriptions and individuals' capabilities and skills.

3.2 OVERVIEW OF P3O MODELS

Chapter 1 introduced the concept of the P3O model as the total structure put in place to deliver functions and services across an organization through a single or multiple offices. The P3O model provides a decision-enabling/delivery-support structure for all change within an organization. The most successful are 'service orientated' rather than 'support orientated'.

A key component of the P3O model is a best-in-class Portfolio Office that provides a realistic overall picture of the organization's portfolio, with standardized reporting rolled up into Management Dashboards. This is supported by Centre of Excellence services and functions, assurance (not audit) and delivery services that are accessible to all across the business. The most successful P3O models are proactively working with business leaders to jointly determine the services they should offer to maximize value from investment in programmes and projects.

3.2.1 Functional areas within a P3O model

In this chapter we identify three key functional areas to explain the focus of an individual unit or team within a P3O model. These key functional areas require different competencies, skills and experience and therefore may be divided into separate functional teams within a single office, or individuals may specialize in one or more of the functional areas. The three areas are thus:

- **Strategic planning or portfolio support functions/ services** – these focus on supporting management decision-making and may include alignment with strategy, prioritization, benefits realization management, reporting through Management Dashboards, support for escalated risks, issues, changes and information and the provision of oversight, scrutiny and challenge. They are key functions at the portfolio level but may rely on supporting information from programmes and projects. They may be provided by a separate team within an organization-wide Portfolio Office or exist in a separate business planning or strategy support unit. In large organizations where decision-making is decentralized to local business units, departments or geographical units, they may exist in hub units supporting local decision-making.

- **Delivery support functions/services** – these focus on supporting the delivery of change and may be provided through a central flexible resource pool of delivery staff, with capacity planning and HR management processes. The central pool of staff may be permanent or contract, dependent on local resource management policies and how work is planned. The type of delivery staff within the central pool may be programme or project support people deployed to work on specific programmes and projects as they are launched. Alternatively they may be internal programme or project consultants who are deployed at programme or project start-up to ensure a fast-track and consistent start-up or deployed throughout a programme or project's lifecycle to provide inputs of expertise, e.g. planning and workshop facilitation. In some P3O models, the central pool of delivery staff may also include a pool of professional programme and project managers, deployed temporarily to specific programmes and projects to manage their delivery. In large organizations, delivery staff may be deployed through local hub offices, building on local or business knowledge, ensuring co-located teams and reducing travel time.

- **Centre of Excellence (COE) functions or services** – these focus on the development of standard methods and processes, developing consistent working practices and ensuring they are deployed appropriately and well. They may include capability support through training and coaching, internal consultancy (the creation of standards and help, advice and guidance on their tailoring), knowledge management, tools support and independent assurance. The functions generally exist in a central Portfolio Office, but may have evolved as a separate independent COE office. In a large organization, COE functions may exist in local hub offices, deployed within business units or departments or to support a geographical area of an organization. In such cases, there should be a single source of standards (provided through a central COE) within the organization, but training and coaching in their use, tailoring for local need and assurance of their use may be provided through a local hub office.

3.2.2 P3O model features

A P3O model may be specifically designed for an organization, but more often it grows and evolves organically to meet central or local business goals. Every P3O model should be tailored to suit the organization.

Its size, physical structure, governance structures, resourcing policies and maturity will all play a part in:

- What kind of P3O model should be deployed
- How many separate offices there should be
- What functions and services they offer
- Where the component offices are physically located.

Some key features of P3O models are as follows:

- **Centralized versus decentralized offices** – in many organizations there will be a single P3O unit, sitting in a central corporate function or department, that will perform one or all of the portfolio support, delivery and COE functions. In other organizations there may be up to three central offices, each providing a single organizational focus for the portfolio support, delivery or COE functions. In large organizations or functionally focused organizations with decentralized decision-making and a policy of deploying local resources closest to business delivery, there may be a small central office with portfolio support and COE functions, with delivery functions and local portfolio and COE functions operating out of hub offices. Decentralized models focus support on local need, but care must be taken to ensure adherence to a consistent organization-wide set of standards, albeit with local variations.

- **Permanent versus temporary offices and staff options** – permanent offices will exist to support functions that are required to support ongoing portfolios, senior management decision-making and setting generic standards for all change initiatives. Therefore Portfolio Offices and local hub offices will be permanent offices, generally staffed with permanent staff trained to perform specific functions. In some permanent offices there may be a core of permanent staff supplemented by contract staff to meet peaks and troughs of workload or to provide an input of expertise to develop new standards, etc. When a new programme or project is launched, it may require its own temporary Programme or Project Office. If there is a permanent office (Portfolio Office or hub) with a central flexible delivery team, resources may be requested from there. This has the advantage of ensuring staff trained in organization standards and ways of working are deployed, start-up is fast-tracked and costs kept to a minimum (economies of scale and reuse). However, in some organizations the central pool may not exist or may not be big enough to cope with demand, in which case business staff may be seconded to project roles with support from a COE (where one exists), or contract staff may be engaged. Some organizations may develop a framework agreement with a partner organization to provide all programme and project staff, both managers and support staff. However, whenever contract or framework staff are used, they should, wherever possible, be inducted into the organization's standards and ways of working.

- **Physical versus virtual offices** – the ideal scenario is to have a permanent organization office with staff physically co-located, ensuring team cohesion and consistency of approaches. However, in some organizations, as a result of a lack of physical office space, or an adherence to work/life balance policies that allow individuals to work near their homes, or the location of functional experts with other teams, a virtual model or team may emerge. Where a virtual model exists, it is essential that there is an acknowledged single set of standards, albeit with separate owners for components of the standards. It is also vital that the virtual team communicates often and well, through the use of meetings, central information portals and collaborative working practices. This is covered further in Example Model 4, later in this chapter.

3.2.3 Where should the component offices of a P3O model report?

'Where should a P3O model sit within an organization and where should its component offices report in terms of line management?' is a question often asked, frequently by Programme Offices whose historical location within an IT department has left them constantly striving to prove their worth as a strategic Portfolio Office for all programmes and projects across an organization.

There is no one answer to this question; a P3O model is often made up of multiple offices, each serving a particular business need. However, if the P3O model is to truly add value to an organization, it should ultimately report to a main board director, preferably the Strategy or Business Change Director. If the P3O model is to provide support to the organization's governance for all change programmes and projects, its final point of escalation for decisions, priorities, risks, issues and changes should be the main board.

Where an Organization Portfolio Office exists it should report to a main board director, the Chief Executive Officer (CEO), Chief Operating Officer (COO), Chief Financial Officer (CFO) or Chief Information Officer (CIO). If the Portfolio Office is a hub in a decentralized model, aligned to a division or department, it should report to the Divisional Director.

Where a Centre of Excellence exists (in a separate unit from the Portfolio Office) it often reports to a corporate services function or directorate, aligned to other cross-organizational standards and assurance units such as audit, finance, procurement or communications.

3.3 EXAMPLE P3O MODELS

This section outlines some of the models that are found within organizations, their key features and the factors, in their evolution and success.

Variations on the models described in this chapter may arise out of different organizational factors, including:

- Economic sector, whether public or private
- Size of organization
- Approach to organizational governance arrangements
- Number, size and duration of projects
- Level of organizational portfolio, programme and project management maturity
- Centralization versus decentralization of core services
- Whether the business is driven by local or central investment decisions

- Whether the organization provides opportunities for growing its staff with a strong coaching and support ethos and thereby values a formal Centre of Excellence
- Whether there is a culture of 'quality and assurance' and a mindset of continual improvement in the organization
- Whether programmes and projects are undertaken as internally focused initiatives or the organization delivers programme and project management services to a client base
- Whether there are distinct geographical divisions of the organization.

Another dimension that drives the P3O model is the business goals of the organization. Typical business goals will include the following:

- Improve quality and/or quantity of service provision
- Reduce time to market
- Increase revenues
- Reduce costs
- Improve quality of product.

For example, there is no point in building a model that is focused on supporting a high level of governance if 'time to market' is critical to the organization and the cost of additional governance would cost the organization significantly in sales if it delayed implementation of that critical programme or change.

The example models described in this chapter (see Table 3.1) are found in both private and public sector organizations. This is not an exhaustive list; other models exist, aligned to the local organization culture and business decision and delivery structures.

Table 3.1   Example P3O models and features

Model name	Features
Organization Portfolio Office model	A single, permanent, organization-level Portfolio Office, focused on strategic portfolio support, planning, delivery support and COE functions, with temporary Programme and Project Offices set up to support new initiatives as they are launched
Hub and Spoke model	Large organization model with multiple, decentralized, permanent Hub Portfolio Offices designed to serve specific divisions, geographical regions, business units, departments or functions
Temporary Office model	No permanent office exists; temporary Programme and Project Offices (or individuals with support skills) are set up as new initiatives are launched
Virtual Office model	No physical central office; P3O functions are carried out by business or functional units across the organization
Small Organization model	Very small office or single individual, usually focused on consistency of methods/ training, etc.

Appendix C provides case studies of how these models have been tailored in real organizations.

3.3.1   Organization Portfolio Office model

In this model, there is often one permanent P3O unit, which may be called the Organization Portfolio Office (see Figure 3.1) (other possible variations of its name include Portfolio Management Unit, Enterprise Portfolio Office or Corporate Portfolio Office), that fulfils a variety of purposes including one or more of the following:

■ Organization Portfolio Office – enabling strategy, prioritization, senior management decision support
■ Flexible resource pool of delivery support staff – specialists, coordinators, support officers, etc.
■ Centre of Excellence – standards, assurance, competencies and training.

The services that this model will offer are often linked to the maturity of the organization and where it reports within the organization structure. In an immature organization its services may be limited to providing standards or project management handbooks. In a mature organization it may offer strategic support, internal consultancy and a flexible delivery support pool. It may also work with other organizational departments, e.g. strategy or business planning unit, internal audit, finance or HR, to provide a virtual P3O model.

As programmes or projects are launched, temporary Programme or Project Offices may be set up and support staff can be provided from the central flexible resource pool to help the programme or project manager fast-track the Start-up and Initiation stages. Where there is no flexible resource pool, contract staff may be recruited. These staff need to be inducted in the standards recommended by the Organization Portfolio Office. As the programme or project progresses into implementation, the support staff roles should be revisited to ensure that the central expert pool is being used appropriately and that the programme or project has sufficient (not excessive) support resources.

Support staff within the temporary Programme and Project Offices may be line-managed through the Organization Portfolio Office or the business units themselves.

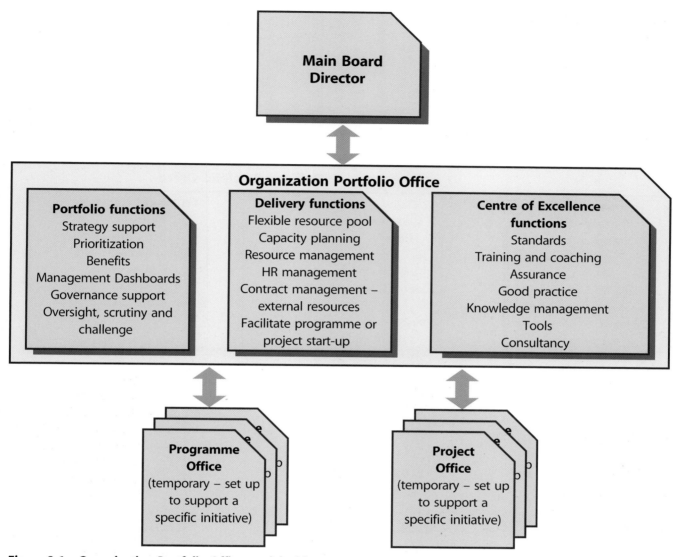

Figure 3.1 Organization Portfolio Office model with temporary Programme and Project Offices

This is a centralized model that can occur in any size of organization, but it is more often found in small to medium-sized organizations with centralized decision-making and key functions co-located geographically. In Appendix C, Case Study 2 (government agency) and Case Study 3 (food manufacturing) illustrate practical applications of this model. Case Study 5 (services) illustrates an organizational model with central flexible resource pools of programme and project managers and project coordinator staff.

The Organization Portfolio Office model often started its life in the IT or technology division or department and has expanded its remit to provide support to all key programmes and projects across an organization as well as IT programmes and projects. It may still be located in the IT division and its services cross-charged across the organization, or it may have matured and be located within corporate services or report to a Strategy or Business Development Director (on the main board), which is the ideal position.

Figure 3.1 shows a single unit responsible for the three functional areas of strategic planning support (portfolio functions), delivery support (flexible resource pool) and standards and capability support (Centre of Excellence functions). However, in some organizations the strategic planning support functions may have evolved in a separate unit under a Strategy Director (see Figure 3.2). Where this occurs, the ideal scenario would be a merging of the two units under a single director. If this is not possible, then the two units should work closely in tandem with each other.

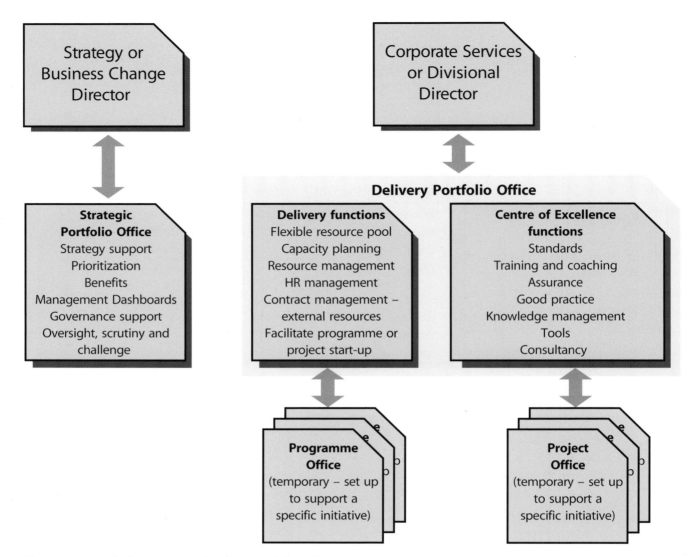

Figure 3.2   Variation on Organization Portfolio Office model, with separate Strategy Office

In Appendix C, Case Study 6 (telecommunications) illustrates the separation of the strategic portfolio functions from COE and delivery functions, a variation on the Organization Portfolio Office model illustrated in Figure 3.2.

Hints and tips

The underlying success factors in the Organization Portfolio Office model are listed in Table 3.2.

Table 3.2   Underlying success factors in the Organization Portfolio Office model

Success factor	Advantages	Consequences of not doing it
Make sure the P3O has a senior management champion with continuity of support	■ Decision-making at senior levels ■ Drives action through other management teams.	■ P3O will not be recognized ■ Processes will not be used ■ If the senior management champion changes before the P3O principles are embedded in the culture, then the vision may change and it's 'back to the beginning' in some cases
Ensure clarity of strategy and direction for management of change	■ Gives direction for prioritization and capacity planning	■ The organization does not have a portfolio of programmes and projects aligned to the organization's goals ■ Too many projects or programmes are started that do not add real value to the organization ■ Pet or rogue projects may be allowed to develop, driven by whoever shouts loudest
Employ a Head of P3O who is highly respected, charismatic and is comfortable working and influencing at all levels of an organization	■ Gives the P3O units gravitas across the organization ■ The Head of P3O is invited to senior planning meetings and able to influence organizational direction	■ P3O requirements are not considered when key restructuring decisions are taken ■ Rolling out standards and methods across an organization will be difficult
Ensure the Portfolio Office is staffed with highly competent senior staff, who have practical experience of running programmes and projects, including the 'war stories and delivery scars', who are also excellent coaches and mentors	■ Ability to empathize with delivery programmes and projects ■ Know what works and the challenges ■ Able to tailor standards and approaches appropriately ■ Respected and listened to	■ P3O seen as admin unit or a 'post box'
Establish a Programme/Project Management Forum – where professionals across the company come together to learn from each other	■ Lessons learned 'in context'– of how enterprise standards translate into reality ■ With an Organization Portfolio Office it is necessary to learn from programme and project managers to ensure standards and approaches remain fit for purpose within the operational environment ■ Changes in industry best practice and how it may be applied within the organization can be easily communicated to the full P3RM community	■ Potential for local Programme Offices or cliques to form with no sense of corporate identity ■ No face-to-face forum for issue (or debate) updates to organizational best practice
Develop and maintain a P3O Blueprint, which is regularly revisited in line with improvements in best practice or changes in organizational focus, structure or business drivers	■ Adds structure and focus to P3O development and delivery ■ Can be used to focus senior management's attention on the added value of the P3O and stop any attempts at cost cutting	■ Without a P3O Blueprint the purpose and services of a P3O may be vulnerable to constant change as senior managers champion changes over time and personal visions intervene
Develop and maintain an intranet or collaboration zone where all P3RM staff can access best practice and standards	■ Single source of access for standards, periodically updated ■ Lessons learned and emerging industry good practice can be centrally applied and easily accessed by all	■ Local standards may evolve and develop Individuals save templates etc. on local drives and do not keep up with changing best practice

3.3.2 Hub and Spoke model

The Hub and Spoke model is a P3O model that describes a system of organizational design where there is a permanent central Organization Portfolio Office (hub) connected to a number of smaller permanent decentralized offices (spokes) with a subset of the centralized office's business objectives, functions and services. These decentralized offices in their turn act as hub offices to the temporary programmes and projects (spokes) they service. All information and processes (connections) are arranged so that they move along spokes to the organization-level hub at the centre. A Hub and Spoke model provides the benefit of scalability for large organizations and supports business ownership by maintaining a level of decentralization.

The Information Hub refers to the centralized element of the Hub and Spoke model for P3O in terms of information flows. It supports highlight and exception-based reporting for projects, programmes and/or portfolios by amalgamating information with the process and information owned by the central office as the Information Hub.

Where the hub services a geographical area, division, department or business unit, it may also perform local prioritization of programmes and projects that feed into the organization-wide prioritization process. It may also provide a local flexible resource pool of delivery staff and tailor organization standards for local use through a local COE function.

The illustrated Hub and Spoke model consists of a permanent central Organization Portfolio Office with Hub Portfolio/Programme Offices, supporting individual business units, and temporary Programme and Project Offices set up to support delivery of individual programmes and projects (spoke offices) – see Figure 3.3.

The Hub and Spoke model is similar to the Organization Portfolio Office model; however, the size of the organization, the divisional split of business interests or geographical spread of sites may necessitate the setting up of separate Hub Portfolio/Programme Offices to focus support at the point of local delivery. This model tends to be an option for larger, more complex organizations, possibly with a multinational reach.

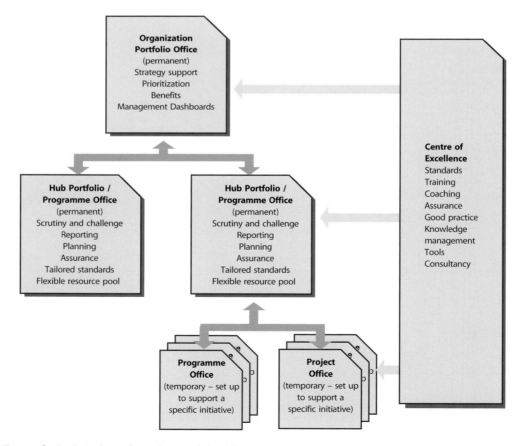

Figure 3.3 Example P3O Hub and Spoke model with permanent Hub Portfolio Offices and temporary Programme and Project Offices

As in the Organization Portfolio Office model, individual temporary programmes and projects may be staffed from the hub's flexible resource pool or staff provided from within the business division or geographical location.

Programmes and projects will use standards and assurance from the corporate COE or the local hub office (acting as a local COE), dependent on its size and maturity.

The local hub office may also provide portfolio functions in setting local priorities, developing divisional Management Dashboards and carrying out capacity planning for scarce technical resources and P3RM resources.

In Appendix C, Case Study 4 (retail) and Case Study 6 (telecommunications) illustrate practical applications of the Hub and Spoke model.

> **Hints and tips**
>
> The underlying success factors in this model are the same as for the Organization Portfolio Office model (see Table 3.2), with the additional factors outlined in Table 3.3.

3.3.3 Temporary Office model

In this model there are no permanent Portfolio or Hub Offices, and temporary Programme or Project Offices are established to support initiatives as they arise.

This is generally an immature model (organizational P3M3 maturity level 1 or 2), found in organizations where a 'programme or projects culture' has not yet been established.

As each new programme or project is launched, it is staffed with local business people, sometimes supplemented by contract staff to bring in additional expertise. There is no central Portfolio Office although there may be an underlying project method, defined on the company intranet or inherent in the culture, in that individuals may have been sent on programme or project management training courses such as PRINCE2 or MSP.

This model suffers from inconsistency of approach on programmes and projects with extreme variations in terms of delivery success, dependent on local business managers' competence.

> **Hints and tips**
>
> The underlying success factors in this model are defined in Table 3.4.

Table 3.3 Additional underlying success factors in the Hub and Spoke model

Success factor	Advantages	Consequences of not doing it
Effective capacity planning and flexible resourcing model	■ Geographic clustering of resources ■ Resources familiar with local business model and working practices, e.g. IT or marketing focus	■ Resources continue to be bought in or may be asked to travel over a large geographical area
Availability of good Hub Portfolio/Programme Office managers using core standards and methods and able to tailor them appropriately to local need	■ Flow down of good practice and standards with localized tailoring and application	■ Local hubs develop their own standards and do not share best practice ■ Transfer of good staff across hubs and divisions requires constant retraining
Develop a Portfolio/Programme Office Managers' Forum – where key staff from Hub Portfolio/Programme Offices meet to ensure consistency of approach	■ Consistency of application of enterprise or corporate best practice ■ Learning from each other how best to apply enterprise or corporate standards	■ Local hubs develop their own standards and do not share best practice ■ Transfer of good staff across hubs and divisions requires constant retraining

Table 3.4 Underlying success factors in the Temporary Office model

Success factor	Advantages	Consequences of not doing it
Develop centrally documented programme or project standards and templates	■ All programme and project managers have a central point to refer to for standards, templates, etc. and don't have to invent their own ■ Consistency of approach and terminology across the organization	■ All programme and project managers act individually and use their own templates. ■ Where there is a large contract P3RM pool, external staff will bring their own kitbags of standards and ignore any internal enterprise or corporate ways of working
Ensure a consistent approach to programme and project management training through the procurement of an approved set of courses and training providers	■ All staff advised to go on similar courses through a standard set of providers ■ Consistent training messages and language	■ Staff may go on any course they like, with inconsistent language and messages ■ Training providers will not be able to tailor courses to local company culture
Develop a Portfolio/Programme Office Managers' Forum – where key staff from Hub Portfolio/Programme Offices meet to ensure consistency of approach	■ Consistency of application of enterprise or corporate best practice ■ Learn from each other how best to apply enterprise or corporate standards	■ Local hubs develop their own standards and do not share best practice ■ Transfer of good staff across hubs and divisions requires constant retraining

3.3.4 Virtual Office model

In this model there is no permanent Portfolio Office or COE function to provide centralized support, assurance and standards, as these functions are embedded in the organization's business delivery units. Temporary Programme and Project Offices are established to support initiatives as they are launched and staffed and supported from within the business units themselves.

This model generally exists in highly mature organizations, where consistent standards are embedded, the P3RM staff are highly competent, and P3O services and functions can be provided across the organization without the need for a physical structure to support them. There is often a Head of Profession for portfolio, programme, risk and project management who liaises with all the professional staff embedded within business teams. This role will also provide the link to strategy and business planning and ensure internal standards continue to be good practice by attendance at best-practice events, seminars, etc. A key feature of this model are Programme, Risk and Project Management Forums, where all P3RM professionals come together at quarterly or half-yearly events to share best practice and learn about new methods and ways of working.

It is becoming more common for a virtual P3O to be developed using external resources and internal collaboration tools, which allows a more community-based involvement with a smaller core team. With the trends in cost reduction, this could be a useful model for an organization to explore further as its P3RM maturity increases.

Hints and tips

The underlying success factors in the Virtual Office model are outlined in Table 3.5.

3.3.5 Small Organization model

In many small organizations the P3O may simply be a single expert person or a couple of people delivering a subset of functions/services to suit local need and culture. Functions and services are typically focused on providing support for an in-house project method through the development of consistent processes and templates, and providing specific hands-on support to key projects. The range of services provided will depend on the skills and areas of expertise of these individuals.

Scaling hints and tips

If you are a very small unit, these models may seem daunting. The key thing to consider is what these models offer in terms of services and functions and who they serve in terms of stakeholders. If you are not carrying out the services and functions highlighted in the models, ask who is doing those things within your organization. The outcome may be the discovery of a network of people who could work more effectively together as a virtual P3O.

Table 3.5   Underlying success factors in the Virtual Office model

Success factor	Advantages	Consequences of not doing it
Ensure a P3RM maturity level of 3 or above (P3M3)	■ P3RM maturity level of 3 indicates an organization with consistent work practices, and a review and continuous improvement culture ■ Centralized training and centralized access to standards are key features leading to consistency of approach	■ Implementing a virtual model when maturity level is less than 3 will not be successful, as there is no embedded projects culture, no consistent application of standards and no centralized ownership
Develop Programme/Project Management Forums	■ To share best practice and share the role of updating and embedding changes to best practice	■ With no face-to-face discussion forum, the base standards and practices may stagnate ■ Any updates without consultation will be seen as an imposition and consistency of approach will disappear over time
Ensure a single point of ownership by senior P3RM professional (Head of Profession for P3RM) for portfolio, programme, project and risk standards	■ Senior professional is outward-facing to look for and consider advances in best practice, but with a good understanding as to how the advances may be applied pragmatically within the organization	■ With no central team to update and coordinate standards, local variations may creep in and all previous good work will be undone
Ensure standards continually developed and embedded through reference to external best practice	■ A single point of reference exists for virtual teams to access that is regularly updated	■ With no central team to update and coordinate standards, local variations may creep in and all previous good work will be undone
Develop a strong underlying programme, risk and project culture	■ Strong underlying programme, project and risk culture means that the whole project team from Project Executive, SRO, Programme or Project Boards, programme and project manager to business teams understand their roles and the reasons behind the consistent approach	■ Without a strong underlying programme, project and risk culture there is a danger that programmes and projects act individually and do not deliver consistent good working practices ■ The training overhead for programme and project managers' bringing boards and business resources up to date may be excessive

3.4   WHAT FUNCTIONS AND SERVICES SHOULD THE P3O OFFER?

3.4.1   High-level functions and services

Each office within a P3O model may deliver a different functional emphasis dependent on the business drivers and customer demands. P3O functions and services are categorized as planning, delivery or COE in Figure 3.4. Permanent Portfolio Offices primarily focus on planning services, whereas temporary Programme and Project Offices focus on delivery services. However, all functions and services may be delivered with a different emphasis by any type of P3O unit (see Appendix F). COE functions may exist in a separate unit or be integrated into Portfolio, Programme or Project Offices.

See Appendix F for a more comprehensive list of functions and services.

3.4.2 Functions and services – point of delivery

A function or service may have a different emphasis in different offices within the P3O model and at different levels of governance, with the key driver being 'adding value at point of service delivery'.

Some functions and services only exist at portfolio level, whereas others may exist at portfolio, programme and project level, but require different input/support requirements.

An example of this is **planning**:

■ At the **portfolio level**, planning is done in terms of designing the programmes, projects and their impact on business operations to meet the strategic objectives of the organization, incorporating them into business plans and then providing support by ongoing prioritization, capacity and resource planning. Answer the questions 'What should we deliver?' and 'Do we have the capacity to deliver and adopt it?'

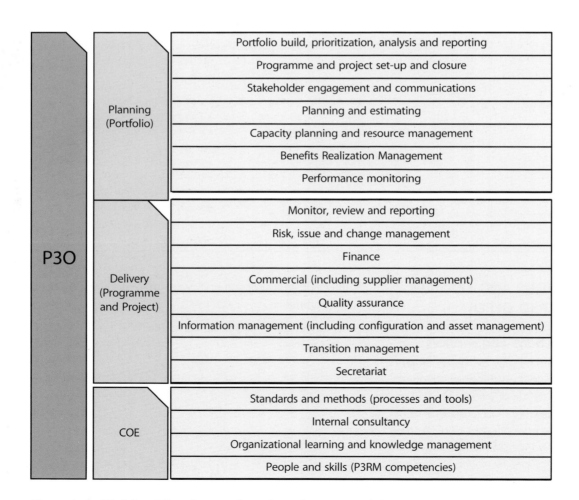

Figure 3.4 High-level functions and services of a P3O model

- At the **programme level**, planning is concerned with understanding the new capability that will be required to realize planned business benefits, how it will be delivered and when, while ensuring that delivery resources are available and economic. It also covers dependency management, both within the programme and to other external factors

- At the **project level**, planning is concerned with developing a plan to deliver the outputs in a timely and cost-effective manner to the required quality, providing planning templates or planning support (tools/techniques/expertise) to create project plans (maybe linked to programme plans, where a project is part of a programme), managing dependencies and ensuring transition plans to business operations are in place.

Another example is **risk management**:

- At the **portfolio level**, risk is considered from a strategic viewpoint, looking at risks that may inhibit the organization's ability to deliver its strategic objectives. The P3O should develop a risk management policy for compliance by programmes and projects based on the organization's own corporate risk policy, identify and manage portfolio risks and liaise with the Corporate Risk department, where one exists. It should also review the risks of programmes and projects to look for common risks that should be managed at the portfolio level rather than individually by programmes or projects. The P3O would also be best placed to evaluate the net effect of these threats and opportunities when aggregated together, and escalate this information to the board or Corporate Risk Management

- At the **programme level**, risk is considered with regard to the ability to achieve the planned outcomes and benefits for a specific business change and the P3O should develop risk management standards for the Project Dossier (if one does not exist at a portfolio level), and develop and maintain the programme's Risk Register, recommending escalation or cascading of risks as necessary. The P3O may also look at risks to stakeholders, benefits, delivery, dependencies and external supplier risks, and proactively review risks across the individual projects to seek out those that should be managed by the programme rather than by individual projects. The P3O may also facilitate risk workshops to ensure consistent application of risk processes across the programme.

- At the **project level**, risk is considered with regard to the delivery of the project's outputs to meet the required objectives on time, cost, benefits, quality and scope. The P3O should provide a standard risk management strategy, process and templates for monitoring risks to delivery of the project outputs through standardized Risk Registers. The P3O may also provide resources to run risk identification workshops or to manage the risk process in support of the project manager and Project Board.

3.4.3 P3O assurance functions and services

Independent assurance services are often offered as part of portfolio, programme or project support. This may take many forms, from coordinating or facilitating Gated Reviews or stage reviews (in UK government, the OGC Gateway Review process) to regular health checks, internal or external audits, or lessons-learned reviews.

Assurance teams may also provide quality assurance to programmes and projects by providing an assurance resource (full or part time) or independent advice/guidance in the Start-up stage to advise on the tailoring of processes.

Whatever the level of assurance service provided, it is essential that it is independent of the programme or project delivery and that there are no conflicts of interest.

The P3O model itself should also be subject to independent assurance and external audit, in particular the external review of COE functions and services to ensure that good practice is being kept up to date with changing industry standards and trends.

Staff across the P3O model may also carry out assurance within a multi-programme/project environment, providing oversight, scrutiny and challenge. Independent assurance external to the delegated assurance from the Programme or Project Board may be requested by Senior Management Boards and may be focused on fulfilment of strategy, impact on business operations, management of dependencies or other areas of concern.

Case study

A Programme Office servicing a large complex programme within a UK government department offers an independent standards and assurance function. This office consists of three individuals who are assigned to projects within the programme. Each assigned assurance resource provides advice/guidance on the standard processes to be used and develops an assurance approach tailored to the individual project – this may consist of Gated Review coordination, health checks, intermediate and final lessons-learned reviews, and advice or guidance on quality criteria and quality reviews. The assurance team is separate from the delivery support team within the Programme Office, ensuring their independence from delivery.

Hints and tips

An assurance function should always be forward-looking and action-oriented (either specific or systemic) to improve the potential for successful delivery, rather than simply auditing what may have happened.

3.4.4 P3O governance functions and services

Chapter 1 introduced the concept of the P3O in an organization supporting governance, through enabling and challenging programme and project data and in some cases scrutinizing the impact of programme or project delivery on Business as Usual (through achievement of strategic goals or least disruption to operational working).

In all the functions and services referred to in Appendix F, each office within the P3O model – whether it be a Project Office (or individual support officer), Programme Office, Portfolio Office or COE – will need to be aware of the nature of governance in terms of who makes what decisions and when, what delegated limits of authority are in place, and what are the rules and routes for escalation and cascading of issues, risks and changes.

Governance will also encompass Business as Usual decision-making bodies, and the relationship between the P3O and these bodies should be defined and rules of engagement with those bodies established. The terms of reference for any office within the P3O structure should encompass responsibilities for the escalation or cascading of risks, issues, changes and decisions, and any reporting function should reflect the governance and information needs of all interested parties.

3.4.5 Non-P3RM functions and services

It is sometimes necessary for a P3O to undertake functions and services outside the P3RM area of operations, either in the interests of business efficiency or because those functions have no other logical home. This may mean providing a secretariat service to Management Boards, looking after travel and accommodation (operational accommodation in addition to project accommodation) or liaising with procurement regarding procurement of equipment or resources.

Hints and tips

Where this occurs it is important to ringfence these administration resources away from the professional P3RM functions in a separate team. If the P3O is seen as an administration unit, it may discourage people from deciding on a potentially rewarding career within a P3O.

3.5 INTEGRATION OF THE P3O MODEL WITH THE WIDER ORGANIZATION

The P3O model does not exist in a vacuum; it must integrate with other delivery agencies, departments and functions within the organization.

A key reason for failure of some permanent P3Os is the lack of integration of the P3O model and the wider organization. The Head of P3O needs to understand who is responsible for the following functions and how the model, and the various offices within it, will interact with them:

■ Strategy development and management, including business planning
■ IT service management (release, change, configuration, etc.)
■ Human resources
■ Marketing/public relations
■ Procurement/purchasing/commercial, including bid management
■ Finance
■ Corporate Risk Management
■ Corporate information security (see section 3.5.1 for further information)
■ Audit
■ Quality
■ Business operations.

The P3O model seeks to provide the governance backbone for all change within an organization, ensuring all decisions are made at the appropriate level with the right facts and in a timely manner. This means that the P3O model needs to work effectively with all bodies across an organization that either make decisions or provide facts and information to allow a decision to be made. Effective governance in programmes and projects therefore requires integration with all other areas of the business.

Just as P3O resources may exist in a matrix management environment with local business line management but with a professional link to an Organization Portfolio Office or COE, so will other professional resources exist within a similar matrix management model.

Clarity is required in terms of roles/responsibilities for delivering functions and services across business areas. For example, financial functions and services may be provided through a temporary Programme Office, but the person delivering the service may be embedded in the Programme Office, with their line management and the standards for financial reporting developed and specified by the Finance department (see Figure 3.5). Embedded resources are temporarily assigned to a programme or project (either full time or part time), but their originating department still controls the processes that they will follow and is responsible for normal line management activities.

3.5.1 Information assurance and P3O

Information assurance (IA) in portfolios, programmes and projects can vary very significantly in its importance. Some organizations such as the Ministry of Defence, the banking

industry and others working with personal or sensitive information may take the view that IA is critical to their business. Others may regard information security as little more than an optional nuisance.

There is another view. IA is based on the three main concepts of **confidentiality, integrity** and **availability.** What these terms mean in general is that information should only be available to those who have a need or authority to see it; that only those with the correct authority should be able to change information; and that the information should be available whenever and wherever the business requires it to be. This last area has implications for most if not all portfolios, programmes and projects.

For any programme or project involving the development or implementation of an information and communications technology (ICT) system, IA is bound to be critical. For many other projects in, for example, engineering or construction, there may be limited implications for IA but they may have some physical security requirements. It is highly likely that any project team will need to consider the business continuity and disaster recovery requirements not only for their project work, but also for the operational system once it has been handed over for live use. This is just one facet of IA, and it needs to be considered early. The potential implications for resources, time and ultimately cost are huge and they have frequently derailed a poorly prepared portfolio, programme, or project.

The P3O has a crucial cost-effective role in providing a number of IA-related resources and management

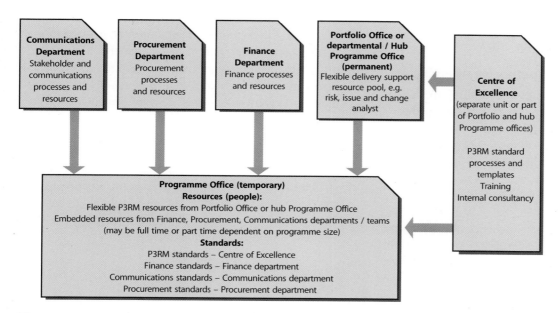

Figure 3.5   Example embedding of resources from a permanent Portfolio Office, COE and business functions into a temporary Programme Office

functions for the support of all areas of the Programme/ Project Management (PPM) environment. Consideration of the IA requirements for the project and its outputs must start at the beginning of the project. Trying to build in IA measures or take remedial action to deal with identified IA issues at the end of the project will never be cost effective or as efficient as building them in during development. The P3O can ensure that an appropriate initial assessment of the IA issues is carried out during the Initiation stage of any new activity, at the latest.

For portfolios and programmes, the role of the P3O is more about setting the overall objectives and then ensuring they are being followed. This might be the establishment of a standard (perhaps using the ISO27000 series of international IA standards, for example) or simply a general security policy statement.

In the scenario where there is a separate IA function or department within an organization, the P3O should engage appropriately with the experts within it and follow a process of embedding IA resources and processes into Portfolio, Programme and Project Offices or teams, as previously discussed with reference to finance or commercial staff.

3.6 ROLES AND RESPONSIBILITIES WITHIN P3O

There are many different roles within any P3O model, some of which are specific to a level of organizational governance (e.g. Portfolio Analyst), others that are specific to a function or service (e.g. Risk Manager). When the P3O office is designed, job descriptions should be identified that are specific to individuals and their skills and competencies.

3.6.1 Skills and competencies of P3O staff

The tone and approach of a successful P3O model or component office within the model is set by the person at the top, so the Head of P3O is a key role. This individual must have the right experience, have influence, credibility and charisma and be able to lead 'from the middle'– manage up, down and sideways. They need to be a good people person, have a good understanding of methods, be a decision-maker, be capable of following a vision and have first-hand experience of programme and project delivery. It is a difficult job to do right and these people are hard to find. Some of the best Heads of P3O have come from varied backgrounds, including business operations management, strategy development or business planning, so an extensive knowledge of P3RM is not necessarily a key competency.

In staffing a P3O office, there should be a matching of roles to individual strengths. Some people are better at detailed work than others; others will have strong interpersonal and coaching skills.

Although good P3RM skills and competencies are essential for some P3O roles, others will require more generic business skills, other functional competencies (finance, commercial) and generic personal skills such as coaching, mentoring, facilitation and presentation skills with the ability to be pragmatic.

There should be a clear emphasis on P3O as a career path in its own right, rather than as a stepping stone to becoming a project or programme manager. P3O staff should have a clear career path mapped out, underpinned by mandatory and desirable skills and competencies with personal and role-focused development plans. Qualifications in P3O-related disciplines are to be encouraged so as to improve the skills, competencies and credibility of the P3O function.

In developing more professional P3Os, staffed by individuals with the right skills, organizations will have to understand that an investment in high-calibre individuals is required. It is more important to have the right number of appropriately skilled people who can interpret and challenge data, rather than a huge number of admin staff who collate data without interpreting it and without making the necessary recommendations to the decision-makers.

The skills and competencies of Portfolio Office staff will need to include investment management, strategic planning and implementation, and business benefits realization. These staff will also need to have the ability to see the 'big picture' view, what is often referred to as the 'helicopter view', and make recommendations based on insightful information. They will need to have political awareness and stakeholder engagement skills, be capable of operating and influencing at Senior Management Board level, and have an understanding of the business challenges and changes required. They should also have credible delivery experience, i.e. they should have run large programmes and projects before, managed risks at a strategic level or operated a business unit, and understand the challenges that change will bring and how to balance change with operational working. Such people are hard to find and should be valued and developed.

Scaling hints and tips

In a small organization with only a single person or a few people dedicated to P3O functions in a central unit, consider how you can expand your headcount and talent-spot for the organization through the use of secondments.

Case study

One organization had an Organization Portfolio Office with a headcount of nine people to support all the projects and programmes across a large multi-division organization. Demand rose significantly as the Portfolio Office began publishing its successes and achieved a reputation for fast-tracking projects through start-up and pragmatic help.

Increasing the headcount was not an option, so the Head of Portfolio Office sought secondments from across the business, talent-spotting good people and gaining agreements from their line managers to fund a 6-month secondment within the Portfolio Office. These 6-month secondments were invariably extended to a year, or 18 months in some cases, as the value of the practical experience was appreciated.

The business units gained by having their people intensively trained, coached and given practical experience, and the Portfolio Office gained by increasing its pool of resources without increasing its headcount. When the staff returned to their units, they provided satellite (or hub) Programme Offices or local project support to their business units, which took the pressure off the Organization Portfolio Office and also provided a flexible resource pool that the Portfolio Office could tap into when workloads peaked.

The secondment process was formally agreed with the HR team and officially sanctioned. An overall business benefit was a general improvement in programme and project management skills across the business and more successful change.

3.6.2 Management, generic or functional roles

The job descriptions in a P3O model or component office may focus on a management or generic role (e.g. Head of P3O) or on a specific function, or be a combination of different functions. The functional roles may, in a larger or permanent office, be allocated to a single person or several people; in a smaller or temporary office, however, these roles will often be combined in a single person's job description.

The role descriptions in Tables 3.6 and 3.7 should be treated as a 'pick and mix' set to create custom job descriptions tailored to the organization's business and customer requirements.

Full role descriptions appear in Appendix A and examples are given in Appendix C: Case study 2 (government agency) describes an organization using functional role descriptions, and Case study 6 (telecommunications) one using generic role descriptions.

Functional-based roles

In a large programme or project each of these roles may belong to a single person, but it is more likely that a single person will take on multiple roles from Table 3.7, aligned to their skills and competencies and the requirements of the programme or project.

Table 3.6 Outline P3O management and generic role descriptions

Role name	Outline description
P3O Sponsor	■ The P3O Sponsor is a senior manager who directs and champions the establishment and evolving operation of the P3O. They will ideally be a member of the main board
Head of P3O (permanent office) – may be called Head of Portfolio Office	■ The Head of P3O establishes and runs the office(s) ■ The role requires strong leadership and management skills coupled with strong P3RM or strategy/business-planning skills to ensure the integrity of the portfolio or programmes and projects. The individual will need to develop and maintain robust relationships with all parts of the business as well as with the programmes and projects, to ensure that all initiatives meet the requirements of the Portfolio or Programme Board. They will also need to work with business areas to identify any gaps in initiatives and to understand what activities are planned to fill those gaps ■ The individual will need to understand the wider objectives of the portfolio and programme, have credibility within the environment and be able to influence others. They must be able to develop and maintain effective working relationships with senior managers, the programme and project teams and any third-party service providers ■ The role will also provide strategic challenge, overview and scrutiny, ensuring alignment with wider policy and strategic initiatives ■ In some organizations the Head of P3O may be a strategic or business planning manager or director
Head of Programme or Project Office (temporary office)	■ The Head of Programme or Project Office establishes and runs the office ■ The role requires strong leadership and management skills coupled with strong P3RM skills to ensure the integrity of the programme or project. The individual will need to develop and maintain robust relationships with all parts of the business as well as with the projects, to ensure that all initiatives meet the requirements of the Programme or Project Board. The individual will also need to work with business areas to identify any gaps in initiatives and to understand what activities are planned to fill those gaps ■ The individual will need to understand the wider objectives of the programme or project, have credibility within its environment and be able to influence others. They must be able to develop and maintain effective working relationships with senior managers, the programme and project teams and any third-party service providers ■ They may deputize for the Programme Manager ■ The role will also provide strategic overview and scrutiny, ensuring alignment with wider policy and strategic initiatives
Portfolio Analyst	■ The role facilitates the development and ongoing management of an optimized portfolio, ensuring senior management decisions lead to the fulfilment of strategic objectives through the delivery of programmes and projects (aligned with Business as Usual objectives) ■ They develop and maintain Management Dashboards
Programme or Project Specialist (internal consultant)	■ The Specialist plays a proactive role in the promotion of programme and project management methods, roll-out of good project management practice, and monitoring certain projects. They provide a consultancy service to programme and project managers or Programme and Project Boards across the organization or department. This consultancy may take the form of coaching, help, advice and guidance, or be of a specific nature in the form of facilitated workshops. At the beginning of a project, the Specialist should work with the programme or project manager and the business to help define an appropriate level of governance and structure management for the programme/project and decide on the level of support and the type of services required. They may provide a tailored series of workshops, which may include elements of programme/project start-up advice, risk analysis, project scoping, planning, tailoring of methods, etc.
Programme or Project Officer (may also be referred to as Programme or Project Coordinator or Administrator, dependent on level of responsibility)	■ The purpose of the Programme or Project Officer is to improve the planning and delivery process by collecting, and maintaining, data in a consistent form. It is the responsibility of Programme or Project Officers to implement guidelines, procedures and templates to collect and maintain this data and provide hands-on delivery support to a programme or project

Table 3.7   Outline functional-based P3O roles

Role name	Outline description
Benefits role	■ The role provides a benefits-realization support service to programme managers, business managers and business change managers
Commercial role	■ The purpose of the Commercial role is to ensure the organization carries out the role of Informed Customer and all commercial/procurement practices and decisions meet designated standards and offer the organization 'value for money' ■ The role may be a P3O role but is more likely to be embedded in the P3O, with formal line management from the Commercial, Procurement or Purchasing function ■ It may also exist within a virtual P3O model
Communications and Stakeholder Engagement role	■ The Communications and Stakeholder Engagement role ensures a Stakeholder Analysis is created and regularly maintained, and a communication plan is designed and implemented successfully. In high-profile P3O offices this role may manage relationships with the media
Information Management role	■ The Information Management role is the custodian and guardian of all master copies of the portfolio, programme or project's information. The role takes on the duties of Configuration Management ■ This role should work closely with any Information Assurance (IA) department or function, as well as those in the Issue and Change Control roles
Consultancy and Performance Management role	■ The role provides internal consultancy and expertise in P3RM and organization processes ■ It seeks to continuously improve performance of the portfolio, programme and projects within an organization ■ It also creates, maintains and disseminates good practice
Finance role	■ The Finance role establishes a professional Finance function within the portfolio, programme or project to ensure the timely provision of funding and effective financial control ■ The role may be a P3O role but is more likely to be embedded in the P3O, while maintaining formal line management from the corporate Finance function
Issue role	■ The Issue role takes the lead in ensuring that the portfolio, programme or project has effective processes in place to identify, monitor and resolve issues. Should be closely aligned to the Information Management and Change Control roles
Change Control role	■ The Change Control role takes the lead in ensuring that the portfolio, programme or project has effective processes in place to identify, monitor and deliver changes. Should be closely aligned to the Information Management and Issue roles
Planning role	■ The Planning role is responsible for facilitating the development and maintenance of the portfolio, programme or project plan and dependency logs
Quality Assurance role	■ The Quality Assurance role leads the work to ensure that the new products or services delivered by the portfolio, programme or project are fit for purpose and are capable of delivering the benefits required by the relevant board/management level
Resource Management role	■ The Resource Management role ensures that current and future programmes and projects are equipped with enough staff of the right skills, at the time they are needed, and that those resources are used as efficiently as possible
Risk role	■ The Risk role takes the lead in ensuring that the portfolio, programme or project has effective processes in place to identify and monitor risks, has access to reliable and up-to-date information about risks, and uses the appropriate controls and actions to deal with risks ■ The role should ensure that all risk management practices are consistent with the corporate risk management policy and strategy
Reporting role	■ The role provides a reporting service to the portfolio, programme or project – collates base data and generates reports to multiple audiences through aggregated data

(continued)

Table 3.7 Outline functional-based P3O roles (continued)

Role name	Outline description
Secretariat/ Administrator role	■ The role provides portfolio, programme or project administrative support ■ It may also provide a secretariat function for the relevant boards
Tools Expert role	■ The role is an expert in software tools to support the change environment. The role may provide support to the P3RM community to configure software or provide training and coaching in their use. ■ Examples of tools may include Enterprise P3RM software, planning, risk, document management or collaboration tools.

Scaling hints and tips

In a small P3O the roles are more likely to be generic and multifunction, so consider whether the generic job descriptions fit what your organization requires of you. If not, build your own job descriptions by picking the key elements from the functional role descriptions. The role descriptions can also help you refine your own job descriptions, or help you refocus on tasks and activities that would make better use of your skills and time. Also, if your small team is not carrying out all the functional roles, find out who in the organization takes on those roles and build links with them or their departments.

3.7 SIZING AND TAILORING OF THE P3O MODEL

The most common question asked when designing a P3O model is, 'How big should it be?' followed by, 'How many people at what levels?'

A P3O model may service a single programme, a number of programmes or the full organization portfolio of change. The detailed design and size of individual offices within the P3O model will need to take account of the size and capabilities of the organization and the characteristics of the programmes it will serve or enable. The design and size will also depend on the P3O vision and the business drivers it is set up to serve.

Staff numbers within a P3O model across an organization may vary from a single person to more than 100 (when including delivery resources), although on average it is between 5 and 10 people. High-performing organizations with mature P3Os are more likely to have larger units, with specialized roles allied to a specific function or service.

Sizing a permanent Organization Portfolio Office or hub office will be different from sizing a temporary Programme or Project Office. When putting in place services for a temporary office, resources may be taken from a flexible resource pool within a hub office; engaged on a temporary basis from the contract market or engaged as a Work Package through a framework agreement with a management or P3RM consultancy company.

The following options should also be explored:

■ It may be more appropriate to provide services to a small programme or project by upgrading an existing Programme Office to a hub (for instance where the programme does not justify enough support resource to form a viable Programme Office in its own right) rather than establishing a dedicated Programme Office.

■ The Programme Office may be either partly or wholly virtual. Use should be made of existing corporate resources where possible.

Designing a P3O completely by formula should not be attempted, as no formula can fully cater for the nuances of any given organization structure or programme. However, it is possible to develop a starting point for a debate over the shape and size of a P3O on the basis of programme value and size characteristics.

Where an organization has a mature permanent Portfolio Office or Hub and Spoke model in place with flexible resource pools, the number of staff and costs are likely to be lower as experienced P3O staff are not required to go through the organizational processes' learning curve and will provide a more cost-effective and efficient service.

The P3O Sizing Model can be undertaken across portfolio, programme and project levels. Where modelling does not demonstrate value for money for a particular project or programme to have its own office, then these could be consolidated among a number of projects or programmes to create a hub office.

3.7.1 Sizing Option 1 – Programme value

Overall, the cost of the Programme Office may range between 3% and 5% of the total programme value. This is a figure covering the life of a programme, rather than an annual one. Within this figure the level of Programme Office provision will vary as the programme progresses.

3.7.2 Sizing Option 2 – Programme size

Table 3.8 indicates the size of a temporary Programme Office based on the number of programme staff supported. The figures in Table 3.8 represent average numbers at the point when the programme is established and going through to implementation; numbers may fluctuate during Initiation and throughout the life of the programme, depending on the number of projects being supported at any moment in time and where they are in their lifecycle.

The numbers take into account:

- Management reporting overhead
- Basic IT tools
- P3M3 maturity level being between 2 and 3.

Adjustment may need to be made for:

- Higher or lower organizational P3M3 maturity levels
- Additional roles taken on
- Programmes spread over multiple locations
- Complex or novel programmes
- Programmes with a large number of third parties

- Programmes with complex finances or complex Benefits Realization Plans
- Large number of projects
- The need for short-term resource required for peak loading, e.g. set-up, acceptance, ends of tranches
- Programmes with complex stakeholder and communications requirements.

3.7.3 Sizing Option 3 – by function

Another method for sizing a P3O is to list all the functions the P3O will deliver and estimate the number of hours or days each activity will take, along with the competencies and skills required. For example, providing the secretariat function for each board may take 3 days' effort per month, developing and populating the Management Dashboard may take 2 days per month, etc. By adding all the hours/days per activities required and level and skills of resource required, a P3O resourcing requirement can be developed.

The size of the office and the activities it carries out will vary through the lifecycle, so the exercise should be carried out at least twice, once in Definition and second at the start of Implementation. The sizing for some functions, such as reporting, may be driven by the number of projects or programmes within the portfolio at any point in time, whereas other functions may be driven by the number of meetings.

An example of a P3O Sizing Model based on Option 3 is shown in Figure 3.6.

Table 3.8 Average headcount in P3O, based on size of portfolio or programme

Unit	Headcount						
Programme	30	60	120	200	300	500	1000
Programme Office	3	4	7	9	12	17	25
% Programme Office staff	10	7	6	5	4	3	3

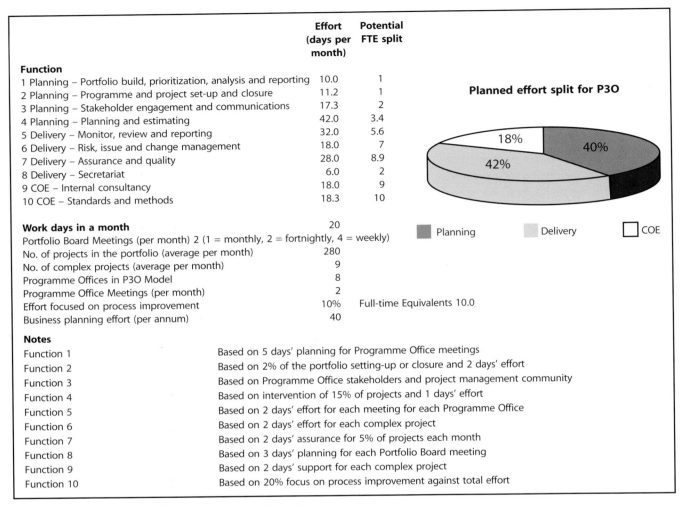

Function	Effort (days per month)	Potential FTE split
1 Planning – Portfolio build, prioritization, analysis and reporting	10.0	1
2 Planning – Programme and project set-up and closure	11.2	1
3 Planning – Stakeholder engagement and communications	17.3	2
4 Planning – Planning and estimating	42.0	3.4
5 Delivery – Monitor, review and reporting	32.0	5.6
6 Delivery – Risk, issue and change management	18.0	7
7 Delivery – Assurance and quality	28.0	8.9
8 Delivery – Secretariat	6.0	2
9 COE – Internal consultancy	18.0	9
10 COE – Standards and methods	18.3	10

Planned effort split for P3O

18% 40% 42%

Planning Delivery COE

Work days in a month	20
Portfolio Board Meetings (per month) 2 (1 = monthly, 2 = fortnightly, 4 = weekly)	
No. of projects in the portfolio (average per month)	280
No. of complex projects (average per month)	9
Programme Offices in P3O Model	8
Programme Office Meetings (per month)	2
Effort focused on process improvement	10% Full-time Equivalents 10.0
Business planning effort (per annum)	40

Notes

Function 1	Based on 5 days' planning for Programme Office meetings
Function 2	Based on 2% of the portfolio setting-up or closure and 2 days' effort
Function 3	Based on Programme Office stakeholders and project management community
Function 4	Based on intervention of 15% of projects and 1 days' effort
Function 5	Based on 2 days' effort for each meeting for each Programme Office
Function 6	Based on 2 days' effort for each complex project
Function 7	Based on 2 days' assurance for 5% of projects each month
Function 8	Based on 3 days' planning for each Portfolio Board meeting
Function 9	Based on 2 days' support for each complex project
Function 10	Based on 20% focus on process improvement against total effort

Figure 3.6   Example P3O Sizing Model (option 3)

3.7.4 Temporary Programme or Project Office size throughout the delivery lifecycle

The size of a temporary Programme or Project Office will also vary throughout its lifecycle, which is where the use of flexible resource pools through Hub Portfolio/ Programme Offices adds real value.

In the mobilization stage (Start-up/Identification and Initiation/Definition) of a project or programme, there is a need for internal consultancy to facilitate establishing and tailoring standard processes, initiate the reporting cycle, develop plans, and fast-track the team and facilities set-up. This could be provided through the temporary engagement of planners, internal consultants (to facilitate collaborative start-up, planning and risk workshops) and assurance staff (to establish a quality strategy and plan) to work alongside the programme and project managers.

As the programme or project progresses into implementation and delivery, the need for a full-time planner reduces as the programme or project manager takes ownership and accountability for the update of the plan; however, some planning support may still be required. The need for internal consultancy reduces to a coaching role (where required), but the assurance role should continue on a part-time basis to provide continuity, lessons-learned support, ongoing health checks, Gated Reviews and advice. During the delivery stage, dependent on the size, complexity and innovative nature of the programme or project there may be a need for generic support from specialists or support officers or functional-based support from a finance, communications, commercial, risk, issue or change perspective.

As the programme or project progresses into closedown and post-implementation review, the delivery resources are no longer required, but internal consultancy may be required to facilitate independent lessons-learned reviews and evaluations. Also, HR professionals may be required to ensure all professional development/appraisal information has been captured and programme or project staff are returned to their 'day jobs' or back into the flexible resource pool with least pain to individuals.

One of the most common problems found when reviewing temporary Programme Offices is that their programme support staff pool is too big. This is often because the number of staff is established at mobilization (Initiation/Definition) and then instead of releasing some of these staff as the programme or project manager takes ownership of delivery, they are kept and 'found work to do' or they do the project manager's job for them.

There are various solutions to this problem, depending on local culture and staffing policies:

- Set up Hub Programme Offices with flexible resource pools, which can be used to mobilize programmes and projects and provide delivery support throughout the lifecycle. The advantage of this is a trained core of people who understand 'the way we do things around here' and require little or no training.
- Engage consultancy support in the mobilization stage (Initiation/Definition) of a programme or project – this may be from a Centre of Excellence or through Work Packages procured from external management or P3RM consultancy companies (through a framework agreement). This approach may also ensure adherence to standards, but requires any external consultancy company to be trained and familiar with local standards.
- Engage contract staff to assist in the mobilization stage (Initiation/Definition) – this is the least preferred options as these staff are not trained in local standards and often bring their own set of templates and processes, which leads to a lack of consistency across programmes and portfolios.

Case study

A large temporary programme of change was operating within a government agency. The programme had a Programme Board (with SRO), Programme Manager and six discrete projects, delivering key strands of the capability. There was also a strong business change implementation team, a Design Authority and a separate stakeholder engagement and communications team (see Figure 3.7).

The Programme Office supported the programme through its lifecycle and engaged additional external consultancy support through a management consultancy for the first crucial 100 days to:

- Fast-track start up
- Establish procedures
- Develop a programme plan (with dependencies)
- Initiate the reporting cycle
- Establish information management
- Develop a strategy for quality output
- Initiate risk, issue and change management
- Engage with the departmental Centre of Excellence to provide good-practice standards and templates
- Provide facilitation support for kick-off workshops.

While the external consultancy team supported the mobilization of the programme with the Programme Office manager, a parallel internal recruitment exercise took place to build the core support team. This team had to carry out a set of functional activities on behalf of the programme and the projects. However, the projects were providing admin resources to support themselves. The Programme Office therefore recruited senior individuals to fulfil the functional roles. These individuals were also permanent members of staff who could be made available, so the functional roles were tailored to meet their strengths and expertise.

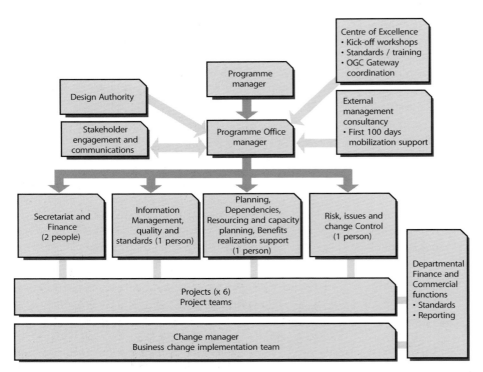

Figure 3.7   Government temporary Programme Office with external mobilization support

Additional case studies can be found in Appendix C, with a variety of organizational models and solutions.

3.8   MATURITY AND EVOLUTION OF THE P3O MODEL

Developing the right P3O model with the correct mix of functions and services will take time.

Any P3O model must take into account the Portfolio, Programme, Project and Risk Management (P3RM) maturity levels of the organization it serves (as defined in P3M3).

P3Os reorganize on a regular basis, some because of a change of P3O Sponsor, others as a result of changing business priorities as well as evolving organization P3RM maturity.

As the organization, or individual divisions/departments within it, matures in its approach to P3RM, so the functions and services of the P3O model will need to evolve to ensure it continues to add value. The planned implementation lifecycle of a P3O model needs to recognize the requirement to continually improve and refine service provision to match or drive the improvement in capability maturity of the organization in P3RM over time. This can be undertaken using either

a continual improvement approach or as a step-change programme to improve already operating functions or services (see Chapter 4).

The Head of P3O must be careful to maintain a stable environment of incremental improvements with periodic change rather than constantly changing the scope or approach to the functions and services provided.

In an immature P3O model the services and functions offered are often limited to data gathering, reflecting one or more of the following factors:

- Lack of senior management sponsor/support to the P3O model
- Limited funding available
- Lack of competency of P3O team members
- Lack of competency of programme or project managers or business change managers
- Lack of commitment of business owners or senior management into the need for project, programme or portfolio management discipline
- Low level of understanding of the senior management role in sponsoring business change
- Lack of appetite on the part of senior managers for decision support information.

In a mature P3O model, individuals will possess the competencies to offer a wider range of functions/services and be capable of challenging and using the data gathered to inform decision-making. Functions and services will standardize information to aid roll-up and consolidation, enabling portfolio reporting, analysis and decision-making.

Hints and tips

Where an organization is striving to climb the maturity ladder and rise from maturity level 2 (repeatable) to level 3 (defined), a P3O is essential to provide the following:

- **Common language** – providing consistent definitions and usage of P3RM related terms, to avoid confusion or misrepresentation
- **Information management** – providing a central hub for the collection, analysis and amalgamation of information on a highlight and exception basis for all programmes and projects within the portfolio or about a specific programme or project
- **Organizational focus** – providing a central point of function and service ownership for the development of standards, policies and methods and ensuring they are disseminated, have the commitment of stakeholders, are used appropriately and are continually improved to meet the needs of the different groups. Note that this does not mean that the P3O will own all of the processes (these will be managed by a number of areas) but that the integration of the business processes across the organization is efficient and effective
- **Training, skills and competency development** – ensuring consistency for training, skills and competency development, owning a corporate training strategy for P3RM and providing logistical support to training courses, coaching/mentoring, etc.
- **Centre of Excellence role deployment** – consistency of approach
- **Quality assurance** – organization assurance that programmes and projects have suitable quality plans and measures
- **Tailoring** – providing guidelines and support to the tailoring of methods and standards to different scale, levels of risk and complexity of programme and project delivery
- **Systems and tools** – design, development and operational management of tools and systems (whether manual or automated) to assist implemented functions or services.

The evolution is often linked to the business planning cycle as evolution may require more resources in the form of people or facilities with a subsequent increase in budget. Any increase in budget has to be matched with a similar uplift in the benefits delivered due to the increased maturity.

As the P3O model evolves through levels of maturity from administrative support to developing standards, methods and competent staff, through a tracking and assurance role to an oversight, scrutiny and challenge role, care must be taken that the services the P3O offers and the people within the P3O don't become 'process and templates focused'.

P3O models should provide services to help programme and project communities grow and improve rather than tracking failure by looking for things going wrong and criticizing the programme and project managers for incorrectly completing templates. P3O staff should be reviewing and challenging the content of documents and templates and offering help where data quality is low.

More mature P3O models experience a higher success rate and are more likely to develop into true enterprise service offices, serving the whole organization and all staff involved in change.

P3O models need to be allowed to evolve and mature if they are to add real value to an organization's programme and project management capability and improve returns on investment.

As P3O models mature they are significantly better at promoting effective sponsorship, improving accountability, developing competent staff and demonstrating value. They also gain more acceptance among their stakeholder communities and are able to access more appropriate funding, ensuring their ongoing survival and the subsequent improvement in organizational portfolio, programme and project performance.

How to implement or re-energize a P3O

4

4 How to implement or re-energize a P3O

4.1 PURPOSE OF THIS CHAPTER

Just as the implementation of a project or programme should follow a lifecycle, so should the implementation of a P3O model. After all, it is a change to the organization; there will be a defined budget, expected outcomes and timescale to deliver.

It is recommended that the implementation of the P3O model is run at least as a project but preferably as a programme with appropriate governance; a P3O Sponsor is in place to act as Project Executive or SRO; and an appropriate lifecycle and processes are followed. The nature of the change the P3O model will bring will be widespread, affecting multiple stakeholder groups, requiring changes to business processes and relationships and also requiring a shift in mindset and behaviours. For these reasons it is recommended that the change is run as a programme using MSP principles, processes and products and this chapter reflects that approach.

However, in some organizations programme management may not yet have been adopted or the change may be limited to a simple office set-up in the first instance, in which case the design and implementation of the P3O may be managed as a project. In small organizations where the P3O unit is simply one or two individuals, the P3O implementation may simply be managed as a series of small business changes, being delivered as part of Business as Usual.

Whatever the approach taken, it is important to have a good understanding of the problems you are intending to solve or the opportunities you want to maximize, supported by a vision of the future P3O provision and a time-phased plan to achieve that vision. It is also important to engage effectively with stakeholders, communicate well and keep a focused eye on benefits. So even if the P3O model is being implemented as a project or Business as Usual change, some elements of MSP are well worth incorporating in the approach to be taken, including the Vision Statement, Blueprint, Benefits Realization Management, and Leadership and Stakeholder Engagement.

Chapter 2 discussed understanding the problems to be solved or opportunities to be maximized and how to engage senior management commitment in supporting a new or re-energized P3O. It set the scene for this chapter by defining the 'Identify P3O' process, considering the Business Case, Vision Statement and outline Blueprint for the future P3O provision.

This chapter takes the Business Case and Vision Statement created in Chapter 2 and develops them through the design, planning and delivery processes. It also provides checklists, techniques and processes that may help an organization develop a plan to design and implement a P3O or re-energize an existing one.

These include:

- A P3O implementation lifecycle for establishing/improving capability and the role of the P3O model, based on MSP principles and processes
- How to apply the maturity model P3M3 in understanding the current state of the P3O service provision, the maturity of the organizational environment into which it will deliver and how to set targets to enable establishment and prioritization of the Project Dossier or project deliverables (for start-up, improvement and recovery of underperforming P3O models)
- Guidance on example timeframes for levels of maturity and projects (e.g. P3O start up) within the programme
- An understanding of implementation success factors and key threats to delivery
- Consideration of organizational change issues, including how to engage P3O stakeholders effectively
- The need for ongoing periodic review and lessons learned
- The requirement to integrate with the yearly business planning cycle for a permanent P3O unit such as a Portfolio Office.

Also highlighted are the differences in lifecycles between permanent P3O models and temporary units. The latter are set up to support specific programmes or projects and may only exist for the lifetime of that programme or project. Some Programme Offices that start out as temporary may evolve into Hub Portfolio/Programme Offices taking on the more permanent support requirements of a rolling portfolio of programmes and projects.

> **Note**
>
> The optimal mature P3O model may not be achieved through a single tranche Blueprint: there may need to be multiple tranches of benefit delivery with intermediate Blueprints along the journey to maturity.

4.2 LIFECYCLE TO IMPLEMENT OR RE-ENERGIZE A PERMANENT P3O

Figure 4.1 shows a typical lifecycle for the implementation or re-energizing of a permanent P3O model. As discussed earlier we will be using MSP principles, processes and products in describing this lifecycle. The 'Identify P3O' process in the lifecycle in Figure 4.1 is covered in Chapter 2 – Why Have a P3O? It covers the need to understand what your existing P3O provides, if anything, and defines the future P3O through a Vision Statement and outline Blueprint. It also provides guidance in developing a Business Case to justify the investment in the P3O and provide an ongoing reference point for the value it will add to the organization.

This chapter describes the remainder of the P3O lifecycle, once the outline Business Case has been approved, from the design of the Blueprint through to closure and evaluation.

The Definition of the programme (or project) to implement a permanent P3O model requires careful planning to design the future-state P3O Blueprint and develop governance strategies to ensure that it continues to align with strategic objectives.

4.3 DEFINITION

The key activities within Definition are as follows:

1   **Team** – establish the team
2   **Vision** – refine the Vision Statement
3   **Stakeholder** – develop Stakeholder Analysis, Stakeholder Engagement Strategy and Communication Plan
4   **Blueprint** – develop the P3O Blueprint
5   **Benefits** – develop Business Case, Benefits Profiles and Benefits Management Strategy
6   **Risk** – develop Risk Register and Risk Management Strategy

Hints and tips

■ These activities are not sequential and may happen in parallel with each other
■ All Definition activities are scalable: for a small organization or small P3O operation, the approach should be tailored to suit local need and available resources.

4.3.1 Definition activity 1 – Establish the team

It is critical that the right mix of capabilities are in place or accessible for the team to ensure that a pragmatic P3O model is defined and implemented. Fundamentally, a core team with capabilities in strategic and business analysis, portfolio, programme and project management is required, with the associated specialist knowledge around processes and principles.

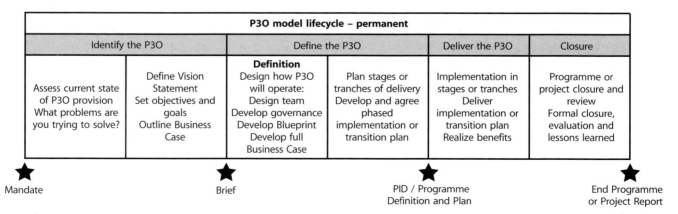

Figure 4.1 Permanent P3O lifecycle

The members of the team set up to establish or transform the P3O model may also be the individuals who will form the core team working within the model going forward, or may be a mix of long-term staff and interim resources.

Scaling hints and tips

In a small organization, or where the P3O unit may consist of one or two people, there may not be a formal implementation team. However, it is important that the individuals who will operate the P3O are given appropriate support, coaching or training, including interim external support, to enable them to be effective in implementing the new P3O functions and services. Also find out who else in your organization has complementary or similar skills and competencies and work closely with them to develop collaborative working.

The following checklist provides a guide as to the additional skills and competencies that may be required:

- **Process:**
  - Portfolio, programme and project planning and scheduling
  - Financial management
  - Enterprise Architecture processes and principles
  - Portfolio management
  - Governance design and implementation
  - Procurement
  - Contract and supplier management
  - Strategic management
  - Portfolio, programme and project assurance
  - Requirements management
  - Benefits management
- **Organizational:**
  - Organizational design
  - Roles and responsibilities development
  - Organizational change management
  - Training
  - Mentoring
- **Technology:**
  - PPM software installation, configuration and training
  - Project scheduling software
  - Spreadsheet and database design and development
  - Knowledge management systems
  - Web portal development

- **Information:**
  - Performance Management
  - Management reporting
  - Governance secretariat
  - Information and knowledge management
  - Enterprise Architecture modelling
  - Strategic planning.

In terms of identifying potential candidates and appointing roles, it is important to mix those with knowledge of the organization's current practices and culture, where these are in place, with specialist skills to ensure that a balance of new and current ways of working is available to the P3O programme.

Where the P3O model cannot be developed by internal staff, either owing to lack of the right skills and competencies or because resources are unavailable, it will be necessary to buy in external expertise to fast-track the programme or project through the Blueprint design and into implementation. When engaging external consultants or contractors, ensure they will work together as a coherent team, with complementary skills and experience. An early deliverable should be the engagement or appointment of the permanent Head of P3O, so a skills transfer can take place from the external supplier and the Head of P3O can have input into the design of the P3O Blueprint from an early stage.

The use of Expert Reference Groups or focus groups (both internal and external) is strongly recommended as it enables input across the multiple specialist areas of knowledge required within the scope of a P3O.

4.3.2 Definition activity 2 – Refine the Vision Statement

Ensure that the outline Vision Statement developed to start the P3O change programme (see Chapter 2, Figure 2.3 for an example Vision Statement) is refined to include a high-level view of the outcomes that will be achieved across process, organizational, technology and information areas once the programme is completed. This will be critical as a marketing tool to communicate the goals of the programme across the wider organization and build momentum, as a significant number of staff may be impacted.

4.3.3 Definition activity 3 – Stakeholder analysis, engagement and communications planning

As with any change programme that affects multiple stakeholders, it is essential to understand who the members of the stakeholder community are, who will be affected or impacted by the changes, who will be 'winners' and who may be 'losers'. Thus:

- Carry out a Stakeholder Analysis of all those involved in or impacted by the P3O model development or improvement programme. These will include senior managers, business unit managers, programme and project management delivery community, P3O model staff (old and new), external suppliers and business process owners of linked units

- A key success factor is to enthuse a champion (P3O Sponsor) – a senior manager with authority, influence and charisma who can sell the P3O vision and engage commitment across the organization at all levels, particularly at senior manager level, as well as obtaining investment funds

- Develop an effective communication plan to educate stakeholders of the value of the P3O, make them aware of the services the P3O will or does offer and engage their commitment and enthusiasm for the new world that will follow the P3O model roll-out. However, do not underestimate the amount of resistance likely to be encountered. The P3RM community who deliver change are often the most resistant to change themselves

- Do not just communicate what is being done (or could be done): develop a marketing plan for the P3O, develop a 'brand' and a slogan or strapline, use 'selling tactics', advertise successes (using facts and numbers), use case studies, leaflets, posters and desk drops to announce what the P3O does and has achieved. Use all available media, particularly intranets, portals, internal newspapers and team briefings to get the message across

- Finally, don't just communicate once – use regular Programme/Project Management Forums to share lessons learned, coach people in new approaches, tools and techniques and make the P3O the first port of call when an issue arises.

Scaling hints and tips

Even small P3O units with one or two people need to understand their stakeholders, whom they serve, whom they work with and whom they impact upon. Does the organization understand what you do? Do they recognize your successes? If you don't tell them, they won't know. Raise your profile and develop a clear understanding of your stakeholder community: you might be surprised where future support may come from. However, be aware of the consequences. One organization successfully marketed itself across a new division and was overwhelmed by the response and increased requests for help – this led to bringing in temporary staff for the short term while a formal Business Case was developed to plan for future expansion of the unit.

4.3.4 Definition activity 4 – Develop the P3O Blueprint

The key to designing a quality P3O Blueprint is understanding what organizational issues need addressing and why portfolios, programmes or projects are failing to deliver the right outputs and outcomes in a timely manner.

The Portfolio, Programme and Project Management Maturity Model (P3M3 – see Figure 4.2) provides a meaningful way to understand the underlying issues and to assess and document the current state of the organization in relation to portfolio, programme and project management. It also provides guidance in terms of the specific outcomes that an organization may wish to achieve to improve capability maturity led by the P3O staff.

It is also important to understand the maturity levels of the environment in which the P3O model will be operating, in order to build a robust implementation or transition plan with tranches of delivery. For example, there is no point in designing a P3O model underpinned by tools to automate processes if the organization is at level-1 maturity and does not have a basic understanding of the key processes.

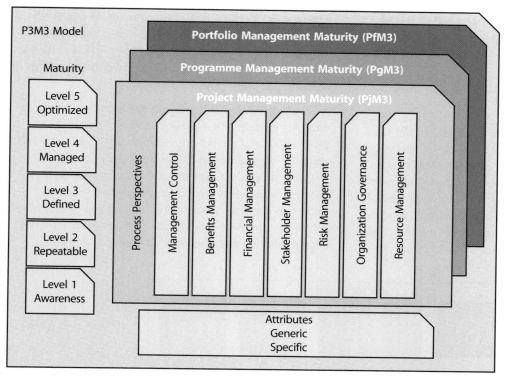

Figure 4.2   Overview of P3M3 model

Remember that not all organizations will be reaching for level-5 maturity; it is important to set a realistic level of maturity and the associated outcomes based on a fit-for-purpose approach.

It is also important to understand the P3O's role in the issues raised concerning any failure to deliver and its role in the ultimate success of portfolios, programmes and projects. This involves reviewing the current P3O status: what functions, if any, are performed; who is supported by current P3O practices; what are the current organizational skill sets; and are there any cultural barriers in place such as credibility issues. It is essential to understand who values the P3O services, who does not, and why. This is covered in more detail in Chapter 2.

It also involves understanding and critically reviewing how 'best of breed' P3O models are operating in similar industries or sectors.

The Blueprint will describe the future state of the P3O model, either to be met in a single tranche of delivery or through multiple tranches. It should include sections on:

1   Processes

2   Organization

3   Tools and technologies

4   Information flows

5   Operational costs and performance levels.

Blueprint section 1 – Processes

Define and agree which functions and services will be required to address the issues you are facing and to meet future expectations of the P3O model. Appendix F provides a useful checklist of functions and services focused on the different levels and types of offices within the P3O model. Use the tables in Appendix F as a 'pick and mix' guide to identify which functions and services are required immediately and which may be aspirational for future tranches of delivery as the organization and staff, both within and outside the P3O, mature over time. This helps in developing a phased implementation plan.

In terms of delivering the functions and services, it is important to understand how they will be implemented and operated, i.e. whether a manual process or an automated process/tools approach will be used. This may evolve over time, with an initial manual business process or simple tool approach using spreadsheets eventually evolving into an organization-wide integrated tool.

At this stage it is important to define 'what' functions and services the P3O will contribute to and 'which' functions or services the P3O will own as part of the P3O model. It is not important to define 'how'.

Consider using pictures, process models or swimlanes to demonstrate processes, interfaces, roles and responsibilities. You are more likely to gain the attention of senior managers and other users of the P3O model if the key processes within the P3O model can be described in a single A4 picture.

Blueprint section 2 – Organization

Governance

The underlying goal in establishing the P3O model is to bring structure to decision-making and business change practices across an organization, with clear line of sight from strategic goals down to local change decisions and working practices. It is important to note that practices will already be in place within the organization, which may not be structured to deliver optimum value to the organization.

In designing the P3O, a key outcome will be a joined-up governance model that enables a clear strategic understanding of priorities, progress, key risks and issues, thereby enabling confident decision-making with points of accountability at all levels.

A simple technique to determine the future governance model is to start with a generic model of portfolio, programme and project organization (see Figure 4.3) and align the organization to these roles and responsibilities. It is also important to understand the organization's business governance structures and decision-making bodies, as decisions made within the change environment will impact on Business as Usual. The governance model should describe who makes what decisions and when,

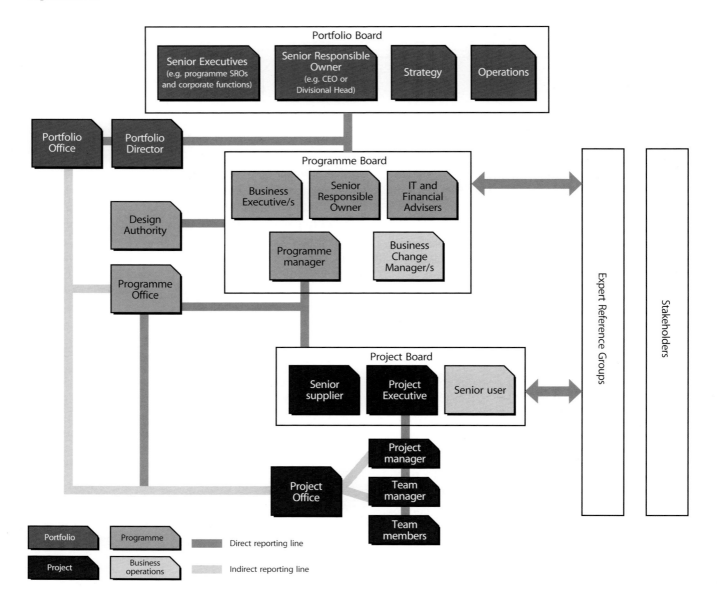

Figure 4.3 Generic portfolio, programme, project and P3O model organization, consisting of the Portfolio Office, Programme Office(s) and Project Office(s)

who may be impacted by those decisions and what the rules for delegation of authority and escalation of risks, issues and changes will be. This will help define the P3O stakeholder community, provide the basis for a communications plan and provide points of reference and formal accountability when issues arise within the portfolio, programme or project governance structures.

Once the conceptual governance model is developed and agreed within the P3O Blueprint, then it is more easily subsequently translated into a functional model (i.e. giving names or positions to governance structures and accountabilities). The component offices of the P3O model should sit within the overall organization governance model.

P3O model organization, roles and sizing

Once it is agreed where the component offices of the P3O model will sit, where they will report and whom they will serve in terms of customers, the P3O model itself should be designed in terms of reporting lines, centralized versus decentralized reporting, roles and responsibilities.

The functions and services that are owned by the P3O model, or that the P3O contributes to at portfolio, programme or project level, will drive the role types, the organizational components and the number of staff required to operate the P3O services and functions.

When building the P3O staffing plan, first define the staff skills profiles, assess the current staff (if a P3O exists) or the staff that are available, and define an action or development plan to fill any gaps. Consider options for training, mentoring or coaching for existing or new staff. Buy in short-term help to fast-track the set-up stage.

Finally, don't neglect relevant qualifications for staff within the P3O model, to give credibility to the people and the services they provide. In addition:

- For an in-depth look at P3O models, sizing, services and functions and the roles/responsibilities within them, see Chapter 3
- For roles and responsibilities, see Appendix A
- For case studies, and for example P3O models that may be appropriate for tailoring to your organization, see Appendix C
- For an in-depth look at services and functions and how they are implemented in different levels of the P3O model, see Appendix F.

Organizational relationships

The P3O model will require commitment from other parts of the organization to undertake parts of processes, comply with policies and standards, and potentially integrate their processes with the P3O.

It is important that any changes to current practices within other parts of the organization as a result of developing or enhancing a P3O model are documented and agreed.

Determine who will be the business process owners and who will be the contributor to the business processes. The P3O may be either, but it is necessary to be clear as to which. See section 3.5 for further information on integrating with other business units.

Culture

It is important to document and agree the type of P3O culture that the organization should strive for in developing the P3O Blueprint. Some characteristics that may be required for an effective P3O model include:

- Information sharing
- Focuses on learning rather than blame
- Value focus to all activities
- Innovative
- Service focused
- Proactive analysis rather than data collection
- Pragmatic approach, flexing where appropriate
- Facilitates rather than directs
- Manages to objectives
- Believes in continuous improvement through lessons learned.

It is also important to understand the organization culture into which the P3O model will be delivering and adapt the approach and communications to suit that culture.

Case study

A government agency already had in place several programmes, which had evolved local processes over time. The agency decided to set up an Organization Portfolio Office to provide overall portfolio-level support and encourage consistency in the way the programmes were managed and controlled.

Taking account of the current culture meant that the Portfolio Office did not impose strict new processes and templates on the Programme Offices from day 1, but allowed them to continue in much the same way as before while setting out a series of minimum principles with mandated elements for investment proposals, Business Cases and reporting. All mandated elements were those necessary to allow ease of roll-up of information and presentation of that information to the Agency Investment Group by the Portfolio Office.

Moving towards a culture where all processes and templates were consistent was achieved over time by setting up a working group of all Programme Office representatives and selecting the best from across all programmes. Because the programme staff felt they were creating their own solution rather than the Portfolio Office imposing it on them, acceptance and adherence was high.

Blueprint section 3 – Tools and Technologies

Types

The tools and technologies that support the P3O business processes and information flows may be as simple as documents, forms, spreadsheets and databases, or much more sophisticated. It is important to note that tools and technologies should not necessarily be limited to schedule management or planning-and-control-related software. Consideration should also be given to the level of integration to limit or remove data duplication at the project or programme manager and team levels.

Chapter 5 gives examples of tools and technologies that should be considered when developing the Blueprint.

Organizational Maturity

It is critical to match the P3RM capability maturity of the organization with the sophistication of the tools and technologies to be employed in achieving pragmatic solutions.

In relation to supporting organizational capability maturity improvements with P3RM tools, the guide shown in Figure 4.4 provides a list of P3M3 attributes across each perspective where P3RM tools may support achievement of the overall capability across portfolio, programme and project management.

It is important to note that this list is not exhaustive, but may be used to derive specific requirements for the organization.

P3M3 perspectives

P3M3-specific attributes supported by P3RM tools

Management Control

- Lifecycle control
- Gates, stages and tranches
- Change control
- Issue control and management
- Progress monitoring
- Clarity of end state
- Interventions and redirection
- Configuration Management

Benefits Management

- Benefits management process and workflow management
- Benefits management information and Benefits Realization Plans
- Benefits profiling, categorization, ownership and measurement
- Management of benefits realization activities
- Business Change Management
- Business Performance Management

Stakeholder Management

- Stakeholder identification and analysis
- Structured engagement cycles
- Regular and effective communications
- Sophistication in the use of channels and message delivery
- Processing and actioning feedback

Organizational Governance

- Initiative optimization
- Strategic alignment of initiatives
- Governance process and workflow management
- Existence of control boards
- Approvals and authorization
- Control and reporting structures
- Legislative compliance
- Compliance and integration with corporate standards
- Assurance for project and programme compliance
- Alignment between PPM and organizational hierarchy

Financial Management

- Financial reporting and monitoring
- Integration to business planning cycle
- Actual budget and forecast P3RM expenditure
- Staged funding release
- Financial tolerances setting process
- Financial management information on costs and benefits
- Investment management process and workflow management
- Project proposal management, financial appraisal and business cases

Risk Management

- Enterprise-level visibility of risk exposure due to P3RM
- Tracking of resource and budgetary implications of risks
- Risk categorization, assessment and audit
- Risk Registers, tracking and management
- Risk management process and workflow management

Resource Management

- Resource optimization of resources across initiatives
- Resource-management process and workflow management
- Capacity and capability building
- Supply chain management
- Resource monitoring, estimation and forecasting of utilization
- Utilization and efficiency
- Integration of operational and P3RM needs

Figure 4.4 Aligning P3M3 attributes with P3RM tool capabilities

Blueprint section 4 – Information flows

It is important to document the proposed reporting requirements for the future-state P3O model. This will need to integrate with the organizational component of the Blueprint and align to the requirements of:

- Governance groups, e.g. Senior Management Board, Divisional Boards, Programme and Project Boards, steering groups
- Components within the P3O model (e.g. between Portfolio, Programme and Project Offices)
- Programme and project delivery groups
- Corporate support functions, e.g. finance, audit, quality, procurement, marketing and communications
- Benefit owners
- External (if required).

The Blueprint should also describe the need for alignment to the principle of management by exception and the use of highlight and exception-based reporting. At this stage, the detailed contents of these reports is not required, but will be detailed in the subsequent initiatives to deliver the capability. However, a high-level overview of the content of Management Dashboards will add value and commitment.

An example of an information flow for a P3O model is shown in Table 4.1.

Case study

A European public sector organization launched a multimillion-euro project, which was more than 70% financed from European restructuring funds. The reporting requirements were extensive, with more than 10 different reports plus 70 other documents for different institutions – including 2 central government institutions – each month. Each report had to adhere to a strictly defined format, containing various items of information, including extensive financial data. The reports were so complex that the project team designated a separate person to prepare each of them. The designated report owner was also responsible for data gathering from five different team managers, report preparation and report distribution.

Soon, problems occurred. Team managers were tired of giving practically the same information to different people. Reports prepared by different people, based on information collected at different times, tended to be incoherent and the lack of joined-up timing meant that there was no single consistent view of progress. The source information was incorrect or inadequate, as team managers tended to give it just to get rid of the people asking for it. As a result, some of the reports were rejected, causing financial problems for the project – payment tranches were suspended.

An external consultant was brought in to examine the issues and propose a solution. The conclusion, agreed across the project team, was to use PRINCE2 reporting formats and processes, supported by the introduction of a Project Office to manage reporting.

Each team manager was obliged to prepare monthly Checkpoint Reports in a predefined format (containing all the necessary information to feed the multiple stakeholder reports). Those reports were collected by one person who, using simple IT tools, was able to transfer and amalgamate this information into reports in the formats required by the different institutions.

The benefits of this were clear:

- Less cost – one person instead of ten
- Better team morale – especially among team managers
- Reports contained accurate and coherent information from a single source, aligned to a single point in time
- Subsequent payment tranches are executed without delay.

Table 4.1 Example P3O information flow

ID	Report name	Accountability	Report recipient	Meeting and report frequency
Portfolio level				
1	Portfolio Report – Management Dashboard with supporting papers, including benefits reviews	Portfolio Director or Portfolio Office manager	Senior management	Monthly
2	Portfolio Risk and Issue Papers, for resolving portfolio conflicts across the business units, and specifying significant assurance-related risks or issues for programmes and projects	Portfolio Director or Portfolio Office manager with contributions from business units, programmes and projects as required	Senior management	By exception
3	Escalated Project and Programme Risk and Issue Papers	Project and Programme Boards	Senior management (tabled through Portfolio Director)	By exception
4	Mission Critical Business Cases	Senior Responsible Owners	Portfolio Board	As required
5	Operational Business Plans (describing core and changes to core business)	Business Unit Managers	Strategy group P3O	Annually or as necessary
Programme level				
6	Business Unit Portfolio Report – Management Dashboard and supporting papers	Hub (divisional, department or business unit) Programme Office	Business unit senior manager P3O	Monthly
7	Escalated Project and Programme Risk and Issue papers	Project and Programme Boards	Business unit senior manager	By exception
8	Business unit Portfolio Risk and Issue Papers, for resolving portfolio conflicts within the business unit, and specifying significant assurance-related risks or issues for programmes and projects within the business unit	Business unit Programme Office with contributions from Project and Programme Boards	Business units senior manager P3O	By exception
9	Benefit Reviews	Business change managers	Business unit senior manager	As documented in Benefits Management Strategy

(continued)

Table 4.1 Example P3O information flow (continued)

ID	Report name	Accountability	Report recipient	Meeting and report frequency
Project level				
10	Project Mandates	Idea generator	P3O	As required
11	Project Business Case	Project manager	Project Executive P3O	On acceptance of Project Mandate into approved programme or portfolio
12	Highlight and Exception Reports	Project manager	Project Executive P3O	Highlight Reports may be monthly or fortnightly on acceptance of Project Business Case
13	End Project Report	Project manager	Project Executive P3O	On agreed completion of the project
14	Post-Project Report	Project Executive or nominated Business Owner	Business Unit Manager P3O	Defined time after project completed when benefits and original Business Case investment can be assessed
15	Risk and Issues	Project manager	Project Executive	As required
Transition Management				
16	Benefit Profiles	Business Case generator or business change manager	Business Unit Programme Office P3O	In parallel with Business Case and updated periodically
17	Transition Plan	Programme or project manager, with contribution by senior user or business change manager	Project Executive P3O	When approaching readiness for implementation of business change

Blueprint section 5 – Operational costs and performance levels

It is important to design and implement P3O metrics or performance indicators to measure how successful the P3O model has been and show improvement over time, linked to specific service improvements – these are necessary to maintain continued support for the P3O and justify the investment in its set-up and ongoing operation. Keep the performance measures simple or no one will bother to collect or maintain them. Ensure they justify the ongoing existence of the P3O model.

Some general success measures that may be used to determine the effectiveness of the P3O model over time are:

■ **Number of programmes and projects delivered to plan** – measuring the effectiveness of the P3O model in providing decision support and achieving plans

■ **Number of programmes and projects rejected, deferred, re-scoped and cancelled by stage** – measuring the effectiveness of governance in ensuring that poor business change investments are stopped in a timely manner

■ **Average programme and project delivery timescales** – measuring the effectiveness of the P3O model in increasing throughput by reducing average programme and project lifecycles and improving predictability of delivery timescales

■ **Variance between budget and actual total investment in P3RM and total benefits realized** – measuring the outcomes of the P3O model in facilitating programme and project delivery and ensuring there is a focus on measuring and realizing benefits

- **Cost of risk mitigation against level of residual risk (risk treatment)** – measuring the effectiveness of risk response actions against the reduction in inherent risk of the portfolio
- **Audits of level of compliance to processes** – measuring the effectiveness of the P3O model in having fit-for-purpose approaches that are used by the programme and project community
- **Number of programmes and projects delivering non-red Gateway Reviews (UK government)** – measuring the reduction in red Gateway assessments, including reduction in the number of red specific recommendations in the action plan and Delivery Confidence Assessments
- **Staff turnover** – measuring staff morale and individual's alignment to the P3O model. Exit interviews can also be used to supplement this success measure
- **Staff development** – measuring spend on staff to improve the P3O model, level of qualifications across the resource pool and metrics on matching skills to programmes and projects (both within the P3O model and the programme and project delivery resource pool)
- **Stakeholder surveys** – measuring objectively the level of stakeholder satisfaction in the operation of the P3O model – is it delivering the services its customers want and need, and is it perceived to offer value for money?
- **P3M3 capability maturity model assessment** – evaluating the change in organizational maturity in portfolio, programme and project management as a result of investment in the P3O model over time
- **Post-programme and project reviews/health checks** – measuring the compliance of programmes and projects to the programme and project management frameworks, strategies and policies and the achievement of planned business benefits.

Scaling hints and tips

As a small P3O unit you may feel that setting up performance measures is not a good use of your time. However, consider using performance measures to justify your existence or your future growth plans. Demonstrating value and attributing it to your team's actions is the best way of justifying increased investment. Also consider using some of these performance measures within your own personal objectives to focus attention on your achievements.

4.3.5 Definition activity 5 – Refine Business Case, develop Benefits Profiles and Benefits Management Strategy

The development of the Business Case is covered in Chapter 2 and an example in provided in Appendix B. At this stage in the lifecycle the Business Case should be revisited and refined as a result of further information and further development of requirements.

Develop a Benefits Management Strategy, Outcome Relationship Model and Benefits Profiles as defined in MSP. Even if you are using a project approach (or a series of business process changes being made as part of Business as Usual) to implement the new or re-energized P3O model, it is essential to focus on the benefits the P3O will deliver and formally track these over time, so take time out to understand and adopt these MSP processes and products.

In creating Benefit Profiles and developing the Benefits Management Strategy, there are significant opportunities to generate commitment and support for the P3O concept and value to the organization. Once the business change areas are understood, undertake a series of workshops to determine the initial, interim and final outcomes to be achieved by progressive transition to the P3O model. This can then be used as an input to determining the planned benefits as a result of the new capabilities delivered.

By spelling out the benefits users will get, they may become champions and can be used to influence stakeholders across the organization. However, care must be taken in recognizing that some current users or current P3O staff may not benefit from the new or revised model and therefore may resist the change.

Some of the benefit drivers (translatable into Benefits Profiles) that a P3O may provide are:

■ **Improved cost savings** – delivering the same capabilities with less business change investment

■ **Improved cost avoidance** – reducing the investment in outputs that do not lead to planned business benefits, and stopping such projects or programmes either before they get off the ground or while they are under way

■ **Increased strategic alignment** – reducing investment in programmes and projects that only provide tactical value to the business goals of the organization

■ **Increased programme and project throughput** – delivering more change through programmes and projects with the same investment

■ **Optimization of benefits** – delivering more business benefits with the same business change investment or, by effectively monitoring and measuring benefits, ensuring Business as Usual puts the effort in to achieving them

■ **Improved portfolio management** – optimizing investment as the portfolio delivers due to improved visibility, decision support and control

■ **Reduction in threats to the organization** – stronger alignment between planned and actual business change investment as a result of reduced expenditure on mitigation of threats, or issue resolution

■ **Maximization of opportunities** – achieving higher returns on investment in business change as a result of identifying opportunities for additional benefits as new capabilities are delivered

■ **More effective use of resources** – less non-productive time for resources and/or reduction in the reliance on external resources in the delivery of new capabilities.

4.3.6 Definition activity 6 – Develop a Risk Management Strategy and Risk Register

It is necessary to develop a Risk Management Strategy for risk identification and consolidation, a Risk Register for the P3O establishment or enhancement programme and a Risk Management Policy for the communication of risk management.

The following are common key areas identified as the most likely sources of threats to the achievement of the Blueprint for the P3O:

■ Lack of continued senior management commitment – success relies on the continued visible support and commitment of investment and required business resources by senior management. Any reduction in the level of commitment will negatively impact the implementation of the successful P3O

> **Hints and tips**
>
> ■ Do not proceed if there is no senior management consensus as to the P3O vision
> ■ Regularly confirm planned benefits of the P3O model and report performance to these goals
> ■ Manage senior management as key stakeholders to programme success.

■ **Resistance to change by impacted staff** – the P3O model will deliver new and consistent processes with goals of improving productivity and eliminating investment in pet projects. Individual project managers could also feel that they will lose control of their projects as a result of this centralized approach. This may result in resistance to change by impacted staff

> **Hints and tips**
>
> Alert the P3O Sponsor to the risk of staff resistance to change as early as possible so they are able to take proactive measures at a senior level to reduce resistance to change, or are prepared to take action when faced with resistance.

■ **Lack of common language amongst programme team or impacted staff** – given the multitude of approaches to portfolio, programme and project management, stakeholders may have difficulty understanding the different terms used in establishing the P3O model, which may impact on the quality of outputs or lead to resistance to change

> **Hints and tips**
>
> Agree alignment to global standards (such as PRINCE2, MSP, P3M3 and ITIL), provide awareness training and adopt a common glossary to ensure that all staff are at the same level of understanding.

■ **Managing the implementation of the P3O model as a project** – managing the implementation of the P3O model as a project may not recognize the complexity associated with this business change and may leave the integration across the organization to the Head of P3O, significantly reducing the potential for success. The delivery of the P3O model and realization of its planned business benefits is a complex business change programme that requires iterative refinement of the capabilities to be delivered and associated activities. It also impacts upon numerous business units and business change principles across the organization

Hints and tips

Build consensus around the concept of the P3O model across the organization in advance of any activity.

■ **Overly focusing on toolsets** – significant benefits can be achieved by the adoption of P3RM solutions (and other software applications) to provide process automation and improved visibility and control. Implementing sophisticated tools in an immature organization or implementing tools that need a significant investment in time and money to embed into the organization can severely impact the successful delivery of programmes and projects

Hints and tips

■ Investigate existing common tools across programme and project delivery staff (e.g. spreadsheets or Microsoft Project) and investigate a solution that builds on this to reduce the investment in embedding new tools and allows for functionality to be added over time as capability matures
■ Equally, recognize when to move off manual approaches and achieve the benefits of process automation through toolsets at the appropriate level of capability maturity.

■ **Overly focusing on processes and templates** – The introduction of portfolio, programme and project management processes and their associated principles at a detailed process level may focus programme and project delivery staff on process compliance rather than the achievement of business outcomes. Some P3Os get a bad reputation as the 'template office', focusing on the use of the right form rather than the quality of the information gathered, and are seen as an additional burden rather than a source of help

Hints and tips

Focus on communicating 'process principles' rather than 'processes' (supported by appropriate training in portfolio, programme and project management) to assist staff in balancing what is required to achieve governance (e.g. gating), decision support (e.g. project or programme status reporting) and transition to new ways of working. Develop tailoring guidelines to allow the programme and project delivery community to flex processes based on the levels of risk, complexity and size of programmes and projects and develop minimum mandatory compliance to key governance principles.

■ **Initial lack of quality of portfolio or programme information** – when moving to a higher level of amalgamated information, there needs to be an acceptable level of project standardization or commonality. Generally, moving from an unstructured to a structured P3O model will mean that when information is initially brought together for amalgamated reporting, it is of poor quality or missing

Hints and tips

Ensure that data quality improvement or alignment activities are included in the transition plan to introduce amalgamated reporting.

■ **Lack of capacity of impacted staff to absorb change** – as project management and programme management methods focus on numerous principles as well as processes, implementing all at once, or rolling out a toolset in one implementation, can fail because of the inability of impacted staff to understand and comply with new ways of working

- **Physical P3O becomes de-facto owner of business change** – this is especially relevant where the P3O owns delivery resources (such as project managers or business analysts) that are then provided to the business, combined with weak governance arrangements. Essentially, where the P3O may be providing more efficient resource allocation of skills and competencies across programmes and projects by maintaining a resource pool, the P3O is subsequently blamed for failing to deliver outputs or outcomes or attain benefits realization goals, i.e. they take on an implicit ownership of the business change outcomes.

4.4 PLAN STAGES OR TRANCHES OF DELIVERY

Around half the P3Os created are restructured or closed down with a 2-year time frame. Accordingly, it is important to adopt an incremental approach to reduce the adverse impacts of a 'big bang' implementation and to demonstrate benefits to senior management from the investment. Early benefits can also be used to fund later tranches of delivery, so the P3O evolution becomes self-financing.

Each P3O model implementation or improvement will have its own unique combination and phasing of initiatives to achieve the future-state business model (as defined in the Blueprint). As stated previously, the priority associated with these should be driven by the largest capability gaps identified through a P3M3 assessment and what matters most to senior management.

Design the implementation or improvement plan so that the first tranche of delivery contains early critical improvement. Go for early benefits that achieve demonstrable improvements, and consider those deliverables that are simple to implement and instantly create senior management visibility and credibility. For example, create a Portfolio Register – a list of all programmes and projects being undertaken by the organization, their link to strategy, value, key stakeholders and delivery timeframe. For the first time the senior management team will bee able to see all change in the organization, and it often comes as a shock.

Following on from that, carry out a rationalization exercise to identify duplications of effort or initiatives that may be counter-productive. Add exception-based reporting through a Management Dashboard to the portfolio toolkit, and senior managers will buy into your value and continued existence. The investment cash released by stopping projects that should never have started in the first place will provide funding for the subsequent tranches of P3O service roll-out.

The Project Dossier for a P3O programme to improve capability maturity may include the design and establishment of specialist products for:

- Organization governance model for business change
- Business planning or strategy translation framework
- Physical P3O units (including functions and services)
- Existing programme and project portfolio identification and optimization
- P3O metrics and reporting
- Project and programme gating model and framework
- Project and programme delivery model and framework
- Portfolio Management Model and Framework
- Management metrics and amalgamated (highlight and exception) reporting model and framework
- Competency management and career management model and framework
- Requirements management model and framework
- Supplier management model and framework
- Functional models and frameworks (such as Risk, Benefits, Configuration, Quality and Financial Management)
- Training, coaching and mentoring model
- COE community model – sharing best practice and lessons learned
- Toolset/s implementation/s
- Assurance model
- Continual improvement model.

Scaling hints and tips

■ For a small P3O unit consider a 3-year phased performance improvement plan with single deliverables rather than tranches of change

■ Rather than delivering full processes and templates, consider setting principles and minimum mandated standards that are pragmatic and can be tailored.

By way of example, Figure 4.5 provides an outline plan based on this Project Dossier for an Organization Portfolio Office type of P3O. Operating in the private sector, it has a baseline level of capability maturity above 1 and is targeting an improvement towards level 3.

Key sensitivities that may impact on the development of your own Project Dossier include:

■ Existing capability maturity and targets
■ Priorities for capability development
■ Ability to embed change as a result of the culture of an organization, or other business changes impacting on staff
■ Functions and services to be embedded as a result of the P3O added value
■ Pace of change requirements
■ Resource capacity
■ Management commitment
■ Scale of the portfolio
■ Level of need to achieve early benefits to secure continued momentum
■ Risks to delivery and planned benefits.

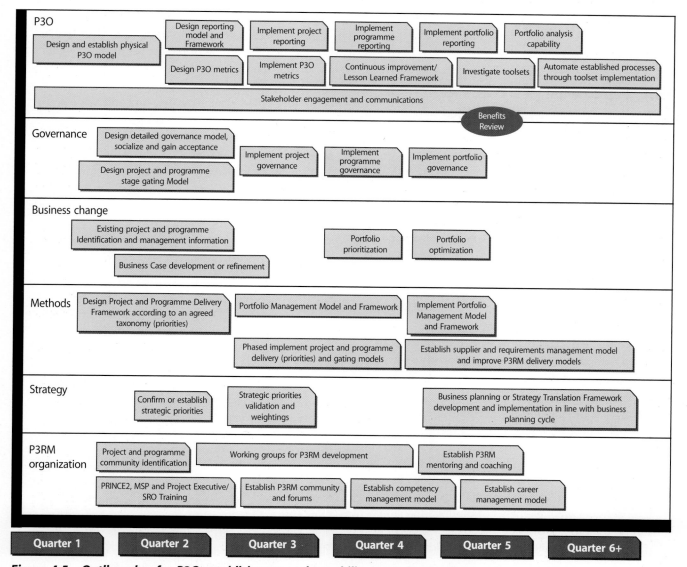

Figure 4.5   Outline plan for P3O establishment and capability maturity development programme

Note that all elements of the Blueprint are implicit in this plan, i.e. process, organization, tools and technologies, information flow and performance.

This plan is also based on achieving early benefits in terms of providing visibility as to the business change initiatives being undertaken across the organization and justifying their continued investment through Business Case development or refinement. Equally, early benefits are achieved through PRINCE2, MSP and senior management training (or similar methods) to provide improved potential for successful delivery.

4.5 IMPLEMENTATION OR TRANSITION OF NEW OR ENHANCED P3O CAPABILITY

When implementing services or functions, consider the detailed activities for each service or function as defined in Appendix F: Functions and services.

When implementing tools and techniques, consider detailed approaches and considerations as detailed in Chapter 5.

4.5.1 Implementation success factors

The following points should be considered when defining implementation success factors:

■ Consider how tranches can be grouped, for example into three-month blocks of design and implementation. The subsequent three months can be spent embedding and building organizational capability in the new ways of working whilst the next three-month tranche is being designed and implemented. This illustrates a key MSP principle by demonstrating early value

■ Ensure that a common glossary is used by all design and implementation projects to ensure that a common language is being used

■ Ensure that a Stakeholder Analysis is done early and that a communications plan is developed to ensure consistent messages are being given to all impacted stakeholders

■ Project and programme delivery frameworks are generally delivered before portfolio management frameworks, as it is often necessary to get a level of project standardization in place to roll up quality decision-support information to the portfolio level. However, if portfolio management is a key priority then consider what elements of portfolio management can be established without the building blocks of good programme and project information flowing up

■ Obtaining a baseline view of the current portfolio is a key enabler to the majority of subsequent projects to enable visibility and determine the scale of the challenge and should be undertaken early. Although this information will generally be of poor quality, it will assist in determining gaps for subsequent activity

■ Consider how a 'proof of concept' or a 'pilot' approach can be applied before full implementation, to maximize the likelihood of success; this may involve:
  ● Trialling new ways of working on a project or sub-set of the portfolio
  ● Running practices such as revised reporting in parallel to current approaches until confidence is achieved in the quality of the decision support information
  ● Focusing efforts where the most gains are to be made, e.g. top 20 projects

■ Look for examples of good practice (or pockets of excellence) operating within the organization and develop standards around these to roll out further. Use the programme or project teams as champions to roll out their best practice

■ Consider developing manual processes to validate whether they work effectively and add value and then automate them as a subsequent step once the process is proven

■ Bring impacted stakeholders along the capability development journey; train them early in key principles such as PRINCE2 and MSP (or similar methods) and then use that knowledge in working groups for alignment and tailoring.

Scaling hints and tips

Use the pool of programme and project managers as members of your extended team to develop new services and tools. One organization had a small Hub Programme Office with a team of four permanent staff members. The manager of the Programme Office agreed with the Head of Programme and Project Management that each programme and project manager in a team of 25 would provide 25 hours of their time per year to support the Programme Office. This time was recorded and contributed towards their bonus entitlement at the end of the year. The Programme Office manager found herself very popular at year end, with project managers volunteering time to develop tools or run workshops to enable them to hit their personal targets. The project managers also found the time spent with the Programme Office helped them address their own development needs, keep up to date with best practice and improve their skills.

4.6 PERIODIC REVIEWS AND LESSONS LEARNED

As a minimum, at the end of each tranche of delivery, carry out a review of progress to date and the lessons that have been learned. Use these to inform the approach to the next tranche. Use the P3O's Gated Review process to provide governance through a 'go' or 'no go' gate, demonstrating that you believe in and practice your own processes.

4.7 PROGRAMME CLOSURE AND POST-IMPLEMENTATION/BENEFITS REVIEW

The P3O model implementation or improvement programme may have a long-term lifecycle or may enter a period of continual improvement supported by a performance improvement plan.

However, where a specific programme has been developed to set up new P3O capability, formal closure and post-implementation and benefits reviews are to be recommended. This offers an opportunity to move from transition to making the P3O capability 'Business as Usual' and allows time for reflection and review – asking the question, 'Was it worth it?'

External consultants or contractors who were brought in to fast-track the improvement programme may be released and the P3O should ensure that full skills transfer is complete before that happens, otherwise the benefits delivered may disappear over time.

Benefits will be realized throughout the programme to implement the P3O model, not just post-programme. Early benefits can be used to gain commitment to later tranches and cashable benefits can be used to fund later tranches.

4.8 INTEGRATION WITH BUSINESS PLANNING CYCLES

A key input to portfolio planning is to develop a balanced portfolio of programmes and projects with a defined investment budget and balanced set of resources. This should be aligned to Business as Usual priorities and strategic objectives. It therefore makes sense to align the development of P3O capability to the normal organization business planning cycle. In some cases, the P3O may also manage this cycle.

Integrating the P3O with the yearly (or 3- or 5-yearly) business planning cycle also allows for full integration of the P3O model and its benefits into the business budgeting lifecycle. If the P3O model aims to save x%

through stopped projects, then the x% saved should be built into next year's budget for use by other initiatives. This adds impetus to making the planned savings, as the P3O staff will be held to account by senior management.

4.9 THE TEMPORARY P3O LIFECYCLE

Unlike the permanent P3O model described in the previous sections of this chapter, the temporary Programme or Project Office is designed specifically for a finite lifecycle and with a more focused set of stakeholders consisting of:

- Upward – Programme or Project Boards
- Inward – programme or project team members
- Outward – suppliers, permanent Portfolio Office or COE, corporate support functions, etc.

Accordingly, the requirements will be different and varied depending on the size, scale and complexity of the programme or project to be supported.

All programme and project management methods, such as MSP and PRINCE2, will encompass processes and product outlines that delivery support teams such as the temporary Programme or Project Offices will need to follow. These should be referenced in your organization when setting up a temporary Programme or Project Office.

The following sections focus on the key success factors inherent in the definition and set-up, running and closedown of a temporary Programme or Project Office.

4.9.1 Organizational context

As new programmes and projects are launched, temporary Programme or Project Offices may be established to support them at start-up, at delivery and through to closure. Where there is a P3O model in place in the organization with an Organization Portfolio Office or Hub Portfolio/Programme Offices, the temporary office may be resourced from central teams with standards and templates provided by a COE function. In this scenario, the start-up, running and closure of the temporary Programme or Project Office will be a standard function or service provided by the central Portfolio Office team.

Where the organization has a Centre of Excellence but no flexible central pool of delivery support staff, local business resources may be assigned to provide Programme or Project Office functions or they may be sourced from the contract market or through framework partnerships (see Appendix C, Case Study 4 – Retail organization, for a practical example of this). Wherever the resources come from, they should engage with the COE to seek assistance with start-up through facilitated workshops, provision of standard processes and templates, and ongoing assurance or coaching.

In organizations where there is no central Portfolio Office or COE function, the set-up and running of the temporary office will rely on the expertise of the local business team responsible for the programme or project and the maturity of their approach and processes.

4.9.2 Definition and start-up of a temporary office

Design and establish the temporary Programme or Project Office team

A temporary Programme or Project Office may be simply a single person (multi-role, multitasking Programme or Project Officer), or may be resourced with a team of generalists or specialists (see Appendix A for typical roles and responsibilities).

The programme or project team should establish a clear understanding of its stakeholders, the business environment it will be delivering within, the scope it will be delivering and its timescales. This will indicate what type of delivery support skills may be required. Where there are multiple stakeholders with complex communications and reporting requirements, the programme or project may benefit by having a specialist stakeholder and communications role. The programme or project may have complex finance arrangements that may necessitate bringing in a Finance role to act as a programme or project accountant, or it may involve complex supplier contracts or relationships and therefore benefit from bringing in a Commercial role focused on supplier relationships or procurement. Appendix A outlines both generic and specialist functional roles and these should be used to build job descriptions for specific resources within the Programme or Project Office.

The members of the delivery support team may be permanent members of staff drawn from the Portfolio Office or hub or the business unit itself. Specialist functions may be drawn from the Finance, Commercial or Communications/PR departments, bringing with them specialist processes and templates as well as expertise. These specialist roles may be full or part time. Where they are part time, careful negotiation should be undertaken to ensure their time on the team is used to best effect and with the full understanding and commitment of their line manager.

The members of the delivery support team may also be temporary or contract resources, brought in to support the delivery of the programme or project. Do not underestimate or neglect the need to induct these resources both into the organization and into the standards and templates that the COE will provide. Where there are no organization standards, external resources often bring their own from previous assignments; although in the short term this will enable the team to get started quickly, it also leads to inconsistency of approach and lack of organizational learning.

The temporary office will also benefit from an injection of time, expertise and standard approaches from a COE. Internal consultants, tools experts or assurance staff can work with the temporary office to run workshops, establish consistent and tested working practices and collaborative tools and coach any business or external resources in the organization's standard programme and project methods.

Wherever resources are drawn from, and whatever their backgrounds, there will be a requirement for a focused programme or project induction and team building. If a COE exists, it can provide an induction in organization standards and the programme or project manager can deliver a briefing on the scope, timescales, etc. of the programme or project.

A common mistake for the temporary Programme or Project Office is not to consider the planned scale and long-term requirements of the programme or project that it will support. Some programmes or projects start small in terms of resources and over time increase in scale to large numbers. In the early stages, establishing the temporary office with minimal support can significantly impact the programme or project as it struggles to provide support, quality decision-support information and other services. A Programme or Project Office, properly resourced at an early stage, is a key success factor in the start-up and delivery of programmes and projects.

Case study

A multi-year programme to implement improved practices through process optimization and the rationalization of hundreds of legacy systems and interfaces started its lifecycle as a team of five people, identifying the programme and developing outline business requirements. The Programme Office function was undertaken by one person on a part-time basis using an individual scheduling application and manual spreadsheets to track finances. Within a year the team had grown to more than 100 across seven workstreams and the same scheduling methods. Processes no longer represented what was really occurring in the programme, providing senior management with poor decision support on progress. Further, it was taking the equivalent of five full-time equivalents to manage the schedule and the lead time for the report meant that it was out of date by the time it was produced. This impacted implementation timeframes and the cost of the overall programme, as the planning and control processes were never proactively designed to deal with the scale of the programme.

Set up the environment

The Programme or Project Office will need to establish a set of processes to be followed, templates to be used, and ways of working with the rest of the programme or project team and governance board.

It will also have to set up a physical environment, which may range from using existing business facilities to setting up a complete programme or project environment requiring a work space, desks, office equipment, communications infrastructure and software, etc.

Some organizations support 'collaboration zones', which are specially equipped office areas with teamworking tools. These may be used for facilitated workshops or to fast-track the development of plans.

The programme or project may require a common set of tools to be established, to ensure all documents produced may be read and updated by the full programme or project team. A key requirement will be to build a configuration library and establish guidelines for the physical and electronic storage and security of documents. Over and above the normal office tools, planning, drawing and collaboration tools may be required. Chapter 5 should be referred to in planning the tools and infrastructure support.

Where the programme or project is large and would benefit from a tools-based approach to support, consider the need for purchasing tools or developing your own and the timescale to deliver within. An example is the consideration of purchasing and installing tools versus the use of hosted solutions provided by suppliers for the lifecycle of the project or programme. It may be more efficient to use hosted solutions to provide the same capability, which can be provided quickly and cost effectively (because infrastructure, configuration and connectivity are provided by the supplier).

As part of the programme or project start-up, the COE may supply processes, templates and tools and may assist in the setting-up of information portals, collaboration and web-based tools, etc. Where processes and templates are provided through a COE, consider whether they should be tailored to meet the needs of the particular programme or project being supported.

Appendix F gives a comprehensive set of functions and services that may be applicable to a temporary Programme or Project Office. These should be used as a starting point to prioritize what the most effective Programme or Project Office might offer in terms of functions and services.

The COE should also be seen as a source of lessons learned at the start of a new programme or project, and delivery support staff should take advice from the COE on the best way to tailor processes, tools, etc. to meet the needs of the programme or project, on the basis of organizational experience.

Timescales for definition and set-up of a temporary office

It is generally reasonable to allocate up to 10% of the project or programme lifecycle timescale for the establishment of the temporary Programme or Project Office. See Table 4.2 for example start-up timescales.

Table 4.2   Example temporary Programme or Project Office establishment timescales

Programme or project lifecycle	Temporary office set-up time (approx.)
12 weeks	1 week
6 months	2½ weeks
12 months	5 weeks
24 months	10 weeks

4.9.3 Running a temporary office through to delivery

The requirements for information flows and processes will have been developed and agreed in governance strategy documents, and the structure and functions of the temporary Programme or Project Office will be determined in the Project or Programme Initiation Documents for which approval is being sought.

These requirements will drive the temporary Programme or Project Office model and the processes it uses; however, as a guide Figure 4.6 displays the key areas of focus.

Throughout delivery, the temporary office should revisit its processes and ways of working to ensure they remain the best approach and are scalable to current information needs.

The resourcing levels and type of resources should also be challenged at regular intervals to ensure the support roles or any functional roles are still adding value. For example, at the beginning of a large programme there may be a need for functional Commercial roles to support

a programme, but once the contracts are agreed and suppliers engaged, this need will diminish.

It is recommended that process reviews and resource reviews take place between the programme manager and Programme Office manager at the end of each stage or tranche to ensure the resource mix continues to add value and processes continue to be scalable and relevant.

Appendix F should be revisited during delivery, as the chosen functions and services at start-up will evolve as the programme or project moves into its delivery stages or tranches.

Any lessons learned identified during delivery should be fed back to the COE or Portfolio Office at the point the lesson is learned rather than waiting until the end of the stage, tranche, project or programme.

Another consideration during delivery will be the coordination of assurance and review activities. These may simply be regular health checks, formal Gateway Reviews or external audits. Whatever their source, the Programme or Project Office should coordinate all reviews, ensuring all team members are aware of them, providing support

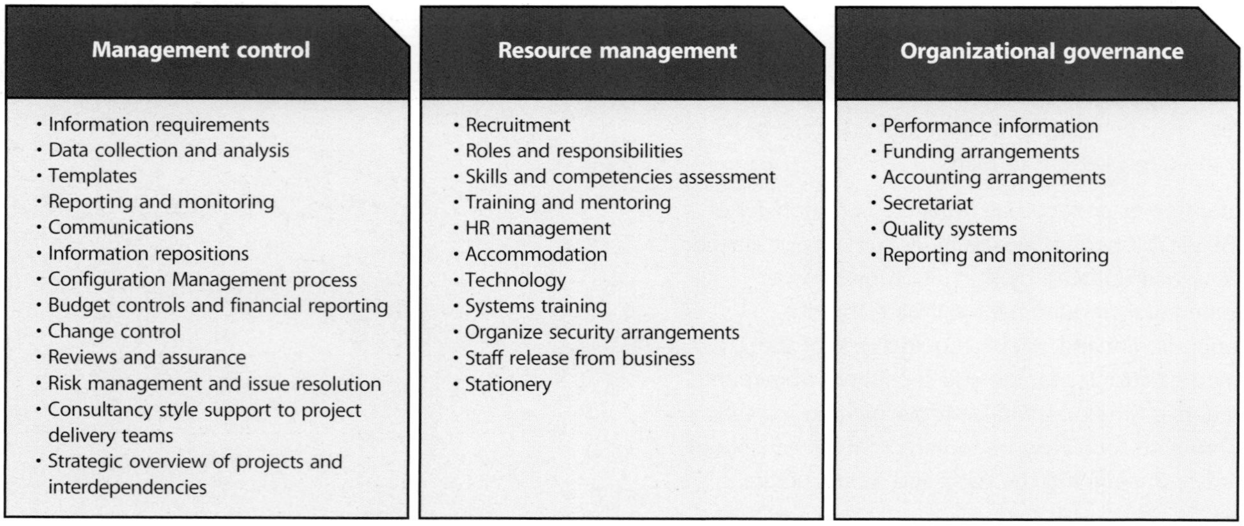

Management control
- Information requirements
- Data collection and analysis
- Templates
- Reporting and monitoring
- Communications
- Information repositions
- Configuration Management process
- Budget controls and financial reporting
- Change control
- Reviews and assurance
- Risk management and issue resolution
- Consultancy style support to project delivery teams
- Strategic overview of projects and interdependencies

Resource management
- Recruitment
- Roles and responsibilities
- Skills and competencies assessment
- Training and mentoring
- HR management
- Accommodation
- Technology
- Systems training
- Organize security arrangements
- Staff release from business
- Stationery

Organizational governance
- Performance information
- Funding arrangements
- Accounting arrangements
- Secretariat
- Quality systems
- Reporting and monitoring

Figure 4.6   Key areas of focus of temporary Programme or Project Office

to external assessors and, on large programmes, providing health checks to the component projects.

4.9.4 Closing down a temporary Programme or Project Office

Closure

Unlike a permanent Portfolio Office, the temporary Programme or Project Office has a finite lifecycle aligned to the programme or project lifecycle itself. Ensure that a proactive and disciplined approach is undertaken, with transfer to operational areas for documentation, contracts, resources and physical accommodation. Ensure that the benefits realization process is transferred to an operational area (if required).

Recycling

A project or programme may have been previously undertaken within an organization and have left a legacy of methods, tools, templates and skills from retained staff as part of a temporary office.

As this capability will have been invested in by the organization for the purposes of supporting the project or programme, it may be possible to recycle rather than re-invent it. This may sound obvious, but there are many instances where there is little or no corporate memory and usable approaches lie dormant, buried deep within an archived project's or programme's documentation.

Provide lessons learned and reusable elements for subsequent temporary offices to draw from. These should be fed back into a COE, where one exists, to ensure a learning organization. Reusable elements may include processes, templates, tools or best practice approaches.

> **Hints and tips**
>
> Always assess the lessons learned by the project or programme or talk to relevant stakeholders when taking advantage of temporary Programme or Project Office recycling to determine how well the office supported the project or programme.

4.9.5 Other considerations

Temporary Programme or Project Office as a trial for permanent Portfolio Office or COE

A common approach is to use the investment in a temporary Programme or Project Office as a trial or proof of concept for a permanent P3O model by subsequently expanding its scope on project or programme completion. This can be a useful way to demonstrate the value of the P3O concept and prove approaches, but it is important to ensure that the subsequent activity to realize this is planned and managed.

Treatment of internal resources

With a temporary Programme or Project Office, more careful consideration needs to be given to building internal competencies and career development for individuals seconded to the project or programme rather than buying in experienced people. A key issue can be a person's temporary elevation in career as a result of a programme or project and a reluctance to return to a lower operational role once the temporary project or programme lifecycle is complete.

Anybody seconded to work on a programme or project, including delivery support staff, should have clear objectives for their role, and these should be assessed in the same way their 'day job' is assessed. It is important to feed back performance information to their line manager and, at the end of their temporary assignment, to ensure their line manager is made aware of any additional skills, knowledge or expertise gained.

A temporary secondment to a Programme or Project Office can sometimes provide a good opportunity for a career change. Managers should look for talented individuals and consider ways of developing their careers for the overall good of the organization.

How to operate a P3O – tools and techniques

5

5 How to operate a P3O – tools and techniques

5.1 PURPOSE OF THIS CHAPTER

The P3O will implement and operate a range of tools and techniques to support consistent delivery of functions and services across the organization.

This chapter discusses a range of common tools and techniques found within a best-in-class P3O model.

5.2 OVERVIEW OF TOOLS AND TECHNIQUES

Tools and techniques may be delivered by a single unit or distributed across the organization in a standard way via the P3O model.

Tools may be used in the following ways:

- **Individual** – where only one person (generally the project manager) uses the tool. There may be multiple installations or instances of the tool across the organization but the relationship is generally one business change initiative to one user. Desktop applications such as project planning software, word processing software or spreadsheets are examples
- **Collaborative** – where multiple people access a single set of information through a tool. There may be multiple installations or instances of the tool across the organization; however, the relationship is one business change initiative to multiple users. Collaboration tools such as web-based portals and applications that share information and processes through a centralized server are examples
- **Integrated** – where multiple people access multiple sets of information that is integrated in some manner through a tool. There will generally be a single installation or instance of the tool across the organization, with partitions for business change initiatives and the ability to link information in a hierarchical manner. The relationship is multiple business change initiatives to multiple users. Enterprise P3RM software, which is distributed across an entire organization, is an example (see section 5.5.1).

Hints and tips

Collaborative and integrated tools may be purchased and implemented by an organization or 'rented' by the organization through hosted services. A critical consideration before implementing such a tool should be the maturity of the P3O. If the P3O is not mature, there is a high probability that the software will only complicate the situation and should not be used. It is critical that the software meets the needs of P3O business processes and not vice versa.

Standard techniques for the P3O may exist:

- Within corporate or P3O standards and policies
- As examples of good practice in knowledge repositories
- With programme and project resources through skills transfer or coaching by the P3O
- Within guides for the use of P3RM templates and standard deliverables
- Through communication of approaches at P3RM communities of practice or forums

5.3 BENEFITS OF USING TOOLS AND TECHNIQUES

The benefits of embedding standard tools and techniques in an organization will vary according to the type of tool used and the maturity of the organization or department that is engaging with or using the tool or technique.

The introduction of tools to support an organization's business processes can ensure a minimum standard is attained. In addition, the tools can help guide inexperienced stakeholders through the process and procedures of an organization, reducing the need to trawl through documents or guides.

Generally, key strategic benefits will include:

- Automation of business processes:
  - Reducing staff requirements to operate P3O functions and services
  - Reducing the overhead on project delivery teams for P3O business process requirements
  - Eliminating or reducing the need for manual data collection, amalgamation, printing and distribution

- **Improved compliance with business processes:**
  - Through the automation of workflows, approvals and governance mechanisms
  - Through the integration of business processes with organization components and information flows for the P3O business model

- **Improved timeliness of decision support information:**
  - Reducing cycle times for the collection of decision support information
  - Improving the response time to potential barriers to successful delivery
  - Providing the opportunity for higher project throughput
  - Providing a structured way to gather information

- **Improved quality of decision support information:**
  - By allowing validation of information automatically against embedded corporate or P3O standards
  - By providing audited business rules around the information compared with manual unaudited processes
  - By allowing for the reallocation of manual processing time to assessing and improving information quality
  - By providing a structured way to gather information and setting expectations for decision support information requirements
  - By being able to introduce automated ways of assessing the health of decision support information for centrally stored information

- **Improved decision-making:**
  - Through the integration of many data elements into central repositories, providing higher visibility and analysis of cross-project or -programme information
  - Through the ability to automate highlight and exception views of information and the hierarchical structuring of information
  - By using structured ways to assess information and make more objective decisions
  - By improved capability to undertake scenario or 'what-if' analysis on the decision support information

- **Improved management across geography:**
  - Through connectivity that allows for improvements to collaboration between project or programme team members

- **Improved staff competencies:**
  - Through skills transfer of structured ways of gathering, analysing and reporting information or undertaking elements of an organization's business change framework

- **Rationalization of legacy systems:**
  - Tools for the P3O that are of an integrated nature may make it possible to rationalize a number of disparate systems.

5.4   CRITICAL SUCCESS FACTORS

Although many significant benefits may be achieved by the introduction of standard tools and techniques to the P3O model, there are also a number of critical success factors. The most significant are as follows:

- **Focus on adding value to the organization rather than the features of the tool:**
  - Marketing materials for tools to support the P3O are predominately focused on features of the tools, integration across these features and level of sophistication, rather than the benefits to the organization or the problems they may solve
  - Research services that provide comparisons of tool providers in the market generally focus on features, ease of implementation and the quality and credibility of the organization behind the tool
  - The introduction of any tool to support the functions or services that a P3O provides needs to be carefully considered as part of the overall P3O Blueprint. Be clear about the value that the tool will provide and then match the tools available with features required

Hints and tips

- Be careful to avoid focusing on 'How can we use this tool feature in our organization?' rather than 'Does our organization need the service or function that this feature supports?'
- The implementation of an integrated tool is an expensive investment that will require significant effort and training. It should therefore be run as a project where the requirements are fully defined, the Business Case is justified and the implementation is planned in detail.

- **Match the sophistication of the tools and techniques to the capability maturity of the organization:**
  - With the move to higher levels of integration and innovation in the features offered by many tools on the market, some of the tools available to the P3O can be quite sophisticated in their functions and usability. Equally, a number of best-practice techniques may be dependent on having basic practices in place or require a high level of competency to be undertaken successfully
  - Because tools and techniques need to integrate with the business processes and information flows and the competencies of resources using them, ensure that the sophistication of the tools and techniques matches the capability maturity of the organization
  - For example, there is little value in implementing a tool with features that support robust benefits management and Resource Competency Management (level 3 P3M3 capabilities) when the organization is not properly defining projects consistently (level 1 P3M3 capability). The tool itself will not drive the organizational capability when more basic capability maturity 'building blocks' are not in place

Hints and tips

The move from individual to collaborative or integrated tools for the P3O model should be considered when the organization reaches maturity level 3.

- **Need for programme and project standardization and data quality:**
  - Introducing tools or techniques with features that prioritize multiple projects based on information provided in costs, benefits, risks, timeframes or strategic alignment is of little value if confidence in the project's data quality is low, which will be the case if a project lifecycle is not in place.
  - Ensure that the governance for programme and project delivery is in place to enable decision-making, and align the software to this decision-making structure

Hints and tips

When moving from manual processes to a higher level of process automation through an integrated tool, do not underestimate the challenges of configuring the system. The quality of existing P3O processes and programme and project information will be the number-one critical success factor in the implementation of the Enterprise P3RM software, so an early activity should be to improve data quality before introducing the tool.

- **Understand the intent of the tool or technique:**
  - Although different industries may have different forms of P3O, they will generally be aiming for similar value from their respective P3O models. However, a number of the tools and techniques available have been developed to meet a specific requirement for an industry or a large client, or are based on assumptions that may hold for one industry but not others. This can create significant implementation or adoption issues when the tool or technique is then offered to the wider market for implementation. For example, a tool that has been developed with construction projects in mind using construction industry language and standards may not be easily adapted to an IT or marketing portfolio environment
  - Understand the portfolio, programme or project management methods that the tool or technique is derived from or developed for
  - Understand the history of the tool or technique and how it can add value before focusing on required features, detailed requirements and adoption. For example, some tools are focused on the provision of sophisticated Earned Value Analysis, which is derived from complex resource-usage modelling when planning or measuring activity. For organizations where there may be regular changes to the baseline, there may be little value to be gained by adopting Earned Value Analysis as a tool or technique

Hints and tips

Undertake a Request for Information (RFI) to obtain the history, key clients and system functions when investigating tools for the P3O.

- **Implement tools as part of an organizational change effort:**
  - Tools suppliers generally focus on accelerated approaches to tool implementation and accordingly provide standard project approaches, frameworks or transition plans for implementing tools
  - Additionally, some integrated tools do not have the same basic project management assumptions that individual tools may provide (generally due to lower sophistication) and it can take time for staff to learn new ways of working
  - As a minimum, it is critical to consider and plan the enabling projects and subsequent projects around the tool implementation project. Ideally, the implementation of tools should be considered as part of an organizational change programme, but it can be successfully run as a stand-alone project. (Refer to Chapter 4 for further information.)

Hints and tips

The timeframe for an organization to become proficient with integrated tools and fully realize the benefits to be achieved can be between 12 and 18 months. The timescale will be dependent on many factors, including size of organization, skill set of existing staff, etc. It may be an appropriate strategy to use appropriately skilled external resources to expedite the tools implementation and then transfer skills to internal staff.

- **Maximize successful programme and project delivery through incremental implementation:**
  - Concentrate the efforts of the programme and project delivery teams by considering how implementation may be incrementally adopted
  - Use pilot projects and early adopters – make sure a communications plan is developed to communicate success to the rest of the programme and project management community
  - The disadvantages and problems associated with a 'big bang' project implementation apply equally to integrated tool implementation

Hints and tips

Consider a proof-of-concept/pilot approach or parallel running of current and new ways of working in those teams impacted by the tool implementation, to provide confidence before 'readiness for service'. Other incremental options include implementing on a feature-by-feature basis or adopting the tool for new programmes and projects only.

- **Agree tool ownership within the organization:**
  - For integrated tools being used across a Hub and Spoke P3O model, it is particularly important that the ownership and accountability for tool operations and improvements is clear (single point of accountability), with agreed processes for tool users to provide feedback and request enhancements.

Hints and tips

Where the P3O model is operating at an organization level, the Portfolio Office or Centre of Excellence is generally the most appropriate owner of an integrated tool, because of the need for project standardization across the organization. Where the P3O model is temporary, the Programme or Project Office supporting it will generally be the appropriate owner.

5.5 P3O TOOLS

The tools that support the P3O business processes and information flows may be as simple as individual documents, forms, spreadsheets and databases, or much more sophisticated. Figure 5.1 shows some of the high-level types of collaborative and integrated tools that may be employed within the P3O model.

These high-level types of tools can have a multitude of features and functions that support the value of the P3O and there is significant duplication among them. Figure 5.2 shows the features and functions of the key tool categories identified in Figure 5.1, aligned to the key portfolio, programme and project management principles and processes that the tools may support.

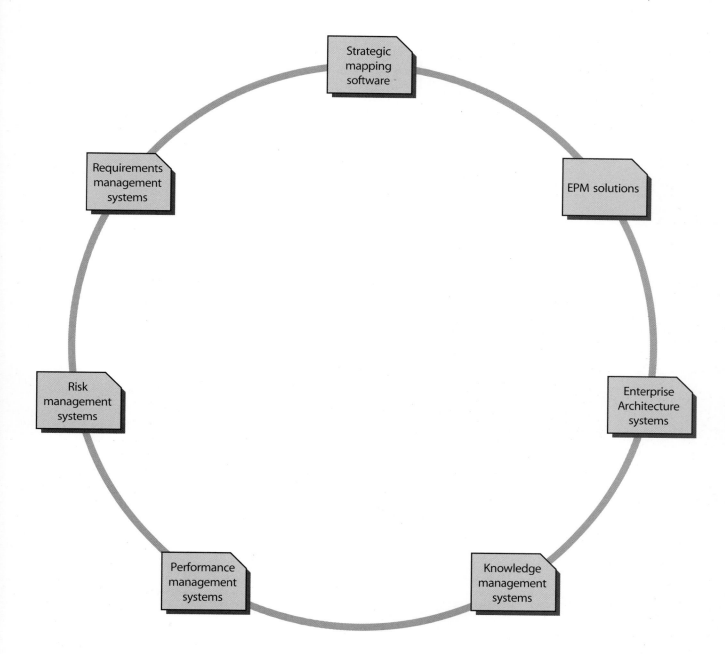

Figure 5.1   Types of collaborative and integrated tools in the P3O model

Portfolio, programme and project management elements

Portfolio level	Organization · Portfolio management approach · Leadership and stakeholder engagement · Benefits Realization Management · Blueprint design and delivery · Planning and control · Business Case · Risk management · Quality management · Integrated programme and project management
Programme level	Vision · Plans · Risks and issue management · Quality management · MSP Transformational Flows
Project level	Information Management · Controls · Management of risk · Change control · Quality in a project environment · PRINCE2 Processes

Tools

Organization
- Skill assessment matrix
- Computer-based training
- Project mgmt
- Programme management
- Risk mgmt
- Org change
- HR software with:
  - Accountability Mapping
  - Roles and responsibilities
- EPM software with:
  - Resource types
  - Governance
  - Workflow
  - Control and approvals

Portfolio management approach / Vision
- Strategic planning software
- Business planning software
- Portfolio registers
- EPM software with:
  - Portfolio schedule and planning
  - Portfolio categorization
  - Portfolio prioritization
  - Portfolio segmentation
  - Portfolio tracking
  - Portfolio review and optimization
- Asset or application portfolio management

Leadership and stakeholder engagement
- Corporate intranet
- EPM software with:
  - Governance
  - Project portal
  - Collaboration
- Survey software
- Email applications
- Stakeholder registers

Benefits Realization Management
- Performance mgmt software
- Business intelligence software
- EPM software with benefits management
- Design/Enterprise Architecture tools with:
  - Business process modelling
  - Business process modelling software

Blueprint design and delivery / Information Management
- Enterprise or Systems Architecture software
- Configuration management software
- Design/Enterprise Architecture software

Planning and control / Plans / Controls
- Simple calendar planners
- Project management Software
- EPM software with:
  - Planning and Scheduling
  - Resource mgmt
  - Financial mgmt
  - Reporting
  - Forecasting
  - Scenario analysis
  - Capacity planning
  - Timesheeting and expenses

Business Case
- Total cost of ownership software
- EPM software with:
  - Proposal management
  - Business case management

Risk management / Risks and issue management / Management of risk / Change control
- Risk registers
- Risk analysis tools such as PERT, Monte Carlo, Event Chaining
- Risk management systems
- EPM software with:
  - Risk mgmt
  - issue resolution
  - Change control
- Design/Enterprise Architecture tools with:
  - Change control

Quality management / Quality in a project environment
- Information or document mgmt software
- EPM software with:
  - Configuration management
  - Document management
  - Version control
- Design/Enterprise Architecture tools with:
  - Configuration management
  - Traceability management
  - Requirements management

Integrated programme and project management / MSP Transformational Flows / PRINCE2 Processes
- Business process modelling software
- EPM software with:
  - Workflow mgmt
  - Standard template repositories
  - Project mgmt guides
  - Knowledge management applications with:
    - Lessons learned
    - Case studies
    - Best practice samples
  - Contract mgmt software
- Estimation software

Figure 5.2   Collaborative and integrated tools mapped to P3RM elements

Note how multiple tools may provide similar functions and the range of coverage across P3RM elements.

5.5.1 Enterprise P3RM (EPM) solutions

The most common integrated tools used in the P3O are Enterprise P3RM (EPM) solutions. These provide a single systems solution for programme and project data collection, maintenance and reporting, allowing for roll-up of information from a single source of data entry (e.g. plan dates) to programme and portfolio levels.

They vary widely in terms of features, levels of integration and levels of innovation; however, core functions are generally provided across portfolio, programme and project management from strategic planning through to programme or project workflow or delivery support (see Table 5.1). A key benefit of these tools is the ability to produce integrated reports for multiple audiences from a single set of data.

Many tools may already exist within operational functions and could be adopted and developed for P3O use.

5.5.2 Selecting and implementing an Enterprise P3RM solution

Table 5.2 provides a checklist of key questions that should be considered when developing a requirements document for the selection and implementation of a P3RM solution.

Table 5.1   Core functions of Enterprise P3RM tools

Portfolio management	Resource management
Strategic planning	Skills matching
Organizational budgeting	Capacity/forward planning
Portfolio identification	Resource assignment
Portfolio analysis	Scheduling, tracking and measurement
Strategic Resource Planning	Timesheets
Strategic Risk Management	
Strategic Issue Resolution	
Portfolio schedule and planning	
Portfolio categorization	
Portfolio prioritization	
Portfolio tracking	
Portfolio review	
Portfolio optimization	
Asset management	

Programme and project management
Workflow and delivery support
Demand management and project collaboration
Governance processes
Benefits management
Lifecycle and stage Gated Review process (e.g. OGC Gateway)
Programme and project guides and support
Planning, management and support
Information and document management
Risk management and issue resolution
Change control
Information portals

Table 5.2   Key questions for developing a requirements document for a P3RM solution

Function	Questions
Strategic	■ How will the P3RM tool/s support the proposed P3O business model?
	■ What is the key objective of the P3RM tool(s)? Has the vendor designed the features around managing mature project Product Breakdown Structure (PBS)/Work Breakdown Structure (WBS), measuring earned value, for a particular environment or around a key client? Does this align with my organization's requirements?
	■ Is the organization planning to use the P3RM solution to support strategic or business planning cycles?
	■ What features are required now and what features may be required in the future as the capability maturity of the organization grows?
	■ Is the current capability maturity of the organization appropriate for a move from individual tools to collaborative or integrated tools?
	■ Am I able to roll out features as capability maturity is built over time? Am I able to easily hide visibility to these features in the interim?
	■ What is the track record of the P3RM tool/s?
	■ Does the organization need to purchase and implement the P3RM tool/s as part of a permanent P3O model or use a hosted or outsourced solution as part of a temporary P3O model (if the requirement no longer exists once the project or programme completes)?
	■ How will senior management respond to new ways of working as a result of the P3RM solution?
	■ What are the organizational change management implications of moving to a P3RM solution? Will I need to move project delivery staff to a new way of operating or will they still use familiar interfaces?
	■ Will there be an impact to successful delivery of the portfolio, programmes and projects as a result of implementing P3RM tool/s?
	■ Is the organization's investment in multiple individual tools and software less efficient and effective than implementing a P3RM solution at an enterprise level?
	■ How will the organization control risk in the implementation approach for the P3RM solution?
Process	■ What frameworks will the organization be aligning the configuration of the P3RM solution to, and can it support portfolio, programme and project methods if required?
	■ What processes can be done more efficiently through the use of a P3RM solution than manually?
	■ What additional benefits can the P3O derive through additional features of the P3RM solution?
	■ What are the priority processes to implement to achieve early benefits?
	■ How will wider organizational processes integrate with processes managed through the P3RM solution?
	■ Will staff involved in capability delivery spend more or less time complying with governance processes and administration as a result of the P3RM solution?
Organization	■ What roles and responsibilities are required to support the P3RM solution?
	■ What skills and competencies are required to maintain and improve the P3RM solution?
	■ Will the maturity of the organization positively or negatively impact the P3RM solution implementation, take-up and realization of benefits from its use?
	■ Are the skilled resources realistically available to operate the P3RM solution in production?
	■ If the organization invests in competency development for current staff in the P3RM solution, how will that impact programme or project delivery and what ramp-up time will be required?

(continued)

Table 5.2   Key questions for devloping a requirements document for a P3RM solution (continued)

Tools and technologies	■ Will the architecture support project delivery?
	■ What licence requirements will suit my organization's approach?
	■ Is there a solution architecture roadmap that I can take (e.g. module based) to align to portfolio, programme and project management capability implementation over time?
	■ Should I buy, outsource or use a hosted solution?
	■ Is the P3RM tool/s easily configurable? Do the tools within the P3RM solution integrate?
	■ What is the cost for customization if required? Am I tied to the P3RM tool/s provider for customization or can I utilize the wider market?
	■ What integration requirements will there be to legacy or line-of-business systems?
Information flows	■ What key questions are being asked by senior management about the portfolio?
	■ What information is required from the programmes and projects to achieve this?
	■ What information does the organization need to monitor to achieve better programme and project outcomes?
	■ Do project delivery staff have to feed information into multiple systems for portfolio or programme management information requirements, or will it be automatically rolled up?
	■ Can data be migrated easily from current systems/approaches into the P3RM solution? Is the data of suitable quality?
	■ Can data subsequently be easily validated to maintain data quality?
	■ What capability is there to provide metrics on the health of the information within the P3RM solution?

5.6   P3O TECHNIQUES

The techniques that support the P3O business processes and information flows can be extremely complex in a mature P3O environment. In contrast, in a less mature environment they may be at a basic, yet effective, level. Techniques may also be used under licence or provided as part of a professional service from a supplier.

The number and focus of techniques that a P3O may use to achieve its Blueprint are evolving and refining even faster than the tools available.

Figure 5.3 lists some of the techniques that may be used within the P3O model aligned to the key portfolio, programme and project management principles and processes that the techniques may support.

Portfolio, programme and project management elements

	Organization	Portfolio management approach / Vision	Leadership and stakeholder engagement	Benefits Realization Management	Blueprint design and delivery / Information management	Planning and control / Plans / Controls	Business Case	Risk management / Risks and issue management / Management of risk / Change control	Quality management / Quality in a project environment	Integrated programme and project management / MSP Transformational Flows / PRINCE2 Processes
Portfolio level	Organization	Portfolio management approach						Risk management		Integrated programme and project management
Programme level		Vision	Leadership and stakeholder engagement	Benefits Realization Management	Blueprint design and delivery	Planning and control		Risks and issue management	Quality management	MSP Transformational Flows
Project level					Information management	Plans / Controls	Business Case	Management of risk / Change control	Quality in a project environment	PRINCE2 Processes
Techniques	• Conceptual, functional and implemented model for governance • P3O sizing model • RACI matrix • Skills maintenance including: - Training plans - Delivery support (P2MM level 3) - Mentoring - Coaching - Induction - Professional development plans	• Prioritization/ portfolio balancing and portfolio analysis • Management Dashboards/ scorecards and reporting • Resource forward planning • Size classification or complexity modelling • Pain/gain matrix • Facilitated workshops • PESTLE • VMOST • SWOT • Porter 5 Forces Model • McKinsey 7-S model	• Stakeholder map • Stakeholder influence and interest matrix • Facilitated workshops • Interviews	• Outcome relationship modelling • Facilitated workshops • Benefits measurements: - Benchmarking - Prototyping - Process modelling - Activity analysis - Questionnaire • Benefits review • Benefits profiling • Cause and effect diagrams	• Models and frameworks for describing business models (current and future state) • Facilitated workshops • Organizational design • Performance monitoring • P3M3 • Benchmarking	• Rich pictures • Earned value • Critical path management • Facilitated workshops • Capacity planning/ resource management • Product-based planning • Resource levelling	• Hypothesis development • Cost benefit analysis • Sensitivity analysis • Activity based costing • Total cost of ownership • Return on investment	• Alignment to risk management standards • Facilitated workshops • Risk potential assessment	• Quality reviews • Assessment of compliance to changed delivery frameworks • Management metrics • Audit • Health checks	• Use of standard industry estimation resources • Facilitated workshops • Delivery frameworks • Gateways • Tailoring guidance to support different scales of risk and complexity for programmes and projects

Figure 5.3   P3O techniques mapped to P3RM elements

Risk assessment

3	Low
2	Med
1	High

Effort requirement

3	Low	< 1 month
2	Med	> 1 month but < 3 months
1	High	> 3 months

Investment driver

Driver number	Driver name	Priority weight	Driver description
1	Service delivery	9	Investment is directly linked to improving service delivery to the organization's customers.
2	Compliance	10	Investment is required to ensure that the organization complies with a change in legislation.
3	Revenue growth	7	Investment benefit is predominantly an increase in revenue or the capacity to increase revenue.
4	Operational risk treatment	5	Investment benefit is predominantly in the treatment of risk to the organization's operations.
5	Productivity	5	Investment benefit is predominantly derived from an increase in productivity.

Figure 5.4 Components of simple prioritization framework

The following sections describe some of the key P3O techniques in further detail.

5.6.1 Portfolio prioritization and optimization

The objective of a portfolio prioritization and optimization technique is to categorize or force-rank, by discussion, the programmes and projects within a portfolio, based on agreed measures (such as strategic alignment, risk, complexity, business benefits, cost, profit and loss impact, or return on investment).

Prioritizing the portfolio is critically important in order to determine where investment should be directed as the portfolio is delivered. Failure to prioritize at the board level will usually result in every project trying to deliver at the same time, using the same resources, which will result in initial chaos and significantly increase the risk of non-delivery. Optimizing the portfolio may involve increasing capacity or reducing commitments.

Its key benefit is in supporting senior management investment decisions using an objective alignment technique

to determine how a project or programme supports and aligns with strategic objectives in relation to others.

Portfolio prioritization and optimization is covered in more detail in OGC's *Portfolio Management* guidance.

This technique can be undertaken periodically (e.g. quarterly) to balance the portfolio against the agreed strategic objectives and refine the weighting of investment.

Key inputs are information on planned or current programmes and projects in the portfolio and an agreed framework for prioritization.

An example of components of a simple prioritization framework is shown in Figure 5.4.

In this example, the portfolio is to be prioritized on the basis of risk, effort requirement and strategic alignment through the investment driver. The priority weight of the investment driver should be determined through facilitated discussions by the P3O with senior or strategy management.

An example of key portfolio information applied to a prioritization model is shown in Figure 5.5.

Unique ID	Project title	Technology risk rate	Complexity risk rate	Benefits risk rate	Delivery risk rate	Total risk rate	Investment driver	Invest driver weight	Pay back <1 yr	+ve ROI Y/N?	Length <1 month = 3 >1<3 month = 2 >3 month = 1	Overall priority score
A	Project A	1	2	2	2	7	Service delivery	9	Y	Y	3	12
B	Project B	1	1	1	2	5	Compliance	10	Y	Y	3	13
C	Project C	2	1	3	2	8	Revenue growth	7	N	Y	3	10
D	Project D	2	1	3	2	8	Operational risk treatment	5	N	N	1	6
E	Project E	2	2	3	3	10	Productivity	5	Y	Y	1	6

Figure 5.5 Example prioritization model

The key output is an assessment of the portfolio against strategic objectives and the determination of relative priorities or a force-ranked list. It is common to find a mismatch between the priority of strategic objectives and the current investment in programmes and projects. This provides an opportunity for optimization of the portfolio by redirecting investment against the investment drivers more appropriately.

Refer to Appendix D for further examples.

Risk/strategic alignment

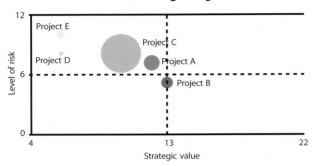

Figure 5.6   Example strategic alignment and risk level diagram

In the example shown in Figure 5.6, it can be quickly determined, on a highlight basis, which of the projects represent high risk and low strategic value. The size of the bubbles reflects the cost of the project, so senior managers can assess where the investment is being spent. The strategic value and risk level numbers relate to the score of each project against a predefined prioritization model scoring system to determine relative worth.

It is important to note that the portfolio prioritization and optimization technique should be validated by the Portfolio Direction Group or senior management team for sensibility.

A number of Enterprise P3RM solutions with capability at the strategic analysis level will provide more automated ways of determining portfolio prioritization and make recommendations on portfolio optimization opportunities using sophisticated calculations.

5.6.2   Management Dashboards

A Management Dashboard should support highlight and exception-based reporting, providing the reader (usually senior management) with the ability to quickly determine if an organization's investment is on track in terms of progress and outcomes or where attention should be focused. A Management Dashboard can be represented as a covering document to the more detailed status reports of a portfolio or programme or can be delivered electronically to provide the ability to drill down to lower levels of detailed information using fit-for-purpose software such as P3RM tools.

The objective of the Management Dashboard technique is to provide key decision-support information across a portfolio using highlights and exception-based reporting, thus providing a rolled-up view of more detailed information. It is generally provided as a top-tier report (exception-based) with links to programme and project information to enable the members of the relevant governance board to drill down to detailed information if required.

Its key benefit is to supplement larger volumes of detailed reporting, allowing the decision-makers to more effectively determine progress and understand where attention and management intervention may be required.

The key input into the Management Dashboard is information and progress reporting from the programmes and projects within the portfolio. It should be highlighted that this technique will only be valuable if there is confidence in the information, and this is directly related to the quality of the programme and project information, P3O processes and skills and the level and quality of the challenge and scrutiny role within the P3O.

When re-energizing or setting up a P3O model or office from scratch, Management Dashboard report templates should be flexible as the requirements are likely to evolve.

An example of a Management Dashboard is shown in Figure 5.7.

Portfolio Management Dashboard sample organization

# Projects at each stage:	Not started	Gate 1	Gate 2	Gate 3	Gate 4	Gate 5	12
		7	6	7	13	5	
# Projects at each status:	Red	6	Amber	10	Green	60	

Project Portfolio Investment Statistics

Total # Projects	76
Total £ Portfolio	£18,425,000
Total Benefit of Portfolio	£14,669,000

By Division

Division A

Total # Projects	9
Total £ Portfolio	£3,539,000
Total Benefit of Portfolio	£5,200,000

Division B

Total # Projects	5
Total £ Portfolio	£148,000
Total Benefit of Portfolio	£150,000

Division C

Total # Projects	22
Total £ Portfolio	£11,030,000
Total Benefit of Portfolio	£5,100,000

Division D

Total # Projects	36
Total £ Portfolio	£3,606,000
Total Benefit of Portfolio	£4,201,000

Division E

Total # Projects	4
Total £ Portfolio	£102,000
Total Benefit of Portfolio	£18,000

Total projects by category

Legend: Compliance, Cost reduction, Customer experience, Revenue/growth, Acquisition

Proportion red, amber and green by project size

# of projects (y-axis: 0, 5, 10, 15, 20, 25, 30, 35)
Project size: Small, Medium, Large
Legend: Red, Amber, Green

Project category by division

(y-axis: 0% to 100%)
Divisions: Div, ADiv, BDiv, CDiv, DDiv E
Legend: Acquisition, Customer experience, Compliance, Revenue/growth, Cost reduction

Project name	Project Executive / Project manager	Approved budget £'000	Priority	Category	Overall	Schedule	Budget	Risks and Issues	Benefits	Project start date	Current stage gate	Next stage gate	Next gate due date	Forecast project end date	Project manager comments	Period 1	Period 2	Period 3	Period 4	Period 5	Period 6	Period 7	Period 8	Period 9	Period 10	Period 11	Period 12
Project A	Project manager A / Project manager A	5,600	1	Compliance	Green	Green	Green	Green	Green		3	4															
Project B	Project manager B / Project manager B	2,400	2	Revenue Growth	Yellow	Green	Green	Yellow	Green		5	-															
Project C	Project manager C / Project manager C	1,200	3	Cost Reduction	Yellow	Red	Green	Green	Green		1	2															

Gate 1 Gate 2 Gate 3 Gate 4 Gate 5

Figure 5.7   Example Management Dashboard

In the example in Figure 5.7, a range of sample metrics and graphs have been used to demonstrate key values. This Management Dashboard demonstrates that this portfolio has a very high weighting in 'cost reduction' projects (more than half of the portfolio and representing the entire Division E project category). This may enable a discussion on whether this is appropriate or whether the portfolio needs to be optimized.

The key output is a populated Management Dashboard that is updated periodically and provided to the relevant governance group as amalgamated decision support information.

The Management Dashboard design and content fitness-for-purpose should be confirmed by each of the decision-making bodies to ensure all individual requirements are satisfied.

A number of P3RM solutions with capability at the strategic analysis level will provide more automated ways of providing amalgamated reporting through Management Dashboards or Balanced Scorecards or reporting using information drawn directly from programmes and projects through a centralized repository.

5.6.3 Knowledge Management

Managing knowledge and learning from change are the keys to success in a professional change management culture. Some specific ways to embed this in the culture are as follows.

Case studies

Create case study material for successful programmes and projects, both internal and customer facing. The case studies should be geared towards 'selling' the value of the professional programme and project management approach and should include details of the benefits actually realized by the customer (internal or external). This requires ongoing reviews and the tracking of benefits to full realization. They should not just be a series of woolly words, but include measurable benefits backed up by facts and figures. The case studies can be used as excellent sales collateral for service-based organizations.

Programme/Project Management Forums

These are half-yearly or quarterly seminars to allow the programme and project management community (including SROs, Project Executives and Project Boards) to meet. The forum should consist of a series of inputs of knowledge, from external speakers, senior managers and programme/project managers. These could be,

for example, presentations, demonstrations of tools or facilitated workshops in syndicates to work through issues. A typical presentation may be from a project team who have just rolled out an innovative solution or worked with a new customer, and should include lessons learned. In organizations where this approach is taken, these forums are generally deemed to be a great asset.

Lessons-learned workshops and dissemination of lessons learned

Lessons learned should be proactively sought and logged from the start of a programme or project, and key lessons learned with suggested action plans fed back to the P3O for consideration and dissemination to a wider audience. At closure of a programme or project (also consider at the end of key stages/tranches), the programme or project manager should commission a lessons-learned workshop from the P3O (to ensure independence) to capture lessons while they are still clear in the team's minds. The lessons collected will provide a valuable resource to other programmes and projects at start-up.

The lessons-learned workshop should consider:

- What went well?
- What could have gone better?
- What should we do differently next time?
- Are there any organizational lessons to be learned?
- What are the key actions that should be taken, who should own them and by when should they be actioned?

Archiving of portfolio, programme and project good practice

At the end of a programme or project the team will have amassed a great deal of material that may be beneficial to future programmes and projects. Any good examples, best-practice documents or innovative solutions should be archived with the P3O for future use. They can provide hints to assist future change initiatives, and help stop re-invention of the wheel. This archive material is a huge asset for kick-starting change and aids the development of junior staff as they can access and learn from the document archive.

Build an external knowledge network

The Head of P3O, or P3O specialists or consultants, should build relationships with P3Os in other organizations or divisions to share knowledge and best practice. The external knowledge network should also be extended to attendance at best-practice seminars or exhibitions,

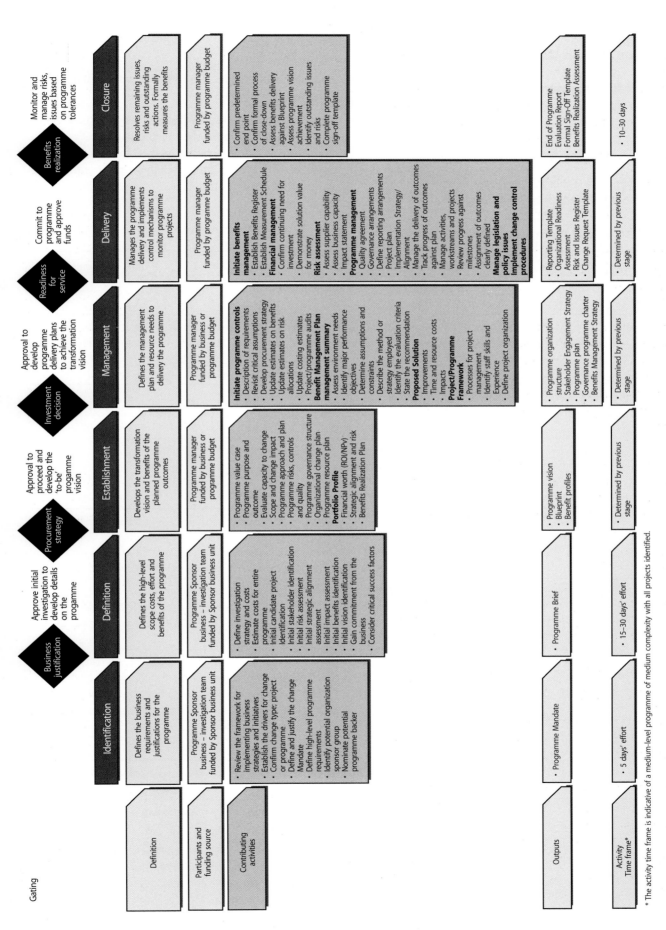

Figure 5.8 Example information portal

* The activity time frame is indicative of a medium-level programme of medium complexity with all projects identified.

membership of special interest groups, best practice user groups and professional associations.

5.6.4 P3O information portal

The objective of an information portal for the P3O is to provide easy access to components of the portfolio, programme and/or project delivery framework to the internal P3RM community.

The key benefit is easier access to key information by all levels of the organization, compared with traditional approaches of detailed policy guides and P3RM handbooks.

An example of the lifecycle within an information portal is displayed in Figure 5.8.

In this example, the key stages and gating requirements for an organization in relation to programme management are provided in relation to a taxonomy of definition, participants and funding source, contributing activities, templates, outputs and recommended activity timeframe.

Table 5.3 Typical facilitated workshops

Name	Purpose/Stage
Business solution	Held during the Initiation stage to brainstorm options and consider options for the programme or project solution
Portfolio priorities	Held during portfolio prioritization process. Identify the strategic drivers or investment objectives and then force-rank each objective by asking the question, 'Is strategic objective A more important or less important than objective B?' Repeat against all strategic objectives until a prioritized order is achieved
Programme/project start-up	Held at any time during Start-up stage or in the early part of the Initiation or Definition to brainstorm the programme or project objectives, scope, timescales, dependencies, risks, etc. Should be attended by board members, programme or project manager, prospective team members
Benefits identification and modelling	Held when determining the key benefits for a programme in the Definition stage. Involves identifying the planned benefits and then determining the dependency network for the identified benefits Can also collect input for Benefit Profile information
Stakeholder identification and communications planning	Held at any time throughout the programme or project, but particularly valuable in the Start-up and Initiation stages of a project or Definition stage of a programme or tranche. Used to identify key stakeholders, understand their influence and impact upon and by the programme or project. The initial stakeholder identification stage may be followed by planning key communications
Risk identification and risk assessment	Held at any time throughout the programme or project, but particularly valuable in the Start-up and Initiation stages of a project or Definition stage of a programme or tranche. Used to identify threats and opportunities to the objectives of the activities, assess those risks in open session, assign owners and actionees, and monitor activities
Planning	Held at any time throughout the lifetime of a programme or project. Particularly useful during the Initiation stage of a project or Definition stage of a programme or tranche as the solution is clarified and detailed plans are sought. May also be useful during a long implementation stage, which has been split into management stages, each of which requires a next stage plan
Problem solving	May be held at any time to resolve issues, generate solutions, to consider options for assessing change requests or exceptions.
Lessons learned	May be held as a workshop to brainstorm all lessons learned from a programme or project, held at closure or end of stages, or at start-up
Training	May be held periodically throughout the lifecycle to maintain the appropriate level of skills required to achieve outputs and outcomes
Blueprinting	Held at the programme definition stage of a programme and periodically throughout the lifecycle in line with tranches or significant change control. Involves translating the vision into how it will impact the organization's business model in terms of its processes, organization, tools, information and managing a view as a programme progresses

Other examples of information portal taxonomies may include detailed policies, requirements by programme governance theme or project management principle, samples of good organizational practice or education packs.

This technique is ideally delivered by means of an intranet site with links to the required templates or more detailed guidance.

5.6.5 Facilitation – workshop techniques

To be successful, programmes and projects require a shared understanding of their objectives, teamwork and effective decision-making. Programme and project decisions by their nature are contributed to by groups of people in meetings or workshops. However, the ineffective management of workshops can lead to wasted management time and effort and the demotivation of the participants. Therefore, managing workshops is a key skill in the programme and project environment and the P3O is ideally placed to provide an independent facilitation role.

Table 5.3 shows a list of typical workshops held during the programme and project lifecycles, which may be independently facilitated by a P3O specialist or consultant.

Managing workshops

The effective facilitation of groups of programme, project and non-project staff is a key skill for P3O specialists or consultants.

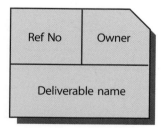

Figure 5.9   Example Post-it note from planning workshop

Example: Planning workshop

A planning workshop is useful when developing a programme, project or stage plan. Attendees should be key stakeholders in the programme or project or individuals who have been involved in similar initiatives in the past and have an understanding of what needs to be delivered. It should be held during the Start-up or Initiation stages of a project. The workshop should be facilitated by the P3O where possible and the programme or project manager should be an attendee. Key props are a large piece of brown paper, Post-it notes and marker pens. The session should start with an understanding of the scope and objectives of the programme or project as understood to date. Where the planning workshop is being undertaken as part of a programme or project Start-up workshop or Definition workshop, the Programme or Project Brief should already have been developed before the planning session. Where a stand-alone planning workshop is held, the audience should be given a copy of the brief before the workshop, to set the scene.

The group will then be facilitated to brainstorm the key deliverables and write each one on a Post-it note. The Post-it notes are then placed on the brown paper in a logical time and dependency sequence. Where possible the group should identify teams/ work streams within the project and place the Post-it notes in 'swimlanes'. When the sequence has been established and gaps identified and resolved, the diagram should be completed by drawing lines to show dependencies between work streams (swimlanes). The next step is to identify key decision or management review points and identify them by marking red 'milestones'.

By examining the flow diagram, the project team should be able to identify when meetings should be held, both with the project team and the Project Board, and these can be marked on the plan. If the 'right' participants are attending the workshop, it may be possible to assign owners to deliverables.

The final output should be a deliverable flow diagram, which can be converted to a Visio or PowerPoint diagram for communication to the programme or project team and board. A simple Post-it note would just identify the deliverable name, a reference number and owner (see Figure 5.9). An agenda for a planning workshop should be developed as a standard template.

5.6.6 Skills development and maintenance

The objective of skills development and maintenance is to ensure that the appropriate competencies are available across the organization to match against portfolio, programme or project, or requirements.

The key benefit of this is to ensure resources are allocated to P3RM roles with the appropriate level of skill. It also allows individuals to understand what their current skills are and what development opportunities they may require.

For the P3O the benefits include providing an input into training needs analysis and assisting forward planning of resources against skills and competencies as well as capacity.

The key inputs are a Skills Assessment Framework (to assess against) and a skills assessment and accreditation process for relevant staff (either self-assessed or facilitated).

Skills development involves identifying the key skill categories and skills for multiple roles in the organization, the setting of targets for skill level by role and then determining recommendations to close the gaps where they exist. This information can then be rolled up into an amalgamated resource view and represented as part of a Management Dashboard or Status Report.

The skills assessment should then recommend training or capability development opportunities aligned to P3O services or functions (e.g. training, mentoring, coaching, computer-based training, etc.).

Competencies	Assessment	Required level	Competency development
Generic skills			
Leadership	3	2	Mentor candidate
Teamwork	2	2	Skill level matched
Interpersonal skills	3	3	Skill level matched
Risk management	1	2	Assurance to provide lessons learned
Communication	3	3	Skill level matched
Influencing	1	2	Mentoring required
Desktop skills	1	1	Skill level matched
Facilitation	2	3	Mentoring required
The business environment			
Financial management	1	1	Skill level matched
Business case development	3	2	Mentor candidate
Commercial business	2	2	Skill level matched
Asset disposal	0	2	Training requirement
Service delivery	0	1	Training requirement
Relationship management	3	3	Skill level matched
Commercial negotiation	3	3	Skill level matched
Programme and project delivery			
Programme management	2	3	Development through progamme value or complexity increase
Project management	1	2	Mentoring or development required
Business change management	2	2	Skill level matched
Benefits realization management	1	2	Mentoring required
Team management	3	3	Skill level matched
Technical skills			
Procurement	3	2	Mentor candidate
Agile development	0	2	Training requirement
Information security	2	3	Mentoring required
Testing management	0	0	Skill level matched

Figure 5.10 Example skills assessment

The key output of the skills assessment is decision support information for the P3O to determine options for professional development and personal support information for individuals to complete personal development plans.

Each organization will have its own set of skills and targets.

OGC has defined a useful standard Skills Assessment Framework and Assessment Guide, which is available through its website.

Tools are commercially available to assess individuals against standard P3RM job descriptions, which provide evaluation of competencies and knowledge against industry bodies of knowledge and benchmarks.

Case study: Tailored Skills Assessment Framework

In this example, the key skill areas were developed around generic skills, understanding of the business environment, contractual relationships, programme and project delivery, technical skills and the legal environment. This may be appropriate for a Senior Responsible Owner/P3O Sponsor role.

The skills assessment involved, determining the level of skills, range from 0 to 3 (see Figure 5.10):

- 0 = If you have NO AWARENESS
- 1 = If you have an AWARENESS
- 2 = If you have KNOWLEDGE
- 3 = If you are an EXPERT.

A number of Enterprise P3RM solutions with capability at the resource management level will provide more automated ways of monitoring and managing skills for P3RM resources and matching competencies to project or programme requirements.

5.6.7 Business process swimlanes

The objective of developing business process swimlanes is to document standard and repeatable business processes with appropriate linkages (often across multiple divisions or business units within an organization) and agreed accountabilities.

The key benefit of this technique is to provide repeatable processes for capability maturity and to set process baselines that can be continually improved through lessons learned.

An example of a swimlane for schedule management in relation to a programme is displayed in Figure 5.11.

In Figure 5.11, the P3O is a temporary structure that has a key role in providing guidelines, receiving and amalgamating schedule information into a programme schedule, undertaking analysis and then updating the Project Dossier as required.

5.6.8 Capacity planning for resource management

The objective of capacity planning for resource management at the portfolio level is to understand the resource capacity and competency supply-and-demand levels and take action to match these appropriately to meet delivery requirements.

Its key benefit is to reduce any barriers to successful delivery of programmes and projects that are due to a lack of resource capacity or competencies across the organization (or division/department).

The key inputs are an assessment of resources available to the P3RM environment (this may be full-time resources or those that contribute to projects on a part-time basis in addition to operational roles), skills assessments and programme and project resource plans.

A sample resource capacity view is provided in Figure 5.12, in both numerical and graphical form.

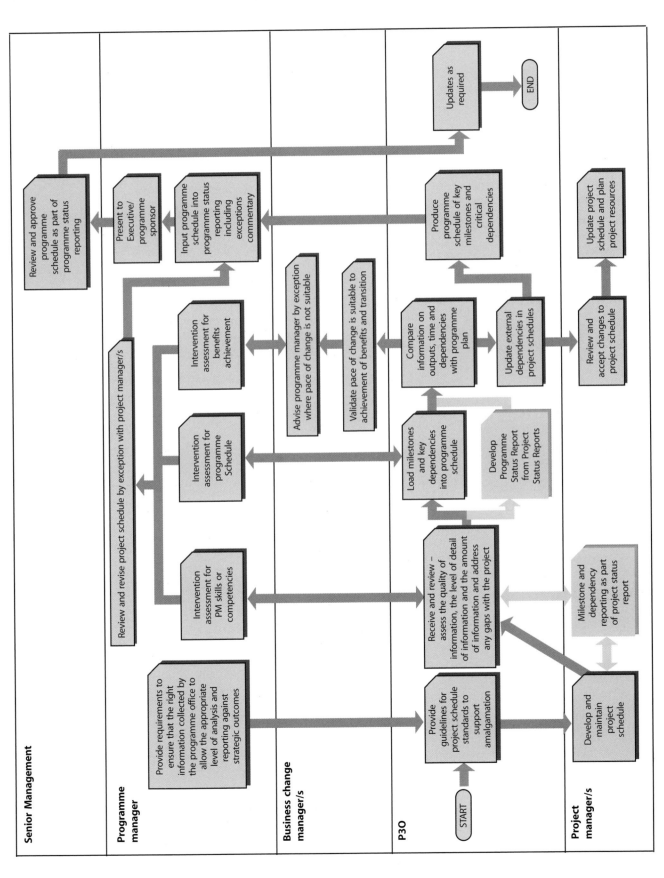

Senior Management

Programme manager

Business change manager/s

P3O

Project manager/s

Review and approve programme schedule as part of programme status reporting

Present to Executive/ programme sponsor

Input programme schedule into programme status reporting including exceptions commentary

Updates as required

END

Review and revise project schedule by exception with project manager/s

Intervention assessment for benefits achievement

Intervention assessment for programme Schedule

Intervention assessment for PM skills or competencies

Advise programme manager by exception where pace of change is not suitable

Validate pace of change is suitable to achievement of benefits and transition

Compare information on outputs, time and dependencies with programme plan

Produce programme schedule of key milestones and critical dependencies

Update external dependencies in project schedules

Review and accept changes to project schedule

Update project schedule and plan project resources

Provide requirements to ensure that the right information collected by the programme office to allow the appropriate level of analysis and reporting against strategic outcomes

Provide guidelines for project schedule standards to support amalgamation

Receive and review – assess the quality of information, the level of detail of information and the amount of information and address any gaps with the project

Load milestones and key dependencies into programme schedule

Develop Programme Status Report from Project Status Reports

START

Develop and maintain project schedule

Milestone and dependency reporting as part of project status report

Figure 5.11   Example swimlane

Project	Resource Types	Period 1	Period 2	Period 3	Period 4	Period 5	Period 6	Period 7	Period 8	Period 9	Period 10	Period 11	Period 12
Project A	Project Manager					1.0	1.0	1.0	1.0	1.0	1.0	1.0	0.5
	Business Analyst					3.0	3.0	3.0	2.0	2.0	3.0	4.0	
	Acceptance Tester								1.0	1.0	4.0	1.0	
Project B	Project Manager	1.0	1.0	1.0	1.0	1.0	1.0	1.0	1.0	1.0	1.0	1.0	1.0
	Business Analyst	12.0	12.0	12.0	12.0	12.0	12.0	12.0	12.0	12.0	12.0	12.0	12.0
	Acceptance Tester						5.0	5.0	5.0				
Project C	Project Manager		0.5	0.5	0.5								
	Business Analyst		1.0	1.0	1.0								
	Acceptance Tester				0.5								
Project D	Project Manager	1.0	1.0	1.0	1.0	1.0	1.0	1.0	0.5				
	Business Analyst		3.0	3.0	3.0	3.0	5.0	5.0	3.0				
	Acceptance Tester						3.0	3.0	3.0				
Project E	Project Manager					1.0	1.0	1.0	1.0	1.0	1.0	1.0	
	Business Analyst						3.0	4.0	5.0	6.0	6.0	6.0	
	Acceptance Tester									2.0	5.0	5.0	
	Project manager demand	2.0	2.5	2.5	2.5	4.0	4.0	4.0	3.5	3.0	3.0	3.0	1.5
	Business analyst demand	12.0	16.0	16.0	16.0	18.0	23.0	24.0	22.0	20.0	21.0	22.0	12.0
	Acceptance tester demand	–	–	–	0.5	–	8.0	8.0	9.0	3.0	9.0	6.0	–
	Project manager supply	3.0	3.0	3.0	3.0	3.0	3.0	3.0	3.0	3.0	3.0	3.0	3.0
	Business analyst supply	20.0	20.0	20.0	20.0	15.0	15.0	15.0	18.0	18.0	18.0	20.0	20.0
	Acceptance tester supply	–	–	–	4.0	8.0	12.0	12.0	12.0	12.0	12.0	12.0	12.0

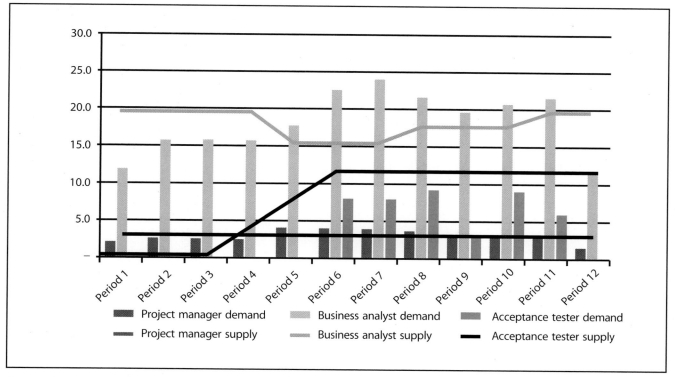

Figure 5.12   Example resource capacity view

In the example shown in Figure 5.12, actions will need to be taken to:

■ Increase the number of project managers (in period 5) or delay Project E until period 9, to smooth out the demand for project managers

■ Investigate actions to deal with the oversupply of Acceptance Testers

■ Investigate actions to match supply and demand of Business Analysts from periods 5 through 10.

Depending on the level of capability maturity in the organization and the capacity of the P3O to undertake the process, capacity planning may simply be an annual baseline for the planned portfolio. This would inform project portfolio phasing to reduce gaps between resource supply and demand for the business year.

It may only be for capacity of key known resource points of failure, or may also include competencies.

As P3O capacity increases and the organization becomes proficient at programme and project planning and control, then capacity planning may involve more frequent assessments based on actual resource experience.

A number of Enterprise P3RM solutions with resource management functionality will provide more automated ways of monitoring and managing resource capacity and competencies against the actual set of P3RM resources, the tasks required across the portfolio, and known constraints (such as time spent by staff on operational work).

5.6.9 Assurance, Gated Reviews and health checks

The objective of assurance, Gated Reviews and health checks is to check the quality of the decision support information being provided to the P3O for amalgamated reporting and to ensure that programmes and projects remain on track to deliver to plan and realize benefits.

The key benefit is in assuring the quality of decision support information being provided to the P3O.

Both PRINCE2 and MSP guidance provides checklists for health checks.

OGC provides guidance on Gated Reviews (OGC Gateway in UK government), which can be adapted to most organizations.

The OGC Gateway guidelines also provide an understanding of Delivery Confidence Assessments, which assess the confidence in the project or programme's ability to deliver its aims and objectives.

5.7 TAILORING OF APPROACHES

The objective of tailoring approaches is to ensure that the proposed project or programme is objectively assessed so that the governance path and requirements subsequently applied to a project or programme are fit for purpose.

Programmes or projects can range from the familiar repeatable-type projects (clarity of objectives, done it before, know how to do it and understand the risks) to highly complex undertakings. The level of governance and control should reflect the risk rating of the programme or project being undertaken.

Programmes and projects should be reviewed as part of the Start-up/Business Case process to categorize them in terms of their business criticality or risk rating. Projects that are high value, long duration, innovative, affect the organization's 'brand', or involve a new customer or new working practices should be regarded as high risk and the governance should be comprehensive with formal controls, reporting, and reviews. Only the most senior programme and project managers should be entrusted with their delivery. At the other end of the scale, repeatable projects delivering off-the-shelf solutions are much lower risk, can be run with a lighter touch and require a lower level of competency from the project manager.

Each programme or project going through Business Case approval should be assessed against a range of criteria to give an overall business criticality or risk factor. Criteria may include budget, timescale, innovation, number of suppliers, type of customer (size, new), brand awareness, size of team, number of business functions involved, etc. Those programmes/projects with a high rating factor would exercise a high degree of governance and control, with an appropriately qualified sponsor, SRO or executive, supported by a board, and the programme and project manager would be accredited and from elite teams within the organization. Those projects with a medium or low rating factor could use a tailored form of the framework with certain elements being mandatory to ensure the appropriate rigour. High-rated programmes and projects would be subject to ongoing reporting to the Portfolio Office or Senior Management Board and also be obliged to engage business change managers to own benefits realization through to conclusion.

A set of tailoring guidelines/matrices should be developed to use programme and project lifecycles and templates appropriately, dependent on the risk factors or importance of the programme or project.

Organizations may develop their own risk ratings based on the organizational risk process.

5.7.1 Project Complexity Modelling

The objective of scaling programme and project governance paths and requirements is to provide the appropriate level of governance to the project or programme once the complexity has been determined.

The key benefit is in providing flexible governance for a programme or project so that the level of governance applied matches the complexity of the project, while still ensuring standardization occurs for portfolio management requirements.

A key benefit of this is ensuring that mandated processes and templates that are required for roll-up of information for governance, escalation and reporting purposes can always take place, while being flexible about the need for other controls.

It is important to assess and continuously improve the governance paths and requirements based on experience to ensure that the governance remains robust and does not create unnecessary bureaucracy.

An example of a tool used to inform the tailoring of approaches for UK government is the Risk Potential Assessment provided in OGC Gateway Reviews. This assessment is a technique provided via a single spreadsheet that rates the degree of complexity for acquisition-based programmes and projects.

An example of a Project Complexity Model is displayed in Figure 5.13.

In this example, the organization has assessed what constitutes complexity for projects and determined 12 key criteria. Analysis has been undertaken to determine the drivers for each of these criteria and their parameters. Weightings have been applied to create an algorithm that categorizes the project as small, medium or large, based on its relative score. Many organizations prefer to use high, medium or low risk or complexity categories rather than large, medium or small. For Project A, the score is large based on the complexity of application systems interfaces and type of data, total project costs and a number of other moderately complex factors.

The key output is decision support for the governance group by the P3O as to the recommended governance process that should be followed.

It is important to note that this technique will require refinement and ongoing review to ensure that the weightings are appropriate to the governance applied and the project outcome.

Project Name: Project A

Project Size: Large

Description	A – 0	B – 10	C – 20	D – 40	Selecct column
Customer (Assess how the solution will impact customers. The impact could be an awareness or it could imply change in behaviour of the customer)	No customer impact	Awareness from customers	Minor behaviour change from customers	Major behaviour change from customers	C
Risk exposure (Assess the risk exposed to the organization and the downstream systems/processes impacts if errors were found in the solution)	No impact	Minor impacts to organization's reputation and downstream processes	Minor impact to organization's reputation but major impacts to downstream processes	Major impact to organization's reputation and downstream processes	C
Internal (Assess how the solution may affect the work process of the business area and any ripple effects to work processes of other business areas)	Within business team	Minor impact to business areas	Medium impact to business areas	Major impact to business areas	B
External (Assess how the solution may affect the work processes of suppliers, partners or other external stakeholders)	No impact to external stakeholders	Requires awareness from external stakeholders	Minor behaviour change from external stakeholders	Major behaviour change from external stakeholders	C
Number of stakeholders (Each stakeholder may represent a group of people either internal or external to the organization. The more stakeholders in the project would imply increased complexity for the project manager)	1 key stakeholder	2–4 key stakeholders	5–10 key stakeholders	11+ key stakeholders	B
Knowledge of technology (If knowledge of the technology is limited, especially if not in house and not easily available, greater risks to the project and would require greater planning)	Well established in the organization	Knowledge is with a number of people in the organization	Knowledge can be sought from the market	Market place knowledge is limited, i.e. is only with the vendor	C
Knowledge of application/business processes (If knowledge of the process is limited with lack of documentation, greater risks to the project and would require more detailed work)	Well established and documented in the organization	Knowledge is with a few of people but well documented in the organization	Knowledge is with a few people but lack of documentation	Knowledge is very limited and lack of documentation	A
Number of IT platforms (Platform refers to the infrastructure, e.g. middleware, operating systems, system software. The more platforms, the more risky and complex will the solution be)	1 key platform	2 key platforms	3 key platforms	≥ 4 key platforms	C
Application systems interfaces and type of data (Assess how the solution may need to integrate with internal systems in the organization and if the data exchange is with external sources)	1 key system and no data interface with external groups	2 key systems and no data interface with external groups	3 key systems; or, with one interface with external groups; or, if the data is of minor sensitive nature	≥ 4 key systems; or, with more than one interface with external groups; or, if the data is of major sensitive nature	D
Number of service providers (The number of providers would be working together to provide the solution)	1 service provider	2 service providers	3 service providers	≥ 4 service providers	A
Total project costs (Total internal and external costs for labour, materials, training, travel, etc. charged to the project for the entire project lifecycle)	Up to £100,000	>£100,000 up to £500,000	>£500,000 up to £2m	> £2m	D
Project completion time (The expected elapsed time before project completion)	Up to 1 month	> 1 month up to 6 months	> 6 months up to 12 months	> 12 months	C

Figure 5.13   Example Project Complexity Model

Roles and responsibilities A

Appendix A: Roles and responsibilities

When designing the P3O and deciding on the right model, job descriptions should be identified that are specific to an individual. The job descriptions may focus on a management or generic role (e.g. Head of Programme Office) or on a specific function (e.g. Finance Officer) or be a combination of different functions.

This appendix outlines a set of management or generic roles and functional roles. The functional roles may, in a larger or permanent office, be allocated to a single person or multiple people; in a smaller or temporary office, however, these roles will often be combined in a single person's job description.

The following role descriptions should be treated as a 'pick and mix' set to create custom job descriptions tailored to the organization's business and customer requirements. This may include addition of the qualifications required to undertake the role, years of experience, skills, key performance indicators and refinement of the responsibilities to align with the organization.

Where a role is aligned to a particular role or service, the reader should also refer to the relevant heading in Table F.1, Functions and Services in Appendix F for a more detailed breakdown of responsibilities.

The following roles are described in more detail in the rest of this appendix:

- **Management and generic roles:**
  - P3O Sponsor
  - Head of P3O (permanent office)
  - Head of Programme or Project Office (temporary office)
  - Portfolio Analyst
  - Programme or Project Specialist (Programme or Project Consultant)
  - Programme or Project Officer (Programme or Project Coordinator or Administrator)

- **Functional-based roles:**
  - Benefits
  - Commercial
  - Communications and Stakeholder Engagement
  - Information Management
  - Consultancy and Performance Management
  - Finance
  - Issue
  - Change Control

- Planning
- Quality Assurance
- Resource Management
- Risk
- Reporting
- Secretariat/Administrator
- Tools Expert.

A1   P3O SPONSOR

Purpose

The purpose of the P3O Sponsor is to champion and direct the establishment and evolving operation of the P3O. The P3O sponsor will ideally be a member of the main board.

The role requires strong leadership and management skills, coupled with authority to champion the P3O set-up and continual improvement. The individual will need to develop and maintain robust relationships with all parts of the business as well as with the programmes and projects, to ensure that the P3O meets the requirements of the main board.

The individual will need to understand the wider objectives of the portfolio, have credibility within the environment and be able to influence others. They must be able to develop and maintain effective working relationships with senior managers, the programme and project teams, and any third-party service providers.

Responsibilities

- Provide leadership by articulating outcomes and energizing people through change
- Secure the investment to implement or re-energize a P3O
- Work in partnership with senior managers in business areas to identify how the P3O could assist in the delivery of their change portfolio
- Provide strategic challenge, overview and scrutiny, ensuring alignment with wider policy and strategic initiatives
- Manage the key strategic risks
- Ensure evolving business needs and issues are addressed effectively.

A2 HEAD OF P3O (PERMANENT OFFICE)

Purpose

The purpose of the Head of P3O (also called Head of Portfolio Office, COE or Hub Programme Office) is to establish and run the permanent office.

The role requires strong leadership and management skills, coupled with strong P3RM or strategy/business planning skills, to ensure the integrity of the portfolio or programmes and projects. The incumbent will need to develop and maintain robust relationships with all parts of the business as well as with the programmes and projects, to ensure that all initiatives meet the requirements of the Portfolio or Programme Board. They will also need to work with business areas to identify any gaps in initiatives and to understand what activities are planned to fill those gaps.

The individual will need to understand the wider objectives of the portfolio and programme, have credibility within the environment and be able to influence others. They must be able to develop and maintain effective working relationships with senior managers, the programme and project teams, and any third-party service providers.

The role will also provide strategic challenge, overview and scrutiny, ensuring alignment with wider policy and strategic initiatives.

In some organizations the Head of P3O may be a Strategic or Business Planning Manager or Director.

Responsibilities

- Develop and implement the terms of reference for the COE, Portfolio Office or Hub Programme Office
- Ensure that the portfolio delivers the organization or departmental strategy
- Ensure the portfolio activities contribute to the bottom-line value of the organization and delivery of benefits from all programmes and projects
- Recruit, develop and retain the Portfolio Office, Programme Office or COE team
- Work with the senior business managers/directors, SROs and programme managers to define and implement the portfolio or programme(s) governance framework
- In conjunction with business owners and programme managers, create strategies for the effective planning, monitoring and delivery of the portfolio
- Assure the overall integrity and coherence of the portfolio

- Support the Strategy Director (Senior Business Manager/Director) in sanctioning programmes and projects for inclusion in the portfolio/programmes
- Maintain close relationships between other key business initiatives that are currently under way, as well as other bodies, to ensure that there are no overlaps in responsibilities
- Provide an ongoing health check of the portfolio/ programme(s) by reassessing whether the programmes/projects continue to meet the overall strategic objectives
- Design, challenge and agree Management Dashboards
- Establish access to policy and strategic information for all programmes and projects
- Scan the horizon for potential policy changes or initiatives and inform the programme(s) and project(s) when policy or strategy changes
- When strategic initiatives are not as successful as expected and fail to deliver the expected benefits, help analyse why, particularly to differentiate between a poor strategic idea and the poor implementation of a good strategic idea
- Provide strategic oversight support for the Portfolio Board
- Establish framework agreements for the purchase, roll-out and maintenance of organization-wide P3RM tools, training and consulting
- Act as owner of programme and project frameworks, templates and procedures; be responsible for ensuring they are fit for purpose and continue to be best practice
- Advise on tailoring the templates and procedures to achieve an appropriate project structure
- Keep abreast of and evaluate the effectiveness of new project management tools and techniques.

A3 HEAD OF PROGRAMME (OR PROJECT) OFFICE (TEMPORARY OFFICE)

Purpose

The purpose of the Head of Programme or Project Office is to establish and run the temporary Programme or Project Office.

The role requires strong leadership and management skills, coupled with strong P3RM skills, to ensure the integrity of the programme or project. The individual will need to develop and maintain robust relationships with all parts of the business, as well as with the projects, to ensure that all initiatives meet the requirements of the Programme or Project Board. The individual will also need to work with business areas to identify any gaps in initiatives and to understand what activities are planned to fill those gaps.

The individual will need to understand the wider objectives of the programme or project, have credibility within the environment and be able to influence others. They must be able to develop and maintain effective working relationships with senior managers, the programme and project teams, and any third-party service providers.

Incumbents must have the ability to deputize for the programme manager.

The role will also provide strategic challenge, overview and scrutiny, ensuring alignment with wider policy and strategic initiatives.

Responsibilities

- Develop and implement the terms of reference for the Programme or Project Office
- Work with the business lead/SRO and programme manager to define and implement the programme (or project) governance framework
- In conjunction with business owners and project (or team) managers, create strategies for the effective planning, monitoring and delivery of the programme (or project)
- Support the overall integrity and coherence of the programme or project
- Support the programme (or project) manager in sanctioning projects for inclusion in the programme
- Support the programme (or project) manager in ensuring that existing initiatives and projects are effectively adopted into the programme
- Support the programme (or project) manager in agreeing project closure
- Maintain close relationships between other key programmes that are currently under way, as well as other bodies, to ensure that there are no overlaps in responsibilities
- Identify dependencies amongst the programme, its projects and other programmes/business change initiatives
- On behalf of the Programme or Project Board, provide an ongoing health check of the programme or project by reassessing whether it will continue to meet the overall objectives
- Report progress to the programme (or project) manager and Programme (or Project) Board via Management Dashboards

- Facilitate end-of-tranche reviews and benefits reviews on behalf of the programme manager
- Set up access to policy and strategic information
- When strategic initiatives are not as successful as expected, help to analyse why, particularly to differentiate between a poor strategic idea and poor implementation of a good strategic idea
- Provide strategic oversight to the SRO, informing the programme or project when policy or strategy changes
- Be responsible for team objectives, one-to-one reviews and evaluation, and the continual improvement of the P3O service.
- Be responsible for workload management of the team and the prioritization of ad hoc work requests versus core team deliverables.

A4   PORTFOLIO ANALYST

Purpose

The purpose of the Portfolio Analyst role is to facilitate the development and ongoing management of an optimized portfolio, ensuring senior management decisions lead to the fulfilment of strategic objectives through the delivery of programmes and projects (aligned with Business as Usual objectives).

Responsibilities

- Provide strategic overview of all programmes, projects and interdependencies, reporting anomalies or areas of concern to senior management
- Analyse the portfolio and make recommendations on the programme/project mix to the decision-makers
- Balance/optimize the portfolio in terms of strategic goal attainment vs delivery capacity/capability and Business as Usual priorities
- Evaluate and help to implement process improvements to improve project workflow and more effective delivery
- Develop and manage the prioritization model
- Develop, maintain and provide expert assistance to the commissioning process whereby programmes and projects are added/deleted from the portfolio
- Facilitate governance/portfolio meetings
- Develop and maintain the Management Dashboard
- Initiate reviews of post-programme and post-project evaluation reports and benefits to ensure the strategic goals have been enabled/met
- Develop and maintain the portfolio plan
- Provide support/information to business planning

- Develop and maintain a Resource Capacity Plan, mapping available resources against programmes and projects
- Develop and maintain the Portfolio Risk Register
- Develop and maintain a Portfolio Dependencies Register
- Assess benefits planning and realization across a number of programmes or projects to identify gaps, overlaps and conflicts, and eliminate double counting in the Benefits Realization Plans of individual programmes and projects
- Develop and maintain key performance indicators (KPIs) for the portfolio
- Scan the horizon for impending strategy or policy changes that may impact on the composition of the portfolio, and communicate an impact analysis to Strategy Board
- Provide an aggregated analysis of Gated Reviews to the Strategy Board
- Review post-stage Gated Review/Gateway improvement plans to ensure key strategic portfolio actions are delivered
- Develop stakeholder strategy and ensure communications are timely and effective
- Liaise with the Finance team re monitoring of financial spend and timing/support for audits
- Provide decision and governance support:
  - regularly review the appropriateness and deliverability of the portfolio
  - review the relative business priorities and risk profiles
  - escalate issues to the Strategy Board.

A5   PROGRAMME OR PROJECT SPECIALIST

Purpose

The purpose of the Programme or Project Specialist role is to play a proactive role in the promotion of programme and project management methods and standards, implementation of good programme and project management practice, and the monitoring of certain programmes or projects.

Postholders provide a consultancy service to programme and project managers or Programme and Project Boards across the organization or department. This consultancy may take the form of advice and guidance or be of a specific nature in the form of facilitated workshops. At the beginning of a programme or project, the Specialist would work with the programme or project manager and the business managers to help define an appropriate

level of governance and structured programme/project management and to decide on the level of support and the type of services required.

They may provide a tailored series of workshops, which may include elements of start-up advice, risk analysis, scoping, planning, tailoring of methods, etc.

Responsibilities

- Provide a centre of expertise and develop consistent standards and procedures, including templates, and guidance in their tailoring across a range of programme or project size, to include:
  - programme/project Initiation
  - risk analysis
  - issue and change control analysis
  - Information/Configuration Management
  - activity- and product-based planning techniques
  - methods and tools
  - quality assurance
  - programme/project organization structures
- Provide a focal point to promote the use and benefits of the programme or project management method, giving a consistent and common approach – develop and lead collaborative learning forums
- Coordinate information about how programmes and projects run the standard programme or project management method, their progress and problems
- Provide specialist high-level planning skills for programmes and projects
- Provide advice and assistance for the appointment of a delegated Programme/Project Assurance function
- Provide briefings to Programme/Project Board members and Programme/Project Assurance staff on their roles and responsibilities
- Provide a fast-track programme/project mobilization support service through collaborative working, facilitated workshops and tailoring of standard approaches and templates
- Review completed programmes and projects to distil good practice and note any factors that unnecessarily adversely affect the duration or outcome of a programme/project, so that they can be avoided in future
- Keep abreast of and evaluate the effectiveness of new programme and project management tools and techniques that support the development and change-management approach

- Carry out health checks on programmes or projects at any time during the lifecycle, when requested by the programme/project manager or Board
- Design and support governance/reporting for programmes or projects
- Build and maintain a register of approved training courses in change, programme and project management and associated disciplines. This register will include details of the courses, the level of person they are aimed at, and the dates when they will be held throughout the year
- Build and maintain a register of P3RM events – exhibitions, forums, seminars, etc. – and publicize them to the P3RM community
- Provide a central coordination point for change management training, both internal and external. Provide an administrative service in the form of booking and organizing courses, both internal and external. This will include the booking of venues and refreshments, liaison with tutors and external organizations, the issuing of delegate lists and course joining instructions, and the management of course fees due
- Build and maintain a repository of good examples of programme and project documentation, e.g. PID, Blueprint, Product Descriptions, End Stage/ Tranche Assessments, Programme/Project Closure Reports, Benefit Profiles, Stakeholder Maps, Quality Management Strategy, Risk Management Strategy
- Build and maintain a library of resources – training aids, DVDs, reference material, manuals, etc.

A6   PROGRAMME OR PROJECT OFFICER

Purpose

The purpose of the Programme or Project Officer (which may also be known as Coordinator or Administrator) is to improve the planning and delivery process by collecting and maintaining data in a consistent form.

Responsibilities

- Implement guidelines, procedures and templates to collect and maintain consistent data and provide hands-on delivery support to a programme or project
- Facilitate the creation and update of programme or project plans as required by the programme/project manager. Identify where cross-project dependencies exist and track/monitor these in support of the programme/project manager

- Implement agreed regular progress-reporting mechanisms for all projects and thereby monitor the routine progress of projects, and assist the programme/project manager in the preparation of the Programme Status/Project Highlight Reports
- Establish and maintain an information management system, manage both electronic and hard-copy configuration libraries. Provide basic training in Configuration Management techniques
- Establish risk, issue and change-control processes and templates, and assist the programme and project team in its delivery
- Manage or facilitate the quality review process for programmes or projects
- Provide a coordination/administration service to a programme or project.

A7   BENEFITS ROLE

Purpose

The purpose of the Benefits role is to provide a benefits realization support service to programmes, business managers and business change managers.

Responsibilities

- On behalf of the SRO, programme manager and business change manager, lead benefits and dis-benefits identification activities
- Develop and maintain an Outcome Relationship Model/Programme Benefits Map
- Facilitate agreement of the Benefits Management Strategy between the SRO, programme manager and business change managers
- Facilitate the agreement of the Benefits Profiles between the SRO, programme manager and business change managers
- Facilitate agreement of the Benefits Realization Plan between the SRO, programme manager and business change managers
- Establish the infrastructure required to implement the Benefits Management Strategy
- Track and report on the realization of benefits by the business
- Work with the business managers or business change managers to identify additional opportunities for benefits realization
- Work with the business managers or business change managers to minimize any dis-benefits
- Assess the impact of change requests for their potential effect on benefits realization

- Assist the SRO in leading benefits reviews
- Regularly review and improve the effectiveness of benefits management arrangements
- Assess benefits planning and realization across a number of programmes or projects to identify gaps, overlaps and conflicts and eliminate double counting in the benefits plan of individual programmes and projects
- Provide scrutiny of a Business Case from a business perspective.

A8 COMMERCIAL ROLE

Purpose

The purpose of the Commercial role is to ensure that the organization carries out the role of 'Informed Customer', and that all commercial/procurement practices and decisions meet designated standards and offer the organization value for money. It may also take on the role of supplier relationship manager, developing efficient and effective relationships with suppliers, outsourcers and partners.

The role may be a P3O role or is more likely to be embedded in the P3O, with formal line management to the Commercial, Procurement or Purchasing function. It may also exist within a virtual P3O.

Responsibilities

- Engage early on with Commercial, Procurement or Purchasing teams to scope the commercial element of the portfolio, programme or project
- Provide ongoing liaison with Commercial, Procurement or Purchasing teams
- Provide liaison with OGC procurement function (in UK government)
- Develop and execute the portfolio, programme or project procurement strategy
- Undertake contracts management, including tracking deliverables against existing contracts and managing any third-party or subcontractor contracts
- Ensure all contracts remain up to date and exit strategies are in place
- Provide analysis of any requests for change that may have a contractual impact
- Coordinate purchase order activity
- Ensure compliance with any applicable organizational, national and international standards and legislation
- Provide commercial expertise/advice to the portfolio, programme teams and constituent projects

- Facilitate relationships between the organization's senior management community, SROs and senior managers within the supplier community
- Take on Supplier Relationship Manager responsibilities (in partnership with Commercial, Procurement or Purchasing department/function), which may include:
  - Facilitating the management of supplier and contractual risk and measure all aspects of supplier performance, instigating remedial actions whenever and wherever necessary
  - Conducting contractual reviews with all major suppliers to the programme or project on a regular basis
  - Managing all aspects and stages of the contract lifecycle on behalf of the programme or project manager
  - Maintaining a catalogue of suppliers, services, products and contracts within the programme or project
  - Providing a single liaison and contact point for all supplier and contractual issues
  - Developing a full understanding of supplier strategies, plans, business needs and objectives
  - Ensuring that the programme or project is working in partnership with suppliers, building on long-term relationships
  - Facilitating the development and negotiation of appropriate, achievable and realistic contracts and contractual targets with suppliers
  - Facilitating the negotiation of 'value for money' services and products with all suppliers.

A9 COMMUNICATIONS AND STAKEHOLDER ENGAGEMENT ROLE

Purpose

The purpose of the Communications and Stakeholder Engagement role is to ensure the effective management of the portfolio, programme or project's stakeholders.

Responsibilities

- Maintain the list of stakeholders and their interests
- Lead the work to identify and document the programme stakeholders (internal and external), their interests and the potential impact on the programme by the programme team, recording the information on Stakeholder Profiles
- Facilitate the formulation of Stakeholder Engagement Strategy and the associated Portfolio, Programme or Project Communications Plan to ensure:

- Awareness amongst all stakeholders of the benefits and impact of the portfolio or programme
- That expectations do not drift out of line from what will be delivered
- Commitment from stakeholders to the changes being introduced – thus ensuring the long-term success of the portfolio, programme or project
- That all stakeholders are informed of progress before, during and after implementation or delivery of project outputs and programme outcomes
- The promotion of key messages from the portfolio, programme or project
- A demonstration of the commitment to meeting the requirements of the portfolio, programme or project sponsors
- Truly two-way communication exists by actively encouraging stakeholders to provide feedback and ensuring they are informed about the use of their feedback to influence the portfolio, programme or project

- Promote opportunities for maximizing the benefits obtained from the portfolio or programme
- Coordinate stakeholder engagement and communication, ensuring effective timing and interdependency management of communications
- Coordinate internal portfolio and programme communications
- Monitor the effectiveness of communications
- Handle press enquiries (providing the point of contact between portfolio, programme or project and the Press Office)
- Establish and maintain any portfolio, programme or project intranet site or information portal

A10 INFORMATION MANAGEMENT ROLE

Purpose

The purpose of the Information Management role (also known as Configuration Librarian) is to act as the custodian and guardian of all master copies of the portfolio, programme or project's information. The role may also take on Asset Management.

The role should work closely with the Security function or department in an organization in order to ensure full information and physical security is considered within a portfolio, programme or project.

Responsibilities

- Ensure key information assets are under Configuration Management and change control, sharing information within the project, programme or portfolio as required
- Create and operate libraries or other storage areas to store products and keep reference materials (such as induction packs) up to date
- Develop and manage document control procedures to cover baseline management, controlled issue of master documents, version control, document history and distribution lists
- Create an identification scheme for all products and assist in the identification of products – naming and filing conventions
- Establish and administer baselines
- Control the receipt, storage and issue of all portfolio, programme or project products
- Maintain a record of all issued copies of products and notify holders of any changes to their copies
- Undertake configuration audits and maintain status information on all products
- Ensure supplier configuration items (documentation and assets) are under control by providing a single point of entry and exit to the programme for such items (working with Commercial staff, as appropriate)
- Seek out knowledge about how to access relevant information outside the Programme Office, other systems in the organization, Internet resources, etc.
- Ensure processes are in place to handle security and confidentiality of programme/project documentation or other assets.

A11 CONSULTANCY AND PERFORMANCE MANAGEMENT ROLE

Purpose

The purpose of the Consultancy and Performance Management role is to provide internal consultancy and expertise in P3RM and organization processes.

Postholders also seek to continually improve performance of the portfolio, programme and projects within an organization. They create, maintain and disseminate good practice.

Responsibilities

- Own P3RM standards and methods, ensuring processes and templates are maintained in line with industry best practice

- Set up and maintain a Performance (Process) Improvement Plan (fed by lessons learned)
- Set up and track portfolio, programme or project metrics to monitor and control performance
- Own the lessons-learned process and action plans, disseminating lessons learned
- Ensure tools/processes facilitate collaborative working across department and organization boundaries
- Run facilitated workshops, e.g. start-up, risk, planning, requirements, lessons learned, benefits mapping
- Undertake mentoring or coaching of portfolio, programme or project staff, including programme and project sponsors/SROs; set up 'buddy relationships' for new/inexperienced staff
- Undertake portfolio, programme or project induction (to purpose, roles, processes, etc.)
- Develop case study material and feed back to COE
- Perform programme and project fast-track start-up and closure assistance (through facilitated workshops)
- Support programme and project 'rescues' through hands-on development and delivery of action plans
- Act as trainer in P3RM for internal courses/workshops
- Act as method specialist/expert in P3RM – provide help, advice and guidance on tailoring
- As Tools Expert (Enterprise Project tools, Risk tool, Collaboration tool, etc.), provide technical leadership, coaching and mentoring on all P3RM tool utilization
- Provide consultancy-style services to programme and project delivery teams at mobilization and throughout the lifecycle of a programme or project, ensuring a common approach is adopted and tailored and good practice is distilled and shared
- Provide business performance monitoring and reporting
- Provide performance deviation escalation management.

A12 FINANCE ROLE

Purpose

The purpose of the Finance role is to establish a professional Finance function within the portfolio, programme or project to ensure the timely provision of portfolio, programme or project funding and effective financial control.

The role may be a P3O role or is more likely to be embedded in the P3O, with formal line management from the Finance function.

Postholders may also assist the portfolio, programme or project manager with budget control.

Responsibilities

- Work with central Finance function to ensure the availability of appropriately profiled funding across financial period(s)
- Administer budget allocations and estimate of future spend
- Develop and maintain the portfolio, programme or project financial controls, paying particular attention to audit requirements
- Review and track portfolio, programme or project costs and, where applicable, revenues (using Earned Value Analysis techniques where applicable)
- Analyse and collect portfolio, programme and project financial information, review and track programme or project costs and (where applicable) revenues; calculate and analyse cost variance
- Support benefits profiling
- Manage invoicing and collection activities
- Prepare monthly financial reports for the portfolio, programme or project manager and for inclusion in status reports
- Create and maintain financial models for the depreciation and amortization of programme and project costs;
- Provide programme Accountancy assistance with:
  - Developing and refining programme and project businesses cases
  - Creating and distributing financial reports
  - Development and maintenance of the Resource Management Plan
  - Advice on cost control and opportunities for savings
  - Adherence to accounting procedures
  - Capitalization of capital assets.

A13 ISSUE ROLE

Purpose

The purpose of the Issue role is to take the lead in ensuring that the portfolio, programme or project has effective processes in place to identify, monitor and resolve issues.

Responsibilities

- Develop and implement the Issue Resolution Strategy, ensuring that the Commercial function leads on contractual issues

- Clearly communicate the Issue Resolution Strategy, and the benefits of following it, to all personnel involved with the portfolio, programme or project
- Establish and maintain the portfolio, programme or project Issue Register
- Register issues for subsequent investigation and resolution, monitoring items identified as requiring action, prompting timely actions and reporting on whether required actions have been carried out
- Ensure that all issues have a nominated owner and actionee
- Ensure that the agreed responses to issues are planned, resourced and implemented
- Communicate to stakeholders, particularly those who are directly affected either by the issue itself or by the response to the issue
- Assess how effective any issue response has been
- Facilitate the regular monitoring and review of all issues
- Proactively examine Issue Registers across the portfolio or programme (within projects) to look for common themes and establish consistent resolution strategies
- Establish and maintain an efficient two-way flow of information between the portfolio, programmes and their projects, regarding issues and their handling
- Facilitate cross-programme/project impact analysis
- Escalate issues to higher authority, e.g. business area management, when necessary
- Liaise with the Information role on Configuration Management.

A14 CHANGE CONTROL ROLE

Purpose

The purpose of the Change Control role is to take the lead in ensuring that the portfolio, programme or project has effective processes in place to identify, monitor and resolve changes.

Responsibilities

- Develop and implement the change control process, ensuring that Commercial functions lead on contractual changes
- Clearly communicate the change control process, and the benefits of following it, to all personnel involved with the portfolio, programme or project
- Establish and maintain the portfolio, programme or project Change Register

- Register changes for subsequent investigation and resolution, monitoring items identified as requiring action, prompting timely actions and reporting on whether required actions have been carried out
- Ensure that all changes have a nominated owner and actionee
- Ensure all changes have appropriate impact analysis, are planned, resourced and implemented through formal Configuration Management
- Communicate to stakeholders, particularly those who are directly affected either by the change itself or by the response to the change
- Facilitate the regular monitoring and review of all changes
- Proactively examine Change Registers across the portfolio or programme (within projects) to look for common themes and establish consistent resolution strategies
- Establish and maintain an efficient two-way flow of information between the portfolio, programmes and their projects, regarding changes and their handling
- Facilitate cross-programme/project impact analysis
- Escalate changes to higher authority, e.g. business area management
- Liaise with the Information role on Configuration Management.

A15 PLANNING ROLE

Purpose

The purpose of the Planning role is to take responsibility for facilitating the development and maintenance of the portfolio, programme or project plan and dependency logs.

Responsibilities

- Define planning standards for portfolio, programmes or projects to enable ease of roll-up of milestone data and dependencies
- Facilitate the design, development and ownership of the portfolio, programme or project plan, ensuring that all milestones and internal and external dependencies are identified, logged and monitored
- Maintain and update plans, advising on forecasted missed milestones, missed dependencies and impact assessment
- Maintain and update resource plans, advising on resource clashes and shortcomings
- Ensure all product-based plans include activities, time and resource estimates for risk mitigation

- Ensure quality review activities and associated time have been allocated realistically
- Analyse interfaces and dependencies between projects and recommend appropriate actions where anomalies exist or there are areas of concern
- Undertake tracking and maintenance of dependencies
- Establish and operate mechanisms to track portfolio, programme or project delivery against the plan; update progress against the plan
- Identify and report deviations and trigger exception reports when appropriate
- Review plans against Business as Usual plans to ensure change can be adopted effectively
- Provide estimating support to the portfolio, programme(s) or projects
- Define and manage time recording processes; use systems/tools to capture actual progress data
- Ensure impending policy or strategy changes are assessed for their impact on the portfolio, programme or project plans or dependencies.

A16   QUALITY ASSURANCE ROLE

Purpose

The purpose of the Quality Assurance role is to lead the work to ensure that any new products or services delivered by the portfolio, programme or project are fit for purpose and are capable of delivering the benefits required by the organization board.

Responsibilities

- Ensure compliance with any applicable organizational, national and international standards and legislation
- Bring together portfolio, programme or project staff of different disciplines and drive the group to plan, formulate and agree a comprehensive Quality Management Strategy and Quality Management Plan
- Establish consistent quality practices and standards, adhering to governance arrangements; monitor performance through gathering relevant data and producing statistical reports
- Ensure tests and procedures are properly understood, carried out and evaluated and that product modifications are investigated if necessary
- Work with the Finance Manager/Analyst to ensure the portfolio, programme or project complies with audit requirements
- Develop bespoke processes, standards and templates (tailored approach) for quality management

- Coordinate quality reviews of portfolio, programme or project documents and deliverables (this could be independent, reporting directly to the board or SRO)
- Provide health checks
- Provide guidance on quality criteria, reviewers and sign-off authority to ensure cross-portfolio or programme(s) consistency
- Work with commercial/purchasing staff to ensure effective interface with supplier's quality systems and oversee the quality review process for contractual supplier deliverables
- Liaise with COE, OGC or other bodies to arrange stage Gated Reviews (Gateway Reviews in UK government programmes and projects), health checks, audits, Common Causes of Failure Certificates (UK government) as required
- Coordinate Gated Reviews and stage reviews and ensure all information is available in a timely manner and quality format.

A17   RESOURCE MANAGEMENT ROLE

Purpose

- The purpose of the Resource Management role is to ensure that current and future programmes and projects are equipped with enough human resources of the right skills, at the time they are needed, and that those human resources are used as efficiently as possible.

Responsibilities

- Provide a capacity planning and resource tracking service across a portfolio or programme(s)
- Capture the resource requirements of the portfolio, programme or project and the P3O itself
- Forecast future resource needs, based on portfolio/ programme/projects plans, close liaison with the relevant managers and (where appropriate) wider business plans and business unit objectives (demand management)
- Provide a view of commitments (of portfolio, programme or project staff) on other programmes/ projects and/or on Business as Usual activities that will impact the ability of a portfolio, programme or project to deliver
- In consultation with Human Resources and others, decide on the best source for the required resources, depending on the long-term requirement for particular skill and its likely availability

- Plan and initiate the acquisition of the necessary staff, in terms of both skill content and quantity, ensuring they are in place at the time needed
- Actively monitor the deployment of staff, arranging new postings (where possible) in advance of assignments ending, to meet staff development needs, and to maintain a good match of skill to role – both delivery and P3O staff
- Work with HR and line management to facilitate succession planning, including knowledge management and leavers' process as required
- Maintain a database of resources, for people and their skills/attributes, location, availability, contact details and lead responsibility for the resource
- Take an active role in the training and development of portfolio, programme or project staff to increase the available skills capability and capacity within the business
- Review the provision of skills audits – do the proposed programme/project staff have the required skills to deliver their role on the programme or project? (delivered through the COE or hub)
- Establish formal mentoring and coaching guidelines and mechanisms
- Provide 'help squads' – supplementary skills to fill shortfalls within the portfolio, programme or project; assist in engaging 'just in time' resources where new requirements surface at short notice
- Manage consultants' and interims' contractual status, closely monitoring use of externals to ensure ongoing value for money and that the requirement still exists
- Where a flexible P3RM resource pool is in place, manage resource planning, data collection and P3RM skills development.

A18   RISK ROLE

Purpose

The purpose of the Risk role is to take the lead in ensuring that the portfolio, programme or project has effective processes in place to identify and monitor risks, has access to reliable and up-to-date information about risks, and uses the appropriate controls and actions to deal with risks. This role should also ensure that these processes are aligned to corporate risk-management policy.

Responsibilities

- Develop a Risk Management Strategy for P3O in accordance with the corporate risk-management policy; clearly communicate the strategy, and the benefits of following it, to all personnel involved with the portfolio, programme or project
- Establish and maintain the portfolio, programme or project Risk Register
- Assist in the identification and ongoing management of risks by running risk workshops and risk review workshops
- Ensure that all risks have a nominated owner and actionee, ensure that risks are proactively managed
- Ensure that the agreed risk responses are planned, resourced and implemented; give advice on appropriate risk responses and contingency planning
- Ensure risks are prioritized and dealt with at an appropriate level of management
- Ensure all project risks that have wider programme implications are escalated and dealt with at programme level, and that any programme risks that have wider strategic implications are escalated to either Corporate Risk Management or the Senior Management Board, and facilitate this escalation process
- Provide cost estimates for all outstanding risks and ensure that risk mitigation costs do not exceed risk occurrence costs
- Communicate to stakeholders, particularly those who are directly affected either by the risk itself or by the risk responses
- Assess how effective any response actions have been and whether the risks identified have actually materialized, including realization of opportunities
- Actively monitor and regularly review all risks on a constructive, 'no blame' basis
- Establish and maintain an efficient two-way flow of information between the portfolio, programme(s) and its projects, regarding risk handling
- Proactively examine Risk Registers across the portfolio or programme (within projects) to evaluate the net effects of common threats and opportunities using modelling or simulation techniques
- Establish consistent mitigation and contingency plans for risks that should be tackled across the portfolio or programme
- Support the sharing of Risk Registers with the supplier community
- Assess and monitor the effectiveness of risk processes and refine as necessary.

A19 REPORTING ROLE

Purpose

The purpose of the Reporting role is to provide a reporting service to the portfolio, programme or project.

It also collates base data and generates reports to multiple audiences through aggregated data.

Responsibilities

- Provide regular reports to boards, including a commentary on performance, coordinating upward aggregation of data/information and reports – Highlight Reports, Programme Status Reports, Management Dashboards, etc.
- Ensure integrity of reports through consistent traffic lights; define and challenge traffic-light status
- Identify and report deviations and trigger exception reports when appropriate
- Develop processes to fulfil the internal reporting needs of the programme, including the development and production of any contractual reports
- Ensure that reporting deadlines are achieved.
- Ensure the reporting process is robust, exception-based and flexible enough to meet the changing needs of the programme or project
- Develop a weekly/monthly reporting calendar with reminders to information contributors
- Implement and manage the weekly and monthly reporting cycle, chasing information as required and challenging the quality of the component data
- Build and maintain an information base of trend data for the programme or project reporting, e.g. rolling traffic lights to ensure 'glitches' are seen as such and not blown out of context.

A20 SECRETARIAT/ADMINISTRATOR

Purpose

The purpose of the Secretariat/Administrator role is to provide portfolio, programme or project administrative support and a secretariat function for the relevant boards.

Responsibilities

- Maintain knowledge/reference library/repository in relation to governance boards, using the approaches set by the Information Librarian

- Support facilities requirements (accommodation, IT support, office equipment), as far as possible matching supply to demand, switching and releasing facilities as necessary
- Support the Resource Management role with the acquisition of resources by maintaining relationships with external organizations that can supply resources: contract agencies for staff, organizations that rent plant and equipment, agencies who rent/let building space (work with the Commercial team), etc.
- Support the Quality Assurance role by liaising with the COE, OGC or other bodies to arrange health checks, audits, third-party reviews and stage Gated/Gateway Reviews, Common Causes of Failure certificates (UK government), as required
- Provide a helpdesk facility for enquiries/issues/problems; record requests for assistance, assign them to members of the P3O team and track the requests to resolution
- Provide admin support to the P3O, including workshop/meeting administration and the establishment and maintenance of the filing system (in conjunction with the Information/Configuration Management function)
- Provide logistical support for training courses (booking rooms, trainers, refreshments and liaising with attendees)
- Provide administrative support for other non-P3RM activities, e.g. travel and hotel bookings.

A21 TOOLS EXPERT

Purpose

The purpose of the Tools Expert is to provide expertise in software tools to support the change environment. The role may provide support to the P3RM community to configure software, or to provide training and coaching in their use. Examples of tools may include Enterprise Programme and Project software, planning, risk, document management or collaboration tools.

Responsibilities

- Examine the market to source tools
- Liaise with tools vendors re requirements specifications
- Liaise with tools vendors re implementation plans and training
- Carry out internal mentoring/coaching in tools
- Advise new programmes and projects in the appropriate use of tools.

Example Business Case B

Appendix B: Example Business Case

This appendix describes a Business Case for a programme or project to develop or enhance a P3O model or office.

B1 AIMS

By (*specify date*) the organization will have a mature (*define desired level of maturity*) P3O that will improve the development of a prioritized portfolio and improve capabilities across the organization to deliver and realize the business change associated with programmes and projects across the portfolio.

The P3O model will improve return on investment across the portfolio by a minimum of x (*specify amount*)%.

The organization will be a learning organization with established programme and project management standards, using highly visible work practices and processes, accountabilities, governance and reporting coupled with appropriately skilled staff and fit-for-purpose technology.

B2 BACKGROUND/REASONS

- Lack of visibility of all change leading to inappropriate investment decisions
- Strategic objectives not being met
- Lack of information to make investment decisions and prioritize funds and resources effectively
- Lack of effective capacity planning leading to top-heavy programme and project resourcing and inappropriate use of scarce technical and business resources
- Lack of consistency in programme and project approaches and methods
- Adverse impact on organization's reputation
- Inconsistent delivery of programmes and projects against time, cost and quality targets – late, over budget, failure to deliver capability or outcomes
- Actual benefits not being realized as specified in Business Cases.

B3 OBJECTIVES

To achieve the stated aims, the P3O will achieve the following high-level objectives for the organization:

- **Portfolio level:**
  - Compile the current business change portfolio and details of potential additional programmes and projects
  - Integrate the current business change portfolio and organizational strategy, identifying opportunities for optimization
  - Establish and maintain the capability to deliver a balanced, prioritized portfolio of change, clearly aligned to organizational strategy
  - Establish and maintain a capacity planning and resource management service
  - Establish and maintain a decision support service through Management Dashboards
  - Coordinate programme and project activity across the portfolio to minimize bottlenecks (e.g. decision-making bodies) and constraints
  - Establish benefits management and strategy realization links to performance measurement

- **Programme level:**
  - Facilitate progress towards the achievement of strategic outcomes for each of the programmes by maintaining a programme management methodology and ensure that it is consistently applied and continuously improved
  - Act as the Information Hub to support effective governance, prioritization and Performance Management towards required strategic outcomes
  - Support strategic governance and senior stakeholder engagement through management reporting at a highlight level or by exception (where required)
  - Support the assurance of the delivery of each programme through Gated Reviews and health checks on behalf of relevant boards
  - Improve cost management approaches across programmes

- **Project level:**
  - Support more effective project delivery through the maintenance of a project management methodology, processes and supporting systems, skills management and the provision of advisory services
  - Support more efficient project management through the centralized management of key components of the project management process across projects
  - Assure the quality of project management outputs through a flexible governance structure to monitor all projects, project health checks and ad hoc assurance of key project management components
  - Enable higher-quality results with more realistic project plans
  - Improve cost management approaches for projects.

B4 COST–BENEFIT ANALYSIS

B4.1 Typical costs

For each cost type, consider both initial or set-up cost and ongoing cost (per year or per programme/project (in temporary unit)) – see section 2.6.2 on running costs.

Table B.1 Cost elements

Cost type	Description
Staff	■ The people employed within the P3O model. Consider salaries, contract rates, and other costs of employment (employer costs). ■ Consider also recruitment and retention costs (training etc.) ■ There may be a mix of permanent and temporary (contract or consultant) staff. What are optimum levels?
Infrastructure	Office space, desks, equipment, collaboration zones (for facilitated workshops, meetings etc.)
Tools	P3RM software, resource management, collaboration, intranet etc.
Training/ development	Include training and development of P3O staff and those who use their services. Include any team-building activity costs.
Consultancy	Initial costs to set up the office or model and ongoing support costs for interim assignments, e.g. workshop facilitation, independent Gated Reviews, etc.

Communications and marketing	Costs incurred in engaging key stakeholders, marketing the P3O services and communicating effectively

B4.2 Typical benefits

Benefits may be those derived from setting up and operating the P3O model from scratch, or those derived from expanding the services of an existing P3O model.

This section may also take into account any cost savings (e.g. staff costs) or income generated (through selling services) to provide a balanced cost–benefit analysis.

Some typical benefits may be:

- **Supporting programme and project management standards** – Projects following a standard lifecycle are more often completed on time, on budget, to the required quality and within scope. We have:
  - Estimated savings = no. of projects × no. of people × average hourly rate × hours saved
  - **Example:** 20 projects × 10 people × £30/hour × 40 hours/week × 4 weeks = £960,000
    - This example assumes time to market will be reduced by 4 weeks for 20 projects. Of course, the additional revenue that can come from new products delivered to market more quickly can make these benefits pale by comparison

- **Identify programme and project risk and resource constraints** – A P3O will require project managers to improve risk mitigation, dependencies, constraints and subsequently impacts on the business. We have:
  - Estimated savings = no. of projects × no. of people × hourly rate × hours saved
  - **Example:** 6 projects × 10 people × £30/hour × 40 hours/week × 11 weeks = £792,000
    - Proper risk identification can result in the cancellation of 20% of projects before the execution phase. In the example above, savings assume 6 projects will be cancelled before execution begins. The time savings are the average for the execution and subsequent phases

- **Development cost improvement** – Tracking and monitoring progress on projects will provide better information to make decisions on the deployment and use of resources and capital. In addition, the significant increase in visibility, cross-functional management support and tracking of these projects will enable the portfolio of projects to accelerate their delivery. We have:

- Estimated savings: average aggregated budget of 60 active projects in portfolio, annualized = £75,000,000
- A 5% annual delivery improvement in time and budget for the projects in the portfolio = £3,750,000

- **Project and programme prioritization** – Delivering unnecessary or inappropriate programmes and projects inhibits the organization's ability to maximize profit, increase its market share and deliver its strategy whilst using scare resources. Prioritization of a portfolio of programmes and projects should lead to the elimination of these unnecessary or inappropriate programmes or projects, with a subsequent cost saving. Thus we have:
  - **Example:** Elimination of 10 projects at an average cost of £600,000 annualized, for a total expected savings of £6,000,000
  - This assumes that the project prioritization process assists management in making the decision not to implement a specific project based on the strategic objectives of a programme

- **Reduction in programme or project start up timescales** – Evidence from organizations has shown that providing a focused programme or project start-up service through facilitated workshops can reduce start-up times by more than 50%. An additional benefit is that a programme or project is better scoped, more realistically planned and stakeholder engagement measurably improves. We have:
  - Estimated savings = no. of projects × no. of people × hourly rate × hours per week × weeks
  - **Example:** 10 projects × 2 people × £30/hour × 40 hours/ week × 6 weeks = £144,000

- **More effective use of resource pool**
  - Evidence has shown that programmes and projects hang on to resources for longer that their natural 'value add' period, e.g. a planner can add value at the beginning of a project but is often retained throughout the lifecycle of the project. Use of a flexible resource pool through a Hub Programme Office means that resources can be deployed and their usefulness/'value add' monitored so that they are only deployed for a minimum time period

- Similarly, where scarce resources exist within an organization, such as technical architects, testers and others, the portfolio can be designed around their availability and optimal usage, thereby reducing overall delivery costs. A side benefit usually occurs as programmes and projects are less likely to be held up awaiting availability of scarce resources or are able to use less expensive internal experts rather than going to the contractor market.

B4.3 Example P3O value metrics – better, faster, cheaper

Table B.2 Value metrics (Gartner, 2007)

Desired outcome	Value objective	Prime metric
Better	10% improvements in benefits delivered per year	% of Business Case benefits delivered
Better	PMO provides value 5 times greater than PMO cost	Satisfaction of IT governance board
Faster	10% faster project completions per year	Average total elapsed project time
Cheaper	10% lower capital spend per year	Average project cost (normalized for size)
Cheaper	10% lower support costs per year	Average ongoing support costs

B5 HIGH RISKS

As mentioned in Chapter 2, there are a number of common barriers that may need to be overcome in order for the establishment of a P3O to be successful. Table B.3 outlines a selection of risk events and possible treatments to counteract some of these common barriers.

Table B.3 Risk events and possible responses

Risk event	Risk response
P3O may be seen as bureaucratic and adding to paperwork burden on delivery resources	Ensure all standards and templates are tailored to the organization, with additional flexing guidelines. Include project teams in the development of the standards
P3O may become a dumping ground for non-portfolio, programme and project activities or people, who don't have a 'home'.	Develop a P3O Blueprint clearly defining its role and responsibilities
P3O staff are seen as administrators with lack of experience to carry out a meaningful oversight, challenge and scrutiny role	Define roles/responsibilities for P3O staff, ensure they are appropriately graded by independent HR assessment and obtain commitment to the seniority of the roles by a senior management champion.
May have problems recruiting the right mix of people in the organization and on the open marketplace (or obtaining appropriate funding for credible staff)	Define roles/responsibilities for P3O staff, grade appropriately to attract the best staff. As part of mobilization consider recruiting consultants or interims to establish best practice and engineer a skills transfer to internal or newly recruited staff
Lack of commitment from senior management to the benefits of P3O	Engage a senior management champion and sell them the benefits and impact on the bottom line. Use the champion to engage the rest of the senior team
P3O may be seen as a resource bottleneck	Ensure processes are seen as fair and workable. Involve current project teams in their development
Lack of career path for P3O staff, programme and project community, resulting in loss of key resources and replacement costs	Ensure that career development is included in the P3O services/functions
P3O may be seen as getting in the way of decision-making and delivery	Engage senior management champion and ensure all P3O processes are clearly aligned to organization governance processes and decision-making bodies
Lack of senior management ownership of portfolio of programmes and projects (similarly, lack of enterprise-level strategy for alignment)	Ensure main board owns the full portfolio of change – hold stakeholder workshops to ensure common understanding of the strategy, the portfolio of change required and the plan to successful implementation of the strategy

B6 INVESTMENT APPRAISAL (TO INCLUDE OPTIONS)

The format for an Investment Appraisal will vary according to the organization, and advice should be sought as to the appropriate format in the organization. Any Investment Appraisal should include costed options to developing the approach being suggested, so that a balanced decision on the return on investment may be made. The organization's Finance department will generally advise on internal standards and policies on Investment Appraisals and provide support to the process to be followed to develop it and obtain agreement. A sample Investment Appraisal form is shown in Figure B.1 below.

	Including redundancy costs	Excluding redundancy costs
Benefits/annual savings/income		
One-off costs		
Annual costs		
Payback period		
Net present value		
Return on investment		
Author		
Business sponsor	Suggested approver should be main board director	

Figure B.1   Example Investment Appraisal form

Model tailoring – case studies C

Appendix C: Model tailoring – case studies

This appendix describes a series of case studies for different models of P3O across a variety of organization types. Each model has been developed to meet a specific business need and some have evolved over several years as the organization's P3RM has evolved or the business drivers and organization structure have changed.

In developing P3O models, consider the organizational context of these case studies and be aware of the success factors in their evolution.

As has been said before, there is no 'one size fits all' solution, but these case studies may give some ideas to implement in similar organizations.

Table C.1   Sample P3O models across sectors

Number	Organization type	Key features
1	International sporting event	Temporary; oversight, scrutiny and challenge, assurance, collaborative
2	Government agency	Permanent Portfolio Office; hub, function-based roles, standards, assurance, delivery support, scrutiny and challenge
3	Food manufacturing	Permanent COE, generic roles, standards and delivery support
4	Retail organization	Permanent Portfolio Office, governance, assurance, standards, business-focused programmes, outsourced Project Office through Work Packages.
5	Services organization	Permanent COE + delivery support unit, flexible resourcing model
6	Telecommunications	Permanent strategic office + COE, Hub and Spoke model with small generic teams focused on business divisions. Flexible resource model

CASE STUDY 1 – OLYMPICS 2012 PROGRAMME OFFICE: ORGANIZATIONAL CONTEXT, MATURITY AND EVOLUTION

The Olympics 2012 Programme Office (Figure C.1) has been established to provide assurance and oversight to the high-level governance bodies. It provides an oversight role of the four key objectives of the 2012 Olympics and their programme and project management delivery organizations. Its key role is to provide a 'critical friend' through scrutiny and challenge, reviewing and reporting performance across the programme, monitoring and measuring progress against delivery plans and an integrated programme plan, and proactively challenging risks, issues and changes across the programme.

It has been set up with a small team of Programme Specialists, all of whom are experts – senior professionals who are able to challenge through experience and knowledge. It does not impose standards on the constituent programmes/projects to deliver the four key objectives but does use common standards for reporting of performance through progress reports, enabling the creation of Management Dashboards for the governance bodies. Reporting to the programme's Senior Responsible Owner, it is empowered to challenge at the highest levels and has encountered a receptiveness and willingness to work together across the programme. Its key driver is putting in the right framework rather than imposing rigid standards.

The Secretariat and Office Administration, Finance and Strategic Communications functions are all provided through separate but linked teams. This allows the central Programme Office to provide a true 'critical friend' role, unencumbered by day-to-day operational functions.

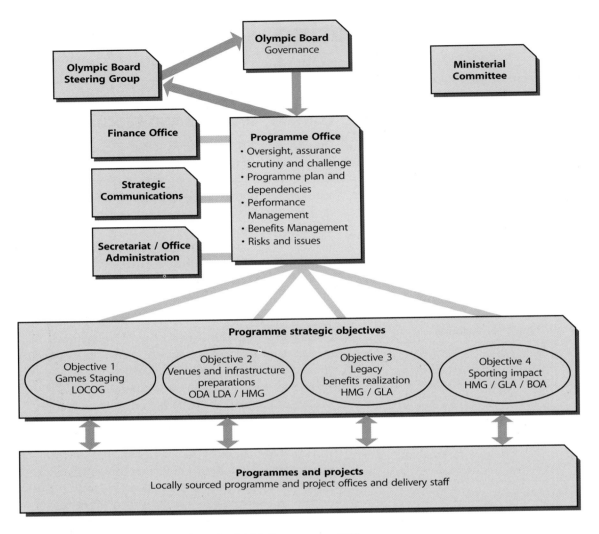

Figure C.1   Case study 1 – Olympics 2012 Programme Office

Hints and tips

A key challenge on a programme of this nature is to ensure good communications across the various delivery strands. The Programme Office does this through a facilitated Programme Managers' Network, which all the Programme Offices attend. A key role of the network is to raise the profile of PPM across the programme and provide the linchpin for good practice and the building of relationships.

A key success to date has been providing ownership and scoping for cross-partner issues and the definition of boundaries of responsibility around issues, providing a central point for the escalation and resolution of aspects

of risk. The Programme Office also provides a professional facilitation service for issue workshops to ensure speedy resolution.

As the programme progresses, it will also own the lessons-learned process and database, capturing overall programme delivery issues to inform future Olympic delivery programmes across the world.

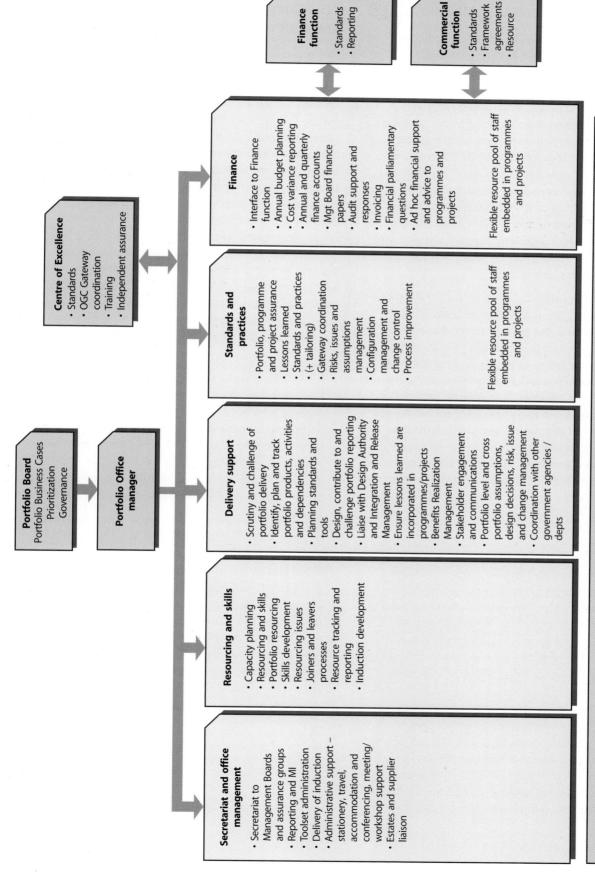

Portfolio Board
Portfolio Business Cases
Prioritization
Governance

Portfolio Office manager

Centre of Excellence
· Standards
· OGC Gateway coordination
· Training
· Independent assurance

Finance function
· Standards
· Reporting

Commercial function
· Standards
· Framework agreements
· Resource

Secretariat and office management
· Secretariat to Management Boards and assurance groups
· Reporting and MI
· Toolset administration
· Delivery of induction
· Administrative support – stationery, travel, accommodation and conferencing, meeting/workshop support
· Estates and supplier liaison

Resourcing and skills
· Capacity planning
· Resourcing and skills
· Portfolio resourcing
· Skills development
· Resourcing issues
· Joiners and leavers processes
· Resource tracking and reporting
· Induction development

Delivery support
· Scrutiny and challenge of portfolio delivery
· Identify, plan and track portfolio products, activities and dependencies
· Planning standards and tools
· Design, contribute to and challenge portfolio reporting
· Liaise with Design Authority and Integration and Release Management
· Ensure lessons learned are incorporated in programmes/projects
· Benefits Realization Management
· Stakeholder engagement and communications
· Portfolio level and cross portfolio assumptions, design decisions, risk, issue and change management
· Coordination with other government agencies / depts

Standards and practices
· Portfolio, programme and project assurance
· Lessons learned
· Standards and practices (+ tailoring)
· Gateway coordination
· Risks, issues and assumptions management
· Configuration management and change control
· Process improvement

Flexible resource pool of staff embedded in programmes and projects

Finance
· Interface to Finance function
· Annual budget planning
· Cost variance reporting
· Annual and quarterly finance accounts
· Mgt Board finance papers
· Audit support and responses
· Invoicing
· Financial parliamentary questions
· Ad hoc financial support and advice to programmes and projects

Flexible resource pool of staff embedded in programmes and projects

Programmes and projects
Standards, governance and scrutiny provided by Portfolio Office
Embedded Assurance and Finance staff from Portfolio Office
Locally sourced programme and project support officers, planners, risk, issue and change analysts

Figure C.2   Case study 2 – Government agency

CASE STUDY 2 – GOVERNMENT AGENCY: ORGANIZATIONAL CONTEXT, MATURITY AND EVOLUTION

This Portfolio Office services a business division within a larger government department (Figure C.2). The government department has a Centre of Excellence with standards and methods, assurance and good-practice teams and Gateway coordinators. The division operates a portfolio of change to meet its strategic objectives and goals, governed through a Portfolio Board aligned to the business and operational functions. The Portfolio Office provides governance support, tracks alignment to other government department initiatives, provides tailoring of COE standards and assurance against the standards, and provides a delivery support and scrutiny/challenge function. It also provides financial tracking and consolidated progress reporting.

Some staff from the Portfolio Office, i.e. for the Finance and Assurance roles, are assigned or embedded in individual programme and project teams. However, individual temporary programmes and projects design and build their own teams including programme and project staff. Programme and Project Office staff carry out Planning, Risk, Issue, Change Management, Information Management and Admin roles. They may be permanent or contract staff and the central resourcing functions considers their utilization as part of an overall resource planning approach. However, in practice the Programme and Project Office teams tend to be too large, as they are taken on for a specific role and not redeployed once their original function has been delivered.

Hints and tips

This model demonstrates two key issues: (1) a lack of centralized capacity planning and (2) individual programmes and projects creating their own teams, which grow over time and can be overstaffed. A strong assurance function is important to ensure that standards and methods are adhered to and tailored appropriately, otherwise roll-up of plans, milestones and progress reports becomes difficult, unwieldy and time consuming. The portfolio team of functional experts need to be empowered to ensure central standards are followed. Wherever possible, a proper capacity-planning function should be in place with a flexible pool of embedded resources, rather than allowing temporary programme/project managers to employ the support staff they want.

CASE STUDY 3 – FOOD MANUFACTURING COMPANY: ORGANIZATIONAL CONTEXT, MATURITY AND EVOLUTION

This organization's Programme Office is a typical single office with a focus on 'doing things right', providing a Centre of Excellence, reporting and a practical hands-on help service across all change in the organization (Figure C.3). Its stated aim is to drive lower costs, reduce uncertainty and increase predictability and success of outcomes. It improves project capability across the organization through developing a standard approach to running projects (based on PRINCE2), working in partnership with project managers to ensure successful delivery of key corporate projects (advice/guidance or practical hands-on support) and adding value by communicating effectively, providing leadership and training in best-practice P3RM. It does not perform the role of a Portfolio Office in that it focuses on programme and project delivery support rather than enabling or supporting business planning, prioritization or overall capacity/capability planning.

Hints and tips

This type of Programme Office has to have a P3O Sponsor who believes in the value it can provide, which may sometimes be intangible. It can be the target for cost cutting as it is sometimes viewed as a 'nice to have' overhead. Ensure performance metrics are built that illustrate the value the unit brings and the impact on the bottom line.

The Head of Programme Office and key staff in this scenario should be senior trusted individuals, who are good communicators, coaches and mentors – they need to 'sell' successful project approaches and overall must have practical experience of running projects. The best Programme Offices of this kind are staffed by former programme or project managers with a flair for stakeholder engagement who have the right level of experience. They must have credibility: all too often Programme Offices are staffed with junior staff, who add little value to the project managers they seek to serve and help.

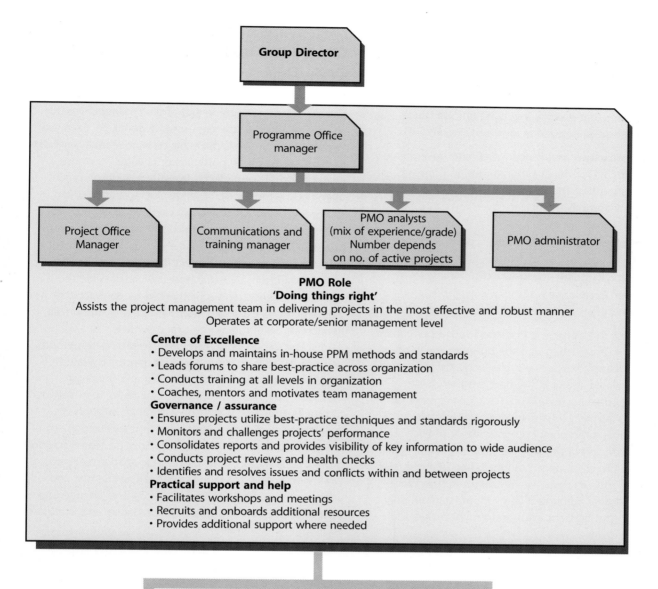

Figure C.3 *Case study 3 – Food manufacturing company*

CASE STUDY 4 – RETAIL ORGANIZATION: ORGANIZATIONAL CONTEXT, MATURITY AND EVOLUTION

The Programme Management Office (PMO) has a number of linked teams that provide a virtual Portfolio Office, including Centre of Excellence functions (Figure C.4):

- **Governance and assurance** – Defining governance arrangements for major programmes and projects and assuring that they continue to meet strategic objectives and have effective governance and plans in place to deliver benefits
- **Group planning and reporting** – portfolio functions of planning, prioritization, alignment with strategy, finance tracking and consolidated reporting
- **Centre of Excellence** – standards/methods, communications and business change.

Each business function has a Portfolio Lead, a permanent member of staff reporting into the business line, who provides a delivery support and challenge function to the Business Lead. Many of the new programmes or projects are outsourced via Work Packages to external P3RM consultancies via framework agreements. In these instances a temporary programme or project function consisting of programme/project managers and programme/project support staff including planners, risk, issue and change analysts, etc. is bought in. The Work Package is closely monitored and support staff are only retained for specific tasks, with bottom line 'value add' being a key driver.

Hints and tips

This model requires good relationships with external suppliers who understand the business and its P3RM standards. The Work Packages need to be focused on outputs rather than roles, so that the onus is on the supplier to provide the more effective set of resources to ensure delivery. Independent assurance from the core PMO team is essential to ensure programmes and project Work Packages provide good value for money and that external resources use internal methods and standards effectively.

CASE STUDY 5 – SERVICES ORGANIZATION: ORGANIZATIONAL CONTEXT, MATURITY AND EVOLUTION

This services company had a very strong Group IT function that provided programme and project management for all key initiatives across the Group (Figure C.5). Each year as part of the business planning cycle, individual business divisions agreed their portfolios of change and these were prioritized centrally by the strategic development team (led by the Group Strategy Director) and ratified by the Group Board. Once the full portfolio of change was agreed, the programme and project management group provided a programme manager per business division, supported by a team of project managers and project support staff from a central pool. Where possible these were permanent staff, supplemented by contract staff where demand exceeded internal supply or authorized headcount. The Programme Office consisted of two teams. The Centre of Excellence team provided methods and standards, help, advice and guidance, facilitated workshops, knowledge management and training. Individual consultants within the COE team were assigned to projects to provide start-up assistance, support collaborative workshops and assist in the development of plans where required. The Delivery Support team provided project coordinators who were assigned to projects to work with project managers, providing secretariat and admin support, Risk Register, Issue Log and Change Log maintenance, plan and report maintenance, and acting as configuration librarian.

Hints and tips

In this model, responsibility for consolidated progress reporting, resource management across the programme and prioritization of delivery into the business environment was done through business Programme Boards consisting of the programme manager, business information manager and senior business managers/directors. Overall optimization of programme and project capacity was done through team meetings between the Head of Programme and Project Management and the programme managers.

The business divisions also ran portfolios of small/medium business-based projects or initiatives. These were often serviced through satellite Programme Offices consisting of project managers and project coordinator roles. The standards adopted by these satellite teams were those from the IT Centre of Excellence and training was provided in their use across the group.

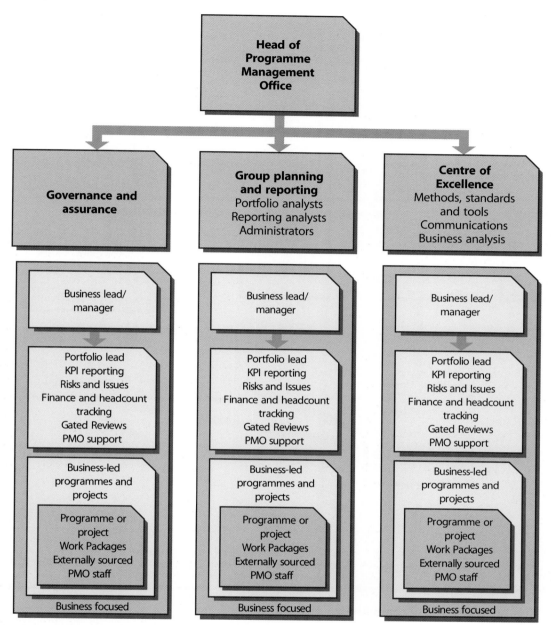

Figure C.4   Case study 4 – Retail organization

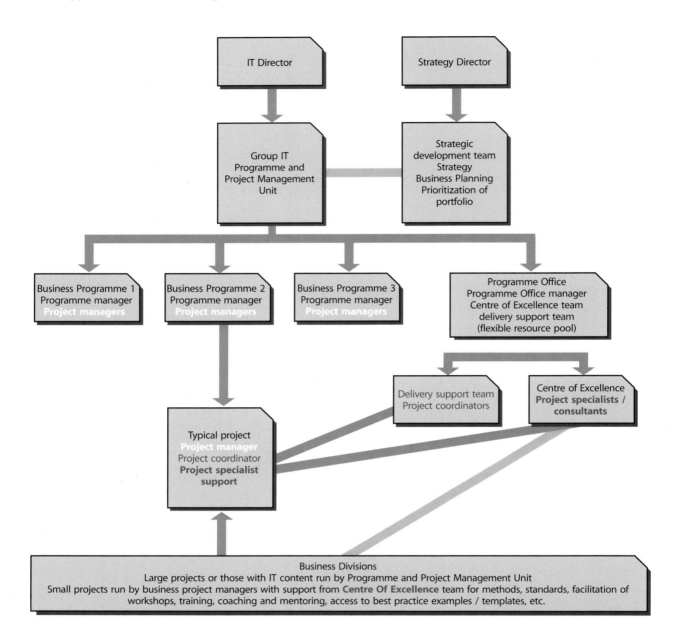

Figure C.5   Case study 5 – Services organization

CASE STUDY 6 – TELECOMMUNICATIONS: ORGANIZATIONAL CONTEXT, MATURITY AND EVOLUTION

This organization has divisions responsible for different threads of the group strategy (Figure C.6). Each division has evolved its own programme and project delivery model, with different gated lifecycles in existence to suit the local business drivers. The Technology Division has a strategic office that manages strategic alignment, approval of Business Cases and prioritization of delivery. Once programmes and projects are approved, the business teams/departments manage their own programmes/projects using staff from central Programme Office and a Programme/Project Management team. The central Programme Office provides Centre of Excellence functions, capacity planning of programme/project staff and centralized consolidated planning and reporting.

Each business team or department (a variable number) is assigned a PMO lead (line managed through central PMO), who is responsible for ensuring central standards are adhered to and tailored, providing the link to the central Programme Office for milestone and dependency tracking and reporting and acting as the point of escalation for risks, issues and changes. The PMO lead has a flexible pool of resources at three levels of competency, consisting of specialists (PPM experts, planning, workshops, knowledge management, etc.), support analysts and administrators (reporting, risk, issue and change, quality reviews, information management and administration). The PMO leads may have line management responsibility for resources in other business teams and meet regularly in a PMO forum to exchange ideas, lessons learned, etc.

The central Programme Office's flexible pool of specialists, support analysts and administrators is composed of 60% permanent and 40% contract staff.

Hints and tips

This model is widespread in private organizations, providing centralized control of standards, assurance and reporting while establishing delivery support resources at the point of delivery. It requires strong leadership from the central Programme Office and continuity of the P3O Sponsor. The PMO leads need to be carefully chosen, trained and coached, with particular emphasis on matrix management techniques. They should also be permanent members of staff wherever possible.

Key successes for this model have been: adherence to a single consistent gated lifecycle, reduction in the numbers of contract staff, centralized capacity planning reducing headcount overall with more control over what the programme and project teams use support staff for (and for how long). Another noted success has been the roll-out of a collaborative approach to project start-up, which has accelerated progress through gates 0–2 of the standard gated lifecycle from nine months to nine weeks on average. This was achieved through the setting up of collaboration zones (physical spaces) around the offices and training the core Programme Office team, PMO leads and specialists in collaborative facilitated workshop techniques.

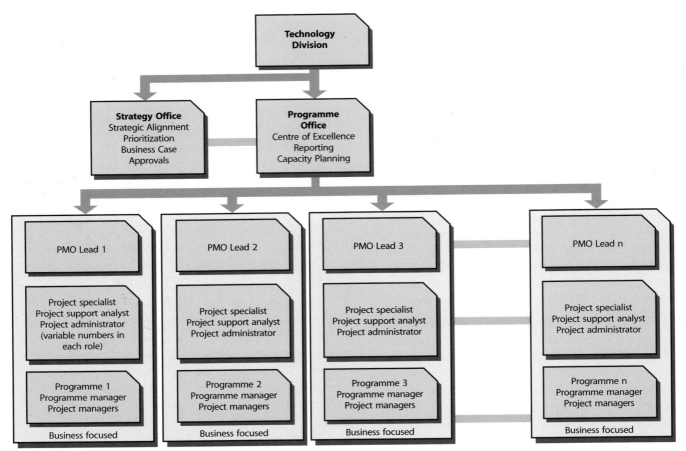

Figure C.6   Case study 6 – Telecommunications

Example tools and
techniques

D

Appendix D: Example tools and techniques

To assist with a number of the concepts described in Chapter 5, an online repository of a sample set of generic tools and techniques has been provided electronically. To access this repository go to www.best-management-practice.com and follow the P3O links.

The tools and techniques are provided as a starting point for tailoring and alignment to the organization's requirements.

The site is designed so that samples of good practice (see example in Figure D.1) can be uploaded for sharing with the wider P3O community. All contributions are welcomed.

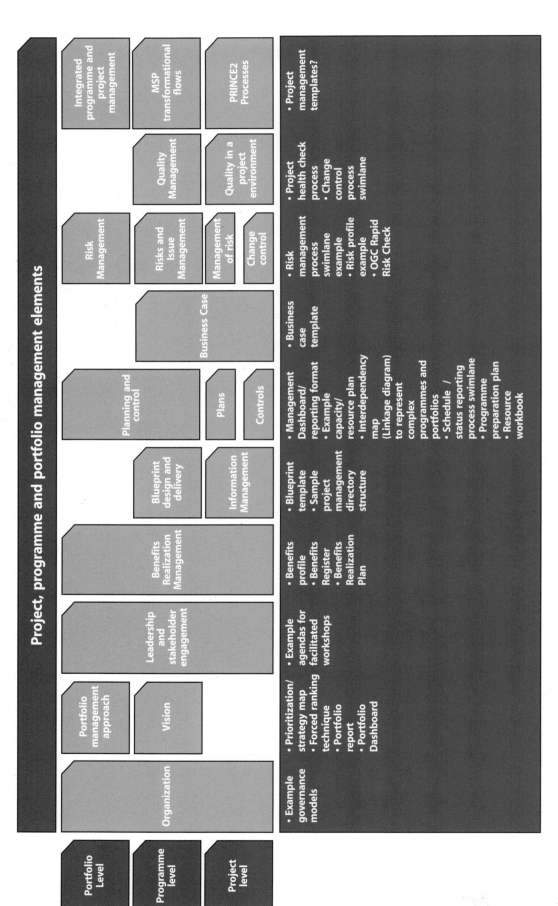

Figure D.1   Sample contents of online repository

P3M3 summary

E

Appendix E: P3M3 summary

The P3M3 model provides a very useful input into the development of a business Blueprint for P3O in terms of current and target portfolio, programme and project management capabilities. It is an excellent tool for measuring the success of capability improvement over time (Figure E.1).

Tables E.1–E.3 provide a summary of the attributes for portfolio, programme and project management (respectively) across each of the process perspectives.

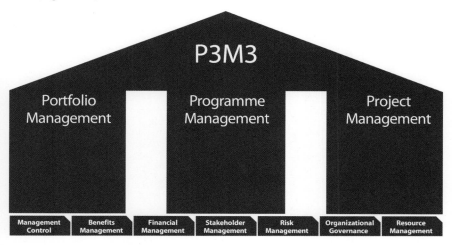

Figure E.1   P3M3 model

Table E.1 Portfolio level (PfM3)

Level	Process	Comment
1	Management Control	■ The organization recognizes the portfolio, but has little or no documented processes or standards for its management, and a limited directory of programmes and projects.
		■ The recognition of corporate or departmental portfolio by the organization is a significant step usually associated with the investment control or Business Case approval process. It is an important first step on the maturity ladder because, by articulating the portfolio, the organization sets out its criteria for prioritization and oversight.
	Benefits Management	■ There is a recognition that programmes and projects exist within the corporate portfolio to enable achieving benefits for the organization. However, this will not translate into a defined benefits realization process.
	Financial Management	■ Portfolio oversight of programmes and projects may be recognized but there is little or no corporate investment control.
		■ There is some financial control but it is often left to budget centres to approve and control programmes and projects according to their own criteria.
	Risk Management	■ There is a growing recognition that risks need to be managed and that, at least for key business initiatives (e.g. cost saving, major site developments), risks threaten success.
		■ There is risk identification (probably in different systems, e.g. spreadsheets, text documents, databases etc.) and maybe some quantification of risk, but little actual management of risk.
	Stakeholder Management	■ The portfolio may be acknowledged, but there is little or no connection between programme and project output, and business outcome and benefits.
	Organization Governance	■ The organization has some inconsistent and informal attempts to align individual programmes and projects to corporate objectives, and there is an ad hoc, inconsistent and ineffective oversight of programmes and projects.
	Resource Management	■ Programme and project resource requirements are recognized but not systematically managed. Resources are planned, developed and allocated in an ad hoc and, usually, project basis.
		■ The symptoms of not having a portfolio approach to resource identification and allocation are all too obvious, but the organization has yet to fully commit to undertake robust corporate portfolio management.

Table E.1 Portfolio level (PfM3) (continued)

Level	Process	Comment
2	Management Control	■ There are some pockets of portfolio discipline within individual departments, but this is based on key individuals rather than as a comprehensive and consistent organization-wide approach. ■ The concepts of Portfolio management will have been grasped by some and indeed there may be local experts. Work will be ongoing to establish a portfolio management approach across the organization through the recognition of an investment cycle, e.g. proposition, feasibility, design, implementation, review, etc. ■ Improved Business Case definition is enabling programmes and projects to be tested against the corporate objectives and priorities.
	Benefits Management	■ The development of the investment cycle will be increasing the awareness and importance of identifying benefits and subsequently tracking whether they have been achieved. However, the realization of benefits is still likely to be patchy, inconsistent and not monitored.
	Financial Management	■ There are some pockets of good Business Case production and some, usually departmental, structures to oversee investment decisions. However, Business Cases are often appraised independently of each other, and real corporate priorities have not been established. ■ Reasonable financial control, Business Case production, procurement appraisal, and investment control are restricted to individuals and departments.
	Risk Management	■ The increasing awareness that the organization bears corporate risk tends to lead to a top-down (perhaps 'knee-jerk') approach to identifying portfolio risk (focusing on major corporate initiatives) that is unconnected to the bottom-up identification of risks in programmes and projects. This often leads to duplication of effort, competing teams, non-optimal allocation of funding, inconsistency and, therefore, the ineffective management of corporate risk.
	Stakeholder Management	■ A portfolio of programmes and projects that serve the corporate objectives and priorities is increasingly seen as the driving force for approval, oversight and Performance Management. ■ The portfolio is tending to be driven by individual programmes and projects, i.e. bottom up.
	Organization Governance	■ Some attempts to recognize the portfolio of programmes and projects, but there is still no overall leadership and direction for the process. ■ Programmes and projects may be initiated and run without full regard to the corporate goals, priorities and targets. ■ It is difficult to establish the rationale for which programmes and projects are funded or approved.
	Resource Management	■ The organization has started to develop resource management processes and improve the identification and allocation of resources to specific initiatives. However, this is likely to be reliant on key individuals and does not assess the wider impact of resource allocation against the wider portfolio. ■ The problems of not managing resources across the portfolio will be greater understood and solutions are starting to be developed in isolated programmes or departments.

Table E.1 Portfolio level (PfM3) (continued)

Level	Process	Comment
3	Management Control	■ Standard portfolio management processes, as well as roles and responsibilities for governance and delivery, are defined, documented and understood. ■ Corporate portfolio management processes have specified owners and there is evidence of use and effectiveness of a portfolio management office. ■ Planning and reporting tools are implemented and used effectively, and portfolio guidelines exist and are actively used. ■ Portfolio management is both defined and established across the organization and defined processes are being used to reduce and manage corporate risk.
	Benefits Management	■ There is a centrally managed framework used for defining and tracking the delivery of benefits across the business operations.
	Financial Management	■ There will be established standards for the investment management process and the preparation of Business Cases. The costs, expenditure and forecasts will be monitored at portfolio level in accordance with organizational guidelines and procedures. There will be defined interfaces with other financial functions within the organization. ■ Portfolio Financial Management is defined and established across the organization, and defined processes are being used to improve investment and procurement decisions, and monitor programme and project budgets.
	Risk Management	■ Portfolio risks are identified, quantified and mitigation plans developed and funded. Risks across the portfolio are continually reviewed and there is reporting to senior management. ■ Robust risk management includes: the identification of strategic, delivery and operational risks; the consistent analysis of risk in terms of probability, impact (on project schedule, cost and quality of deliverable) and timing; the production and funding of contingency plans; and the continual review by knowledgeable experts, risk owners and senior managers.
	Stakeholder Management	■ Stakeholder engagement in the portfolio and individual programmes and projects is taken seriously and genuine authority is extended to appropriate stakeholders. The investment cycle is fully functioning and drives entry to the portfolio, and the importance of business process design is recognized. ■ The portfolio is tending to drive individual programmes and projects, i.e. top down.
	Organization Governance	■ The principles of portfolio, programme and project management are widely understood, practised to a consistent standard, and underpin the governance framework.
	Resource Management	■ Programme and project resources are being managed within defined and well used processes. This allows the organization to increase the targeting and development of resources against corporate objectives. ■ The competent identification of the required resources, skills and experience (especially in the business as distinct from the project team) enables the organization to improve the likelihood of committed resources being released in a timely manner to support the work of programmes and projects.

Table E.1 Portfolio level (PfM3) (continued)

Level	Process	Comment
4	Management Control	■ Portfolio management processes are integrated with those of programme and project management, with programme and project performance capability metrics in place and used.
	Benefits Management	■ The benefits realization and management process is well established and is integrated into how the organization manages itself.
	Financial Management	■ The organization has effective and robust financial control of its investment decisions and the approval and monitoring of programmes and projects. There is proactive, evidence-based management of the portfolio. ■ Financial oversight of the portfolio is corporate-centric rather than programme- or project-centric.
	Risk Management	■ The organization's appetite for risk, and the balance of risk and benefit across the portfolio, are continually reviewed and managed. Senior managers own and oversee the management of risks across the portfolio. ■ Portfolio risk management is embedded within the corporate reporting and management structures.
	Stakeholder Management	■ The organization, as part of the initial planning, readiness preparation and deployment planning, consistently ascertains the current organizational culture and determines the climate and activities required to improve the effectiveness of business change and the generation of ideas. ■ Business areas fully own the transition to new ways of working and, via the corporate portfolio, see programmes and projects as suitable vehicles to effectively manage that transition.
	Organization Governance	■ All programmes and projects are integrated into an achievable portfolio aligned to corporate objectives and strategic targets.
	Resource Management	■ The organization has established effective capacity and capability strategies and processes for obtaining, allocating and adjusting resource levels (including people, funding, estate and tools) in line with medium-term and long-term investment plans.

Table E.1 Portfolio level (PfM3) (continued)

Level	Process	Comment
5	Management Control	■ Potential problems in the programme and project management context are identified and prevented from occurring. There is an awareness of the likely potential and impact of new technology being embedded into the standard programme and project management processes. ■ Quantitative and qualitative measures, and lessons learned, are being routinely used to improve the effectiveness of corporate portfolio management.
	Benefits Management	■ Benefits realization is integral to the development and maintenance of the business strategy.
	Financial Management	■ Financial control of the portfolio is an integral part of the organization's financial control regime. ■ Appropriate financial control is embedded within programmes and projects, and integrated with that for the organization.
	Risk Management	■ The process of Portfolio Risk Management is continually improved, based on analysis of evidence from within the organization and comparison with other organizations. ■ The Corporate Risk Management process is continually improved, and the corporate risk model is refined to align with the organizational culture and corporate objectives.
	Stakeholder Management	■ Continual business process improvements are undertaken in a planned manner, aligned with corporate objectives and priorities, with demonstrable benefits and measurement of the efficacy of programmes and projects. ■ The portfolio, programmes and projects are viewed as the preferred instruments to achieve continual improvement in the organization's business processes.
	Organization Governance	■ The portfolio is proactively managed to ensure that it remains sufficiently dynamic and agile to cater for changes in business direction and priorities. The portfolio is supporting the organization's goals by its use of performance measures, improving quality and productivity, and the effective use of the organization's assets. ■ The governance of investment management has moved from a programme- or project-centric process to a corporate-centric process.
	Resource Management	■ The analysis and management of the portfolio drives the planning, development and allocation of programme and project resources to ever improve the effective use of resources in achieving the corporate objectives.

Table E.2 Programme level (PgM3)

Level	Process	Comment
1	Management Control	■ The programme management terminology may be in use but will be used inconsistently. General approach will be based on project rather than programme level.
	Benefits Management	■ There is recognition of the concept of benefits that can be differentiated from project outputs. Benefits will be developed at a project level with minimal programme control.
	Financial Management	■ Minimal or no financial controls; those that exist are principally related to projects.
	Risk Management	■ Minimal evidence of Risk Management being deployed to any beneficial effect; main focus is on Issue Management.
	Stakeholder Management	■ Programme management is principally seen as an area of activity outside the remit of business operations. Managers may see the programme approach as threatening rather than adding value.
	Organization Governance	■ Informal governance of programmes exists but has undefined linkage to projects and the broader organizational controls. Roles are likely to be notional.
	Resource Management	■ Focus is on project resources being deployed with minimal focus on programme management resource requirements.
2	Management Control	■ General understanding of the concepts of programme management. There is evidence of good examples of deployment but there will be inconsistency and varying levels of commitment. There is a strategic acknowledgement of the value of programme management.
	Benefits Management	■ Benefits are recognized as a key element and differentiating factor for programmes. Focus is likely to be at the project level but initial evidence exists of tracking at a programme level. There will be more detailed definition of benefits.
	Financial Management	■ Financial approvals for projects are evident but the cost of the programme is not being fully accounted for in all cases.
	Risk Management	■ Risk Management is recognized and used on programmes, but there are inconsistencies in approach, commitment and deployment.
	Stakeholder Management	■ Operational and business staff involved with the programme and engaging with the delivery. Engagement is consultative and reactive rather than decision-making
	Organization Governance	■ Programme Management is beginning to take shape but with ad hoc controls being applied and no clear strategic control. Roles and responsibilities will be unclear, as will reporting lines.
	Resource Management	■ Resources are being deployed across the organization but there is little evidence of a consistent approach to acquisition, planning or management.

Table E.2 Programme level (PgM3) (continued)

Level	Process	Comment
3	Management Control	■ There is a consistent approach to programme management controls, with the application of approaches in all programmes. A defined lifecycle exists and there is a active management and application of controls to programmes within it.
	Benefits Management	■ There is a centrally managed framework used for defining and tracking the delivery of benefits across the business operations.
	Financial Management	■ Standard approaches to Financial Management and costs assessments that are tracked through the lifecycle and are deployed consistently across all programmes.
	Risk Management	■ Risk management has a clearly defined process that is followed consistently by all programmes. Framework is based on industry standards and is supported by a toolkit.
	Stakeholder Management	■ Organization and business engagement with the programme approach. Active and regular input into the way programmes are managed, with major focus on the achievement of business change rather than programme delivery.
	Organization Governance	■ All roles and responsibilities documented within terms of reference. Strategic controls being applied consistently with decision-making structures in place.
	Resource Management	■ Planned deployment and effective utilization of resources across the programme, supported by standard approaches to planning and tracking.
4	Management Control	■ Programme management is seen as a key tool for the delivery of strategic objectives by the board. There is acceptance of a common approach, which is supported by management behaviour. Within the programme environment the focus is on improvement, adoption and measurement.
	Benefits Management	■ Benefits management is embedded within the programme management approach and underpins the justification and management of each programme.
	Financial Management	■ Programme lifecycles are being flexed effectively to manage availability of finance and effective decision-making is occurring on the basis of financial evidence.
	Risk Management	■ Risk management works effectively, with active management and avoidance of risks being evident and embedded behaviours.
	Stakeholder Management	■ Extensive engagement with business operations, with an equal focus on business and organization improvement and programme delivery.
	Organization Governance	■ Clearly aligned decision-making processes that adopt and integrate the broader organizational governance and that are transparent to those involved. Programme management responsibilities are embedded within broader role descriptions.
	Resource Management	■ Measurement of resources utilization and proactive engagement to raise and broaden capability, and evidence of improved delivery resulting.

Table E.2 Programme level (PgM3) (continued)

Level	Process	Comment
5	Management Control	■ There is integration between a programme approach and the delivery of strategic aims and objectives. Acceptance of programme management as the optimal approach to strategic delivery is accepted throughout the organization.
	Benefits Management	■ Benefits management is embedded within the organizational approach to change and benefits are assessed as part of the development of corporate strategies.
	Financial Management	■ Financial control is evident throughout the programme lifecycle and a balanced view of risk taking is underpinning the programme governance.
	Risk Management	■ Risk management is embedded in the organizational culture and underpins all decision-making within the programme.
	Stakeholder Management	■ Business operations are integral to the design and delivery of effective programmes. Management methods are integrated within the programme framework. The route to business change and improvement is seen as programme management.
	Organization Governance	■ Programme management is embedded at board level, with clear ownership and control responsibilities embedded within individual directors' terms of reference.
	Resource Management	■ Resources are deployed optimally; there is clear evidence of balancing internal and external expertise, and knowledge is being embedded into the business.

Table E.3 Project level (PjM3)

Level	Process	Comment
1	Management Control	■ Project management terminology is being used by some within the organization but not in a consistent manner and indeed without being understood by all stakeholders. Some projects will be defined, conducted and managed to some extent. ■ Where projects have been defined, the scope and objectives may be articulated to a wider audience with the aim of achieving commitment and support.
	Benefits Management	■ There is recognition of the concept of benefits that can be differentiated from project outputs. Benefits may be cited within some project documentation but will tend to be qualitative or intangible. There will be limited, if any, responsibility for benefits planning and realization. The organization will have difficulty in reviewing benefits and attributing them to projects.
	Financial Management	■ There are minimal financial controls at the project level and a general lack of accountability for monitoring project expenditure. ■ The lack of formal Business Cases will present some difficulties for the organization in fully appraising potential projects, making investment decisions and directing such investments.
	Risk Management	■ Minimal evidence of risk management being deployed to any beneficial effect. ■ A risk management process will not have been established, although some projects will be cognizant of some of the risks that threaten them and these may be documented in an inconsistent manner within project Risk Registers. There will be little evidence of these registers being maintained.
	Stakeholder Management	■ Project management process improvement will be unplanned. There will be evidence of some 'fire-fighting' with perhaps experienced managers being used to rescue projects in difficulty. ■ The project management process is likely to be chaotic and therefore in need of some basic standardization and established baselines on which to consider improvement.
	Organization Governance	■ Informal governance of projects exists but has undefined linkage to the broader organizational controls. Project roles are likely to be notional and terms of reference for the governance structures are unlikely to be fully documented. Planning for business review and governance checkpoints are unlikely to be fully developed. ■ Leadership and responsibilities may not be fully attributable.
	Resource Management	■ There is little recognition of the skills and competencies necessary to deliver projects successfully. ■ As projects are poorly defined, the role of project manager is compromised; project managers are unlikely to get the support and commitment by the organization, to get the resources necessary to accomplish project objectives in a consistent and planned manner.

Table E.3 Project level (PjM3) (continued)

Level	Process	Comment
2	Management Control	■ The concepts of project management will have been grasped by some within the organization and indeed there may be local experts, e.g. experienced project managers working within the organization on key projects. Work will be ongoing to establish a project management approach across the organization through the recognition of a project lifecycle, supported by document templates and some tools and techniques. Such initiatives are likely to be championed by the experienced project managers.
	Benefits Management	■ Benefits are recognized within project Business Cases. There will be some documentation on who is responsible for particular benefits and their realization, but this is unlikely to be followed through. The difference between outputs, outcomes and benefits will be understood by most managers within the organization. The role of SRO in benefits management and realization may be articulated on some projects. Post-implementation reviews (post-project reviews) will be focused on the project activities and deliverables.
	Financial Management	■ Business Cases are being produced in various forms and the better or more formal cases will present the project rationale on which to obtain organizational commitment to the project and take an investment decision. ■ Financial management of projects will be variable, depending primarily on the competency of the project manager. There will be little, if any, evidence that cost considerations are used in, for example, contingency planning and risk evaluation.
	Risk Management	■ Risk Management is recognized and used on all projects, but there are likely to be inconsistencies in approach, commitment and deployment. ■ Key project managers will understand and articulate the purpose and importance of risk management, but there will not be the same level of commitment and understanding across all projects and throughout the organization generally. There will be inconsistencies in the reporting and escalation of risks from projects to other stakeholders within the organization.
	Stakeholder Management	■ Project management process development and improvement actions are not necessarily planned across the whole organization. Strengths and weaknesses will be identified by project managers in isolation and action taken to address specific weaknesses. ■ Project management will be assessed at the local level by individual managers and some improvements will be initiated. There will be little dissemination of good practice between projects and little central control of the improvement agenda.
	Organization Governance	■ Project management from an organizational perspective is beginning to take shape but with ad hoc controls being applied and with no clear strategic control. Roles and responsibilities are sometimes unclear, as are reporting lines and accountabilities. ■ Some projects are perceived as falling outside of the organizational governance arrangements. There is little effective analysis and management of stakeholder groupings and management of their expectations.
	Resource Management	■ Resources are being deployed on projects, but there is little evidence of a consistent approach to acquisition, planning or management of these resources. ■ The organization has started to adopt formal project management methods and perceives the need to familiarize staff with the methods, tools and techniques that are being adopted. ■ Appropriate individuals will be selected for principal project activities based on the project outline or high-level brief. Managers may be recommending some project training.

Table E.3 Project level (PjM3) (continued)

Level	Process	Comment
3	Management Control	■ There is a consistent approach to project management controls across the organization, based on standard processes and methods. This standardization facilitates staff training and development and enables a common set of tools and other support arrangements to be deployed economically and effectively. ■ The project lifecycle will not only focus on project initiation and development activities, but will also have equal emphasis on review and verification activities, implementation and handover.
	Benefits Management	■ There is a centrally managed framework used for defining and tracking the delivery of benefits from the project outputs and in order to achieve the desired outcomes from delivered projects. ■ Measures of success for projects are becoming defined and explicit. Post-project reviews are used to report formally on outcomes, and there may be procedures for periodic reviews of benefits after the project closure. There will be a review of all qualitative benefits to ascertain whether these can be made more tangible and how they might be measured.
	Financial Management	■ The organization will have established standards for the preparation of Business Cases and processes for the management of Business Cases throughout the project lifecycle. Project managers will monitor costs and expenditure in accordance with organizational guidelines and procedures, and there will be defined interfaces with other financial functions within the organization. ■ SROs will have responsibility for each Business Case. ■ Business Cases are likely to be developed by iteration throughout the project lifecycle.
	Risk Management	■ Project risk management is conducted as a defined process that is cognizant of the organization's policy for the management of risks. ■ Inherent project risks are being minimized effectively through project Initiation and Planning stages, while acquired risks are identified throughout the project lifecycle and are either being eliminated or mitigated through viable contingency measures. Risks are being escalated to the appropriate levels within the organization, as necessary.
	Stakeholder Management	■ The organization will have considered project management process improvement in the wider context of organizational improvement frameworks and approaches. A quality management approach will have been adopted and project improvement initiatives defined and managed as a change programme across the organization. ■ Project management processes will be reviewed regularly and information made available to Quality Management.
	Organization Governance	■ Project roles and responsibilities are explicitly documented within terms of reference, including those of governance and control, e.g. Project Board. Strategic controls are being applied consistently with decision-making structures in place. ■ The governance arrangements for projects are clearly defined and embedded within the organization, although the value and benefit of these controls is not being fully realized. Stakeholder involvement is both planned and analysed and the project manager confirms that stakeholder management is in place.
	Resource Management	■ The organization has well defined projects and project managers able to review and assess the resource requirements in relation to project delivery. Project managers will undertake sufficient planning to ascertain their project resource requirements. They will be able to highlight resource shortfalls and indicate individual/team training and development needs. ■ The role of project manager will be a recognized skill within the organization with an associated set of competencies.

Table E.3 Project level (PjM3) (continued)

Level	Process	Comment
4	Management Control	■ Project management is well aligned with the business plans and objectives. Project management has sufficient strategic importance for the organization to ensure that it is integrated with other Business/Strategic planning functions. Project management processes are fully embedded within the organization and there is a move towards more quantitative management and performance measurement.
	Benefits Management	■ Benefits management is embedded within the project management approach. Projects can demonstrate strong business focus and strategic alignment. This will be documented in the Business Case. The organization will ensure claimed benefits are realistic and that they are endorsed by the SRO. ■ Systems will be in place to capture the measurement of benefits and collect information on benefit types.
	Financial Management	■ The organization is able to prioritize investment opportunities effectively in relation to the availability of funds and other resources. Business Cases are evaluated and investment decisions are ratified by the business. Project budgets are managed effectively and project performance against cost is monitored and compared. Cost models are used to demonstrate the efficacy of projects.
	Risk Management	■ Risk management is working effectively and the value of risk management can be demonstrated from the organizational perspective. ■ Business stakeholders are comfortable with the management of project risks and their involvement, as appropriate, in the management process. Project managers are able to demonstrate integration between risk management and their planning and control mechanisms.
	Stakeholder Management	■ The organization has established a continual improvement process by which lessons learned from previous projects are captured and embedded in new projects. There are quantitative goals for project management improvement across the organization. Improvement actions are tracked and measured across all projects, and necessary changes planned and implemented.
	Organization Governance	■ Decision-making processes associated with project performance adopt and adapt the broader organizational Performance Management and governance arrangements. Projects have explicit governance arrangements and clear channels of communication for ensuring stakeholders are informed and commitment remains high.
	Resource Management	■ Resource management for projects is considered at a more strategic rather than tactical level within the organization. There is evidence of resource capacity management, through capacity planning. Resource availability and utilization are being measured and actions taken to ensure the organization has the capacity and capability to meet its project delivery needs.

Table E.3 Project level (PjM3) (continued)

Level	Process	Comment
5	Management Control	■ Project management controls are being optimized to ensure that they are effective and efficient from the organizational perspective. They are regularly evaluated and enhanced so that they remain aligned with business imperatives, strategies and plans. ■ Controls are not only used to monitor existing projects, but the organization uses information feedback to proactively plan and design better control mechanisms for future projects. The level of control is planned in accordance with the criticality and complexity of the project to be managed.
	Benefits Management	■ Benefits management is embedded within the organizational approach to change and benefits being achieved are assessed as part of the development of corporate strategies. ■ Projected benefits are fully documented in Business Cases in terms of a Benefits Management Strategy that is fully supported by a Benefits Realization Plan. Benefits Network Diagrams are likely to be in evidence to analyse dependencies. There is strong evidence that Post-project reviews are performed and trends are established. Lessons learned are fed back into Benefits Realization Planning and other management activities.
	Financial Management	■ Project financial controls are fully integrated with those of the organization. Cost estimation techniques being used at the project level are continually reviewed in terms of actual vs. estimate comparisons to improve estimation throughout the organization. ■ The organization will display effective cost analysis systems, in order to improve future project economy, efficiency and effectiveness. ■ The organization will be able to demonstrate the value for money that is being achieved through its projects.
	Risk Management	■ Risk Management is embedded in the organizational culture and underpins all decision-making with respect to projects. ■ Risk management will be integrated effectively with project planning and estimation, the project management control mechanisms, and the governance arrangements. There will be strong links with Financial Management processes and any risks to project benefits will be highlighted and examined. Project managers will clearly demonstrate the value of risk management in terms of contingency budget savings.
	Stakeholder Management	■ Continual process improvement to the project management processes are undertaken in a planned manner across all projects, with demonstrable benefits and measurement of the efficacy of project management to the quality of projects. ■ There is strong evidence of knowledge management and performance information being used to achieve improvement goals, with quantitative improvements in productivity, project quality and other measures. The organization has an established quality culture and is keen to be contributing to best practice.
	Organization Governance	■ The governance arrangements for projects are taken seriously by the organization, with demonstrable reporting lines to board level and with clear ownership, control and reporting responsibilities embedded within the organization. ■ The governance arrangements for all projects will be explicitly stated in relevant project documentation, including the Business Case. There will be evidence that these arrangements are periodically reviewed for effectiveness, based on lessons learned from project activity.
	Resource Management	■ Resources are deployed optimally, there is clear evidence of load balancing and the effective use of both internal and external resources in accordance with a resource strategy. Project managers will have an understanding of the business processes and business objectives and will be able to assure senior managers that project resources are sufficiently focused on business needs. Resource managers are proactive in identifying future needs and in anticipating future criticality through, for example, technical

Functions and services

Appendix F: Functions and services

This appendix outlines the most common P3O functions and services.

As discussed in Chapter 3, the function or service may take different forms dependent on where it is applied in the governance hierarchy – this is denoted by the different columns in Tables F.1–F.3.

Each row refers to a function or service with the following columns:

- Function or service name, e.g. risk or planning
- Portfolio activities (permanent office)
- COE activities (permanent office)
- Programme or Project Office activities (temporary office)
- Useful tools/techniques relevant to the function or service – may refer or link to other OGC guidance.

Figure F.1 shows a breakdown of functions and services, which have been categorized as Planning, Delivery or Centre of Excellence (consistency of approach, standards, etc.). This is reflected in the table headings in Tables F.1–3.

Hints and tips

Where there is only one office in an organization's P3O model, all functions in all columns should be considered when building the P3O service Blueprint; and in reality Heads of P3O designing a P3O model should use Table F.1 as a 'pick and mix' selection of services to meet local business need and maturity levels.

Keep it simple – it is best to keep the functions and services design simple initially and then build in or add to services and information when their value has been established and the relevant skill sets built up. For example, in relation to resource management and capacity planning first focus on the skills types where the number of resources is severely constrained.

With regard to the content of Tables F.1–3, two special features need to be mentioned:

- **Portfolio Office and Centre of Excellence**: In some organizations there is only one organization-wide office providing both portfolio management and COE functions – often referred to by a single name, e.g. Portfolio Office. In others they are very different offices: the portfolio or strategic change functions may be undertaken by a Portfolio Office or the strategy department, whereas the COE is an office where standards, training, mentoring, coaching process improvement and internal consultancy reside. Tables F.1–3 separate out portfolio and COE functions, but the reality may be a combination of both, so remember the 'pick and mix' rule to meet any organization's needs

- **Hub Portfolio or Programme Office**: A Hub Portfolio or Programme Office (permanent) is often set up to provide portfolio or COE functions and services to a division/agency/department or business unit or function, tailoring them to local need. The hub may also provide a central flexible resource pool for delivery-focused programme and project support staff, enabling improved capacity planning and adherence to standards. The central pool of resources will be allocated to temporary programmes and projects as they launch and may change throughout the programme or project lifecycle. For example, at the start of a programme or project there is a need for a higher level of planning support, but this can be reduced as the programme or project moves into implementation. By creating a central flexible resource pool and resourcing programmes and projects from the central pool, less time will be spent on induction, staff will 'hit the ground running' on standards, and there are opportunities to share staff and lessons learned. In terms of functions and services provided, each Hub Programme Office will reflect local need and be dependent on the size and responsibilities of the organization's Portfolio Office or COE (where these offices exist). There is no separate column in the table to identify Hub Programme Office activities as in reality it may offer a subset of the portfolio and COE activities in addition to providing programme and project activities (through a central flexible resource pool). Again – remember the 'pick and mix' rule.

P3O	Planning (Portfolio)	Portfolio build, prioritization, analysis and reporting
		Programme and project set-up and closure
		Stakeholder engagement and communications
		Planning and estimating
		Capacity planning and resource management
		Benefits realization management
		Performance monitoring
	Delivery (Programme and Project)	Monitor, review and reporting
		Risk, issue and change management
		Finance
		Commercial (including supplier management)
		Quality assurance
		Information management (including configuration and asset management)
		Transition management
		Secretariat
	COE	Standards and methods (processes and tools)
		Internal consultancy
		Organizational learning and knowledge management
		People and skills (P3RM competencies)

Figure F.1   P3O outline functions and services

Table F.1 Planning functions and services

Ref no	Function/service	Portfolio activities (permanent office)	COE activities (permanent office)	Programme or project activities (temporary office)	Useful tools/techniques/references

1.	Portfolio build, prioritization, analysis and reporting	Overall – Supports the planning and management of the implementation of the organization's strategy via a strategic programme or similar, ensuring that critical programmes and projects are well briefed and started on time, remain aligned to strategy, provide regular feedback to Strategy, etc. It does this by:
		
		■ Maintaining a register for current and potential programmes and projects (may be separate registers, subdividing current from potential activity)
		■ Establishing a framework for assessing and comparing programmes and projects against strategic, financial and risk value parameters
		■ Establishing and managing a Gated Review process, including portfolio entry criteria (elements that must be met or commented on prior to an idea being submitted)
		■ Providing decision support to enable the identification, selection and prioritization of new programmes and projects:
		  • Facilitating the choice of the right programme and project mix (workshops/information)
		  • Developing a framework for categorizing programmes and projects
		  • Developing strategy maps
		  • Facilitating outcome-relationship modelling
		  • Developing scenario modelling – to reduce commitments or increase capacity
		  • Quantifying current commitments externally with partners/third parties and internally to existing service levels and operations
		■ Coordinating feedback to the senior management team responsible for strategy so they can measure the success of strategic initiatives
		■ Providing analysis of unsuccessful initiatives to inform future strategic decisions/priorities
		■ Providing tools/analysis for business Capacity Management
		■ Enabling the identification of programmes and projects that cannot be justified – advising on pet projects and challenging divergence from strategic intent
					■ Prioritization Framework/Model
					■ Strategy Maps
					■ Categorization guidelines for programmes/projects
					■ Portfolio baselining/optimization guidelines
					■ Achievability vs Affordability Matrix tool
					■ Design/Enterprise Architecture tools – supporting business Blueprinting
					■ SWOT
					■ PESTLE
					■ MOSCOW
					■ EPM tools with a strategic portfolio planning and analysis focus
					■ Post-implementation Review and lessons-learned techniques

(continued)

Table F.1 Planning functions and services (continued)

Ref no	Function/ service	Portfolio activities (permanent office)	COE activities (permanent office)	Programme or project activities (temporary office)	Useful tools/techniques/references
2.	Programme/ project set-up and closure	On behalf of relevant governance board: ■ Trigger programmes/projects as part of business planning/prioritization ■ Trigger post-programme/project reviews to assess return on investment/benefits for the portfolio	■ Programme or Project fast-track mobilization service – tailoring advice/guidance, templates/processes, facilitated workshops, library set-up ■ Support closure process through independent lessons-learned workshops ■ Capture good-practice examples for inclusion in Good Practice Repository ■ Define/advise on Programme or Project assurance services – delivery, technical, benefits, stakeholders, risk, audit and compliance	■ Programme or Project fast-track mobilization service – tailoring advice/ guidance, templates/processes, facilitated workshops, library set-up ■ Scope management – ensure scope is clear and delineated ■ Support closure process through independent lessons-learned workshops, archiving of libraries, redeployment of resources through flexible resourcing ■ Programme or project accommodation and facilities services	■ Facilitated workshops ■ Tailoring guidelines ■ Standard processes and templates ■ PRINCE2 ■ MSP ■ OGC Policy to Delivery Workshops ■ OGC Achieving Excellence in Construction
3.	Stakeholder engagement and communications	■ Develop Stakeholder Profiles ■ Facilitate the formulation of Stakeholder Engagement Strategies ■ Enable the formulation of Portfolio Communications Plans ■ Coordinate stakeholder engagement and communication, ensuring effective timing and interdependency management of communications across the portfolio ■ Coordinate Internal portfolio communications ■ Monitor the effectiveness of communications ■ Provide answers and briefings to queries/ information requests ■ Support press enquiries (providing the point of contact between programmes and the Press Office) ■ Establish and maintain portfolio intranet site or information portal	■ Define stakeholder engagement and Communications Planning processes and templates ■ Facilitate stakeholder identification and communications workshops ■ Advise on key stakeholders and influencing strategies ■ Be aware of stakeholders with an interest in the organization's delivery portfolio, identify gaps, overlaps and potential conflicts of interest	■ Develop Stakeholder Profiles ■ Facilitate the formulation of Stakeholder Engagement Strategies ■ Enable the formulation of Programme and Project Communications Plans ■ Coordinate stakeholder engagement and communication, ensuring effective timing and interdependency management of communications across programmes and the projects ■ Coordinate Internal programme/project communications ■ Monitor the effectiveness of communications ■ Provide answers and briefings to queries/ information requests ■ Support press enquiries (providing the point of contact between programmes/ projects and the Press Office) ■ Establish and maintain programme/ project intranet site or information portal	■ MSP: ● Stakeholder Maps ● Stakeholder Profiles ● Stakeholder Engagement Strategy ● Programme Communications Plan ● RACI Matrix ■ Collaboration/portal tools ■ Publishing software ■ Web authoring tools

(continued)

Table F.1 Planning functions and services (continued)

Ref no	Function/ service	Portfolio activities (permanent office)	COE activities (permanent office)	Programme or project activities (temporary office)	Useful tools/techniques/references
4.	Planning (and estimating)	■ Facilitate the development of high-level portfolio/ business plan ■ Develop, track and maintain dependencies across programmes within the portfolio and against the strategy ■ Review plans against Business as Usual plans to ensure change can be adopted effectively ■ Develop resource/capacity plans to underpin the portfolio plan	■ Define planning standards for the portfolio, programme and projects to enable ease of roll-up of milestone data and dependencies ■ Provide planning assistance to projects – templates, resources, planning workshops ■ Provide estimating support through experienced staff or estimating database	■ Define planning standards for projects to enable ease of roll-up of milestone data and dependencies ■ Facilitate the development of high-level programme/project plan, including collation of lower level plans into programme/project level milestones ■ Develop, track and maintain dependencies ■ Facilitate the review of plans against Business as Usual plans to ensure change can be adopted effectively ■ Provide estimating support to the programme/projects	■ Enterprise and local planning tools ('what if' scenario planning) ■ Estimating Databases ■ Facilitated planning workshops ■ Planning standards – processes and templates ■ PRINCE2 – product-based planning ■ OGC Achieving Excellence in Construction

(continued)

Table F.1 Planning functions and services (continued)

Ref no	Function/service	Portfolio activities (permanent office)	COE activities (permanent office)	Programme or project activities (temporary office)	Useful tools/techniques/references
5.	Capacity planning and resource management (may include demand management)	■ Capture the resource requirements of portfolio, programmes, projects and the Portfolio Office itself ■ Forecast future resource needs, based on programme/projects plans, close liaison with the relevant managers and (where appropriate) wider business plans and business office objectives ■ In consultation with HR and others, decide on the best source for the required resources, depending on the long-term requirement for particular skill and its likely availability ■ Plan and initiate acquisition of the necessary resources, in terms of both skill content and quantity, ensuring the resources are in place at the time needed ■ Actively monitor the deployment of staff, arranging new postings (where possible) in advance of assignments ending, to meet staff development needs and to maintain a good match of skill to role (as roles vary with programme/project phase) ■ Maintain sufficient management information to enable the above activities and the reporting of resourcing status to senior management ■ Maintain a database of resources, for people, their skills/attributes, location, availability, contact details and lead responsibility for the resource ■ Provide a view of commitments (of programme staff) on other programmes/projects and/or on Business as Usual activities that will impact the ability of the portfolio to deliver ■ Provide resource tracking and capacity planning service across portfolio/programme(s) ■ Facilitate the management of consultants' and interims' contracts – acquisition/contracts engagement/extensions, etc. ■ Provide 'help squads'- supplementary skills to fill shortfalls within the programmes/projects ■ Where a flexible P3RM resource pool is in place, manage resource planning, data collection and P3RM skills development on a wider front, in accordance with a flexible resource deployment model ■ Provide a succession planning service for key roles	■ Assist in the recruitment and evaluation of programme and project managers ■ Provide standard role descriptions for P3RM staff, including support staff and programme/project delivery staff ■ Maintain a database of resources for people, their skills/attributes, location, availability, contact details and lead responsibility for the resource ■ Define a process for selection of key P3RM roles ■ Define strategy for developing/acquiring skills/competencies ■ Ensure HR practices and procedures are aligned to successful operation of programme and project management	■ Capture the resource requirements of programmes, projects and the Programme or Project Office itself ■ Forecast future resource needs, based on programme/projects plans, close liaison with the relevant managers and (where appropriate) wider business plans and business office objectives ■ In consultation with HR and others, decide on the best source for the required resources, depending on the long-term requirement for particular skill and its likely availability ■ Plan and initiate acquisition of the necessary resources, in terms of both skill content and quantity, ensuring the resources are in place at the time needed ■ Actively monitor the deployment of staff, arranging new postings (where possible) in advance of assignments ending, to meet staff development needs and to maintain a good match of skill to role (as roles vary with project phase) ■ Maintain sufficient management information to enable the above activities and the reporting of resourcing status to senior management ■ Work with HR and line management to facilitate leavers' process, including knowledge management, as required ■ Provide a view of commitments (of programme staff) on other programmes/projects and/or on Business as Usual activities that will impact the ability of the programme to deliver ■ Provide resource tracking and capacity planning service across a programme ■ Facilitate the management of consultants' and interims' contracts – acquisition/contracts engagement/extensions, etc. ■ Assist in the recruitment and evaluation of programme and project managers	■ Resource/Capacity Planning tools (part of Enterprise Project tool) ■ Flexible Resource Pools ■ Resources/Skills database ■ Standard role descriptions/templates ■ Resource Capacity Views

Table F.1 Planning functions and services (continued)

Ref no	Function/ service	Portfolio activities (permanent office)	COE activities (permanent office)	Programme or project activities (temporary office)	Useful tools/techniques/references

6.	Benefits management	On behalf of relevant governance boards:
		■ Assess benefits planning and realization across a number of programmes or projects within the portfolio to identify gaps, overlaps and conflicts and to eliminate double counting in the benefits plan of individual programmes and projects
		■ Review post-programme/project benefits against strategic investment decisions
		■ Establish and implement benefits-variance escalation process
			■ Develop standards for benefits management, including processes, templates and tools	■ Facilitate agreement of the Benefits Management Strategy between the SRO, Programme Manager and business areas
				■ Facilitate agreement of the Benefits Profiles between the SRO, Programme Manager and business change managers
				■ Facilitate agreement of the Benefits Realization Plan between the SRO, Programme Manager and business-area business change managers
				■ Track benefit realization on behalf of the business, collating benefits data for reporting purposes
					■ MSP:
					  ● Benefits Management Strategy
					  ● Benefits Realization Plan
					  ● Benefits Map
					  ● Benefits Profiles
					  ● Outcome relationship model
					■ Benefits database/spreadsheet
					■ Radar (spider) diagrams for reporting benefits

7.	Performance monitoring	On behalf of relevant governance board: ■ Set up and track portfolio metrics (KPIs) ■ Set up and track Portfolio Office performance metrics – value proposition	■ Manage portfolio/programme or project Performance Improvement Plan (PIP) template, enabling process and resource (fed by lessons learned) ■ Recommend ways to reduce or shorten project lifecycle times through effective working practices	■ Set up and track programme/project metrics (KPIs)	■ Performance improvement plans ■ Department capability review (UK govt) ■ Standard KPIs/tracking databases ■ Balanced Scorecard ■ Performance Management Systems

Table F.2 Delivery functions and services

Ref no	Function/ service	Portfolio activities (permanent office)	COE activities (permanent office)	Programme or project activities (temporary office)	Useful tools/techniques/references
8.	Monitoring and review	■ Undertake periodic reviews of progress (outputs/outcomes) against strategy and portfolio plans ■ Identify and report deviations (forecast and actual) – advise and trigger exception reports ■ Provide strategic oversight support for SROs and Management Boards (horizon scan for impending policy/strategy changes/new business initiatives and assess impact on portfolio) ■ Perform ongoing amalgamation of data, analysis of portfolio/project selection and delivery performance: ● Provide 'what if' analyses ● Provide 'forward look' – current commitments and track record of delivery ● Provide strategic alignment analysis ● Provide dependency analysis ■ Make a constructive challenge, scrutiny and assessment of overall progress of the portfolio, rather than just the collation of individual reports by: ● Advice and constructive challenge to Management Boards ● Challenging key decisions concerning 'scale of risk' ● Making recommendations on corrective actions and options to Management Boards ■ Identify overcommitment of resources ■ Identify overcommitment of changes to the business ■ Monitor assumptions log ■ Monitor dependency log	■ Develop standards – processes and templates – for monitoring and review ■ Develop time recording systems	■ Undertake periodic reviews of progress (outputs/outcomes) against programme/project plans ■ Identify and report deviations (forecast and actual) – advise and trigger exception reports ■ Horizon scan for impending policy or strategy changes and assessment of their impact on the programme or project ■ Make a constructive challenge, scrutiny and assessment of overall progress of the programme rather than the collation of individual project reports ■ Give advice and constructive challenge to programme and project Management Boards ■ Make recommendations on corrective actions and options to Management Boards ■ Monitor assumptions log ■ Monitor dependency log ■ Implement and monitor timesheet systems to capture actual time spent	■ Timesheet recording tools (Enterprise Programme and Project tool) ■ Earned Value Analysis

(continued)

Table F.2 Delivery functions and services (continued)

Ref no	Function/service	Portfolio activities (permanent office)	COE activities (permanent office)	Programme or project activities (temporary office)	Useful tools/techniques/references
9.	Reporting	■ Report portfolio status to boards – timely and accurate information focused on decision-making ■ Develop and maintain a single comprehensive picture of the portfolio (Portfolio Management Dashboard, Balanced Scorecard) ■ Provide single source of truth for reporting – single report/data feed – consolidated/aggregated reports to different audiences	■ Provide reporting standards, templates, tools and reporting timetable (checkpoints, highlights, programme and portfolio status reports) ■ Define and monitor traffic light status to ensure consistency of reporting	■ Report programme and project(s) status to Programme or Project Boards – timely and accurate information focused on decision-making ■ Develop and maintain a single comprehensive picture of the programme (programme/project Management Dashboard, Balanced Scorecard) ■ Provide single source of truth for reporting – single report/data feed – consolidated/aggregated reports to different audiences	■ Enterprise Project tools ■ Portfolio/Programme Management Dashboard ■ Balanced Scorecard ■ Reporting standards – processes and templates ■ Rules for escalation of data/decisions ■ Definition of traffic light colours for Red/Amber/Green reporting ■ OGC Delivery Confidence Assessments – traffic-lighted assessments (Gateway)

(continued)

Table F.2 Delivery functions and services (continued)

Ref no	Function/ service	Portfolio activities (permanent office)	COE activities (permanent office)	Programme or project activities (temporary office)	Useful tools/techniques/references
10.	Risk management	■ Establish and maintain the portfolio Risk Register ■ Monitor portfolio Risk Register to ensure that all risks have a nominated owner and actionee ■ Monitor portfolio Risk Register to ensure that the agreed risk mitigations are planned, resourced and implemented ■ Communicate with stakeholders, particularly those who are directly affected either by the risk itself or by the risk mitigations ■ Assess how effective any mitigation actions have been and whether the risks identified have actually materialized ■ Actively monitor and regularly 'check and challenge' all risks ■ Establish and maintain an efficient two-way flow of information between the portfolio, programmes and the projects, regarding risk handling and escalation ■ Proactively look across Risk Registers across the portfolio (within programmes and projects) to identify common themes and establish consistent mitigation and contingency plans across the portfolio ■ Proactively examine programme and project Risk Registers for common risks that should be tackled portfolio wide ■ Advise on risk mitigation and contingency planning ■ Support sharing of Risk Registers with supplier community ■ Facilitate risk escalation to higher authority (e.g. Strategic/Business Management) ■ Facilitate independent risk workshops ■ At portfolio level, monitor the organization's total exposure to risk	■ Develop the overall Risk Management Strategy, processes and templates ■ Develop/source/tailor tools for managing risk and train the organization in their use ■ Facilitate independent risk workshops ■ Clearly communicate the Risk Management Strategy, and the benefits of following it, to all personnel involved with the portfolio, programme and projects ■ Advise on risk mitigation and contingency planning	■ Establish and maintain the programme/ project Risk Register ■ Monitor programme/project Risk Register to ensure that all risks have a nominated owner and actionee ■ Monitor programme/project Risk Register to ensure that the agreed risk mitigations are planned, resourced and implemented ■ Communicate with stakeholders, particularly those who are directly affected either by the risk itself or by the risk mitigations ■ Assess how effective any mitigation actions have been and whether the risks identified have actually materialized ■ Actively monitor and regularly 'check and challenge' all risks ■ Agree and maintain an efficient two-way flow of information between the portfolio, programmes and the projects regarding risk handling and escalation ■ Proactively look at Risk Registers across the programme to identify common themes and establish consistent mitigation and contingency plans ■ Proactively examine project Risk Registers for common risks that should be tackled programme wide (+ escalation) ■ Advise on risk mitigation and contingency planning ■ Support sharing of Risk Registers with supplier community ■ Facilitate risk escalation to higher authority (e.g. Portfolio management)	■ Risk tools ■ Risk database/spreadsheets ■ Standard scoring mechanisms ■ M_o_R ■ Risk Potential Assessment (RPA) tool ■ MSP ■ PRINCE2 ■ PRAM ■ OGC Achieving Excellence in Construction

(continued)

Table F.2   Delivery functions and services (continued)

Ref no	Function/ service	Portfolio activities (permanent office)	COE activities (permanent office)	Programme or project activities (temporary office)	Useful tools/techniques/references
11.	Issue resolution	■ Perform logging and tracking to resolution of portfolio issues ■ Proactively examine issue logs across the programme(s)/projects for common issues which should be tackled at a portfolio level ■ Control escalation of issues to higher authority, e.g. strategic or business management	■ Develop the overall Issue Resolution Strategy, processes and templates ■ Develop/source/tailor tools for managing issues and train the organization in their use ■ Facilitate independent issue resolution workshops ■ Clearly communicate the Issue Resolution Strategy, and the benefits of following it, to all personnel involved with the portfolio, programme and projects, including business operations ■ Establish the portfolio, programme or project issue resolution process, ensuring that Procurement/Commercial lead on contractual issues and changes ■ Review effectiveness of issue identification and resolution processes ■ Facilitate cross-portfolio/programme impact analysis workshops	■ Perform logging and tracking to resolution of programme or project issues ■ Proactively examine of issues for links to existing issues, that should be tackled together ■ Control escalation of issues to higher authority, e.g. portfolio or business management	■ Issue database/spreadsheet ■ Issue tools ■ Standard scoring/priority mechanisms ■ MSP ■ PRINCE2 ■ ITIL ■ OGC Achieving Excellence in Construction
12.	Change control	■ Establish and operate change control process for portfolio, ensuring that Procurement/Commercial lead on contractual changes ■ Control escalation of changes to higher authority, e.g. business area management ■ Provide secretariat function to Change Approvals Board (CAB) or Change Control Board (CCB) for the portfolio	■ Develop the overall change control strategy, processes and templates ■ Develop/source/tailor tools for managing change and train the organization in their use ■ Facilitate independent change impact assessment workshops ■ Clearly communicate the change management Strategy, and the benefits of following it, to all personnel involved with the portfolio, programme and projects, including business operations ■ Facilitate cross-programme impact analysis for changes that affect the wider portfolio arena	■ Establish and operate change control process for programme/project, ensuring that Procurement/Commercial lead on contractual changes ■ Manage change control process for business operations whilst programme is still impacted by subsequent tranches ■ Control escalation of changes to higher authority, e.g. portfolio or business area management ■ Provide secretariat function to Change Approvals Board (CAB) or Change Control Board (CCB) for the programme/project	■ MSP ■ PRINCE2 ■ ITIL ■ OGC Achieving Excellence in Construction ■ Change logging and tracking tools

(continued)

Table F.2 Delivery functions and services (continued)

Ref no	Function/ service	Portfolio activities (permanent office)	COE activities (permanent office)	Programme or project activities (temporary office)	Useful tools/techniques/references
13.	Finance (these activities may be provided by the P3O or through Finance staff assigned to work with the P3O)	■ Monitor and report on portfolio spend ■ Calculate and analyse portfolio cost variance ■ Estimate future portfolio spend, challenge cash-flow/spend profile and forecast cash-flow/spend profile as appropriate ■ Manage invoicing and collection activities of portfolio deliverables and activities ■ Prepare monthly financial reports for the Portfolio, Manager/Strategic Board and for inclusion in Management Dashboard reports ■ Work with Finance/accountancy assistance to: 　● Administer and track budget allocations 　● Ensure availability of appropriately profiled funding 　● Develop and refine Portfolio business cases 　● Develop and maintain the costed Resource Management Plan for the portfolio 　● Advise on cost control and opportunities for savings 　● Control adherence to accounting procedures 　● Oversee capitalization of capital assets	■ In conjunction with Finance, develop and maintain the portfolio, programme or project financial processes, controls and templates, paying particular attention to audit requirements ■ Develop Business Case process and templates ■ Provide advice/guidance in developing Business Cases and going through the approvals process	■ Monitor and report on programme or project spend ■ Calculate and analyse programme or project cost variance ■ Estimate future programme/project spend, challenge cash-flow/spend profile and forecast cash-flow/spend profile as appropriate ■ Manage invoicing and collection activities of programme/project deliverables and activities ■ Prepare monthly financial reports for the programme/project, manager/ Programme or Project Board and for inclusion in Management Dashboard reports ■ Work with Finance/programme accountancy assistance to: 　● Administer and track budget allocations 　● Ensure availability of appropriately profiled funding 　● Develop and refine programme and project business cases 　● Develop and maintain the costed Resource Management Plan 　● Advise on cost control and opportunities for savings 　● Control adherence to accounting procedures 　● Oversee capitalization of capital assets	■ Finance planning and tracking tools ■ Net Present Value technique ■ Discounted Cash-flow technique ■ Cost Benefit Analysis technique ■ Earned Value Analysis

(continued)

Table F.2 Delivery functions and services (continued)

Ref no	Function/ service	Portfolio activities (permanent office)	COE activities (permanent office)	Programme or project activities (temporary office)	Useful tools/techniques/references
14.	Commercial (These activities may be provided by P3O or through embedded commercial staff)	■ Liaise with Procurement/Commercial teams on new initiatives to ensure early engagement ■ Support supplier liaison across portfolio ■ Assist in the development of the Procurement Strategy ■ Support contracts monitoring and management ■ Place small orders for portfolio equipment/resources	■ Work with Procurement/Commercial teams to agree standards for purchasing within a programme/project environment	■ Liaise with Procurement/Commercial teams on new initiatives to ensure early engagement ■ Support supplier liaison across programme ■ Assist in the development of the Procurement Strategy ■ Support contracts monitoring and management ■ Place small orders for programme/ project equipment/resources ■ Ensure all programme/project supplier relationships are effectively embedded in Business as Usual with support arrangements and effective handovers of relationships	■ Framework agreements for interim resources ■ Service and Operational Level Agreements ■ ITIL ■ OGC Achieving Excellence in Construction Procurement Guide ■ OGC Policy and Standards Framework
15.	Quality Assurance	■ Ensure compliance with standards/good practice ■ Enable quality assurance of portfolio management products ■ Coordinate quality reviews of portfolio documents and deliverables ■ Oversee the quality review process for contractual supplier deliverables ■ Liaise with internal or financial audit functions	■ Provide a Stage Gate Review or Gateway support/coordination service ■ Provide health checks, assurance or audits through a risk-based approach geared to the programmes and projects that need it most ■ Enable/conduct post-programme/ project reviews ■ Develop, implement and promote a comprehensive Quality Strategy ■ Agree standards and establish clearly defined quality methods for staff to apply ■ Assure the development of portfolio, programme, project quality plans ■ Monitor quality performance ■ Provide guidance on quality criteria, reviewers and sign-off authority to ensure cross-portfolio/programme(s) consistency ■ Analyse feedback from reviews, including Stage Gate Reviews/Gateway, health checks, post-programme/project, audits and lessons learned	■ Work with internal audit and finance to ensure the programme complies with audit requirements ■ Work with procurement/purchasing staff to ensure effective interface with suppliers' quality systems ■ Ensure compliance with COE standards/ good practice ■ Coordinate quality reviews of programme/project documents and deliverables ■ Oversee the quality review process for contractual supplier deliverables ■ Provide quality control for management products	■ MSP ■ PRINCE2 ■ OGC Achieving Excellence in Construction ■ Stage Gating Framework ■ Gateway (including Delivery Confidence Assessments) ■ Health checks ■ OGC Policy to Delivery Workshop

(continued)

Table F.2 Delivery functions and services (continued)

Ref no	Function/service	Portfolio activities (permanent office)	COE activities (permanent office)	Programme or project activities (temporary office)	Useful tools/techniques/references
16.	Information Management (including Configuration Management)	■ Hold master copies of all portfolio information (custodians of the information repository) ■ Establish and administer portfolio baselines ■ Control the issue of portfolio products/deliverables ■ Establish and maintain the index to an electronic library of portfolio information ■ Undertake configuration audits ■ Ensure supplier configuration items (documentation and assets) are under control by providing a single point of entry and exit to the portfolio for such items (working with procurement/commercial staff, as appropriate) ■ Manage archives of portfolio documentation ■ May own Asset Management	■ Develop and implement Configuration Management standards and processes ■ Develop/source tools for Configuration Management ■ Develop/source tools for collaborative working ■ Develop information strategy ■ Develop standard information library structures and templates	■ Hold master copies of all programme/project information (custodians of the information repository) ■ Establish and administer programme/project baselines ■ Control the issue of programme/project products/deliverables ■ Establish and maintain the index to an electronic library of programme/project information ■ Undertake configuration audits ■ Ensure supplier configuration items (documentation and assets) are under control by providing a single point of entry and exit to the programme/project for such items (working with procurement/commercial staff, as appropriate) ■ Manage archives of programme/project documentation	■ Collaboration tools ■ Document Management tools ■ Information library/portal ■ Intranet ■ PRINCE2 ■ ITIL ■ MSP
17.	Transition Management	■ Give assistance to SRO and business change managers with transition management ■ Support sign-off of capability and acceptance into operational running		■ Give assistance to SRO and business change managers with transition management ■ Support sign-off of capability and acceptance into operational running	■ MSP ■ ITIL
18.	Secretariat/Other	■ Provide secretariat service to Management Boards ■ Plan, forecast and manage non-HR resource requirements for both P3O and portfolio (match supply to demand – switch and release resources as necessary) for: ● Accommodation ● IT/tools support ● Office equipment/stationery	■ Work with Procurement/Commercial to establish frameworks for the acquisition of: ● Contract resources ● Plant and equipment ● Facilities/building space	■ Provide secretariat service to programme or project Management Boards ■ Plan, forecast and manage non-HR resource requirements for both programme or Project Office and programme/project delivery team (match supply to demand – switch and release resources as necessary) for: ● Accommodation ● IT/tools support ● Office equipment/stationery	■ Standard agendas/minutes

Table F.3 Centre of Excellence functions and services

Ref no	Function/service	Portfolio activities (permanent office)	COE activities (permanent office)	Programme or project activities (temporary office)	Useful tools/techniques/references
19.	Standards and methods	■ Define and implement governance standards – reporting and information requirements, Financial Management standards (through links to Finance), accountability and escalation routes	■ Develop and implement standard P3RM methods and approaches ■ Develop tailoring/flexing guidelines for standards, methods and approaches ■ Provide link to other standards, e.g. ITIL for Service Management ■ Ensure tools and processes facilitate collaborative working across team, department and organization boundaries ■ Advise on P3RM tools/software ■ Reduce project lifecycles through effective methods	■ Tailor standard processes and templates to the programme or project ■ Set up standards for collaborative working across teams/organizations	■ Standard P3RM processes and templates ■ Intranet ■ Collaborative portal ■ PRINCE2 ■ MSP ■ M_o_R ■ ITIL ■ OGC Achieving Excellence in Construction ■ Stage Gating Framework/P3RM Delivery Framework ■ Gateway

20.	Internal Consultancy	■ Provide advice /guidance on impact of programmes/projects on Business as Usual	■ Execute specialized tasks for programme and project managers
			■ Provide a help desk manned by experts in P3RM to provide knowledgeable responses
			■ Provide facilitation Service (workshops/meetings)
			■ Provide tailoring advice and guidance
			■ Provide project or programme rescues (help programmes/projects in trouble with reviews and analysis, hit squads or recovery plans)
			■ Promote good P3RM within the organization
			■ Advise SROs and Management Boards of appropriate frameworks/governance models
			■ Help programmes and projects 'in trouble' – 'broker' problems and potential solutions, including bringing in external good practice/consultancy
			■ Maintain relationships with experts inside and outside the organization to act as a clearing house for demand for analysis expertise with regard to:
			  ● Business
			  ● Risk
			  ● Organization restructure
			  ● Change management
			  ● Advice on application of best practice
					■ Facilitated Workshops – standard agendas
					■ Tailoring Guidelines
					■ Intranet
					■ Programme/project health
					■ OGC Policy to Delivery Workshops

(continued)

Table F.3 Centre of Excellence functions and services (continued)

Ref no	Function/ service	Portfolio activities (permanent office)	COE activities (permanent office)	Programme or project activities (temporary office)	Useful tools/techniques/references
21.	Organizational Learning and Knowledge Management	■ Undertake trend analysis – through both internal and external monitoring/ reporting ■ Collate post-programme/project reviews and analyse lessons learned for future investment decisions ■ Assess historical perspective of how organization has implemented change previously, based on appetite for change, culture and capacity for change	■ Facilitate lessons learned – process, templates, workshop facilitation, maintenance of information database, dissemination of lessons learned, action plans ■ Develop and maintain good-practice repository (document examples) ■ Develop case study material ■ Enable portfolio/programme/project management/SRO forums/sharing of good practice ■ Liaise/share with P3O in other departments/organizations ■ Perform external networking – attendance at best-practice events, seminars. ■ Maintain knowledge/reference library ■ Develop and run end programme/ project lessons-learned workshops. ■ Enable post-programme and project reviews ■ Develop relationships with other organizations, including delivery partners, and sustain networks to share lessons learned and experience ■ Monitor use of corporate guidance and standards to identify weaknesses and take corrective action as necessary	■ Maintain lessons-learned logs on behalf of the programme or project ■ Liaise/share lessons learned with other programmes/projects	■ Good Practice Repository/database. ■ Programme/Project Management Forums ■ Networking/best-practice events ■ Case studies ■ PRINCE2, MSP, M_o_R, ITIL, workshops or forums ■ Special Interest Groups ■ Topic-specific events ■ Subject/Topic/Technique Matter Experts ■ Knowledge Management Systems

(continued)

Table F.3 Centre of Excellence functions and services (continued)

Ref no	Function/ service	Portfolio activities (permanent office)	COE activities (permanent office)	Programme or project activities (temporary office)	Useful tools/techniques/references
22.	People and Skills	■ Undertake portfolio induction ■ Identify skills/competencies shortages to deliver the portfolio and recommend suitable development	■ Define development strategy for organizational learning in P3RM – training/development needs, courses/modules available, link to training department or external providers ■ Take an active role in the training and development of programme/project staff to increase the available skills capability and capacity within the business ■ Perform P3RM skills assessment and enhancement service: ● Role/skills and competencies matrices ● Independent advice ● Standard development/training plans for roles ● Online skills assessment tools ■ Provide training logistics support – liaise with training providers and internal staff ■ Perform mentoring/coaching: ● Develop guidelines/process/resources ● Organize/match – buddy relationships, secondments ● Provide mentoring to business process owners	■ Undertake programme/project induction ■ Identify skills/competencies shortages to deliver the programme/project and recommend suitable development	■ Intranet ■ Skills/training databases ■ OGC P3RM skills ■ Professional Skills Government (PSG) ■ Online role/skills assessment tools ■ Training courses ■ E-learning modules

Further information

Further information

Association of Project Management *APM Body of Knowledge* (5th edn), APM, 2005

Association of Project Management *Project Risk Analysis and Management guide* (2nd edn), APM, 2004

British Standards Institute *BS6079-2: Project Management Vocabulary*, TSO, 2000

British Standards Institute *BS6079-3: Project Management: Guide to the Management of Business Related Project Risk*, TSO, 2000

Gartner, 'Project Portfolio Management Processes: Keep the People In and the Complexity Out', Gartner symposium, November 2007

Hobbs, B *The Multi Project PMO: A Global Analysis of the Current State of Practice*, White Paper prepared for the Project Management Institute, PMI, 2007

ITIL set of publications under the ITIL banner, TSO, various dates

Kendall, G and Rollins, S *Advanced Project Portfolio Management and the PMO*, J Ross Publishing, 2003

KPMG *Global IT Project Management Survey*, KPMG, 2005

KPMG *International Programme Management Survey*, KPMG, 2002–3

Office of Government Commerce *M_o_R: Guidance for Practitioners*, TSO, 2007

Office of Government Commerce *MSP: Managing Successful Programmes*, TSO, 2007

Office of Government Commerce *P3M3*, TSO, 2008

Office of Government Commerce *Portfolio Management*, TSO, 2005

Office of Government Commerce *PRINCE2: Managing Successful Projects*, TSO, 2005

Office of Government Commerce set of booklets under the Achieving Excellence in Construction banner, various dates

Office of Government Commerce set of booklets under the OGC Gateway banner, various dates

Office of Government Commerce *Successful Delivery Pocketbook*, TSO, 2006 (downloadable)

PMO Executive Council *A Function in Transition: Emerging Organisational Models for the PMO*, PMO, 2006

Project Management Institute *A Guide to the Project Management Body of Knowledge* (3rd edn), PMIC, 2004

Project Management Institute *The Standard for Portfolio Management*, PMIC, 2006

Venning, C *Managing Portfolios of Change*, TSO, 2007

See also www.cabinetoffice.gov.uk/csia and www.cesg.gov.uk for further details on the topic of information assurance

Glossary

Glossary

Aggregated risk

The overall level of risk to the programme when all the risks are viewed as a totality rather than individually. This could include the outputs of particular scenarios or risk combinations.

Assurance

All the systematic actions necessary to provide confidence that the target (system, process, organization, programme, project, outcome, benefit, capability, product output, deliverable) is appropriate. Appropriateness might be defined subjectively or objectively in different circumstances. The implication is that assurance will have a level of independence from that which is being assured.

Benefit

The measurable improvement resulting from an outcome perceived as an advantage by one or more stakeholders.

Centre of Excellence (COE)

A coordinating function for all or part of P3RM ensuring change is delivered consistently and well, through standard processes and competent staff. It may provide standards, consistency of methods and processes, knowledge management, assurance and training. It may also provide strategic oversight, scrutiny and challenge across an organization's portfolio of programmes and projects. It may be a function within a wider scope of P3O or may be the only function of a P3O. This function provides a focal point for driving the implementation of improvements to increase the organization's capability and capacity in programme and project delivery.

Chief Executive Officer (CEO)

Describes the role in a commercial organization with the highest level of authority for the total management of the business.

Chief Financial Officer (CFO)

Describes the role in a commercial organization with the highest level of authority for the management of the financial risks, planning and reporting for a business. This role will generally report to the CEO.

Chief Information Officer (CIO)

Describes the role in a commercial organization with the highest level of authority for the management of

Information Technology for the business. This role will generally report to the CEO but may also report to the CFO in smaller organizations.

Chief Operating Officer (COO)

Describes the role in a commercial organization with the highest level of authority for the development, design, management, and improvement of the open systems that create and deliver the organization's products and/or services. This role will generally report to the CEO.

Cost centre

An accounting term used to describe a division, business unit or part of an organization that does not directly contribute to achieving profit for a company. It indirectly contributes to the organization by providing a service or support function to profit-making parts of the organization.

Dashboard

See Management Dashboard.

Design Authority

A role or function (permanent, temporary or virtual) that provides expert specialist advice or owns some corporate function, service, standard or strategy that will be affected, or a major programme outcome or change that needs to be controlled. This could be an IT or property infrastructure design, or a major service contract; it could also be a business process model or the programme or corporate Blueprint. The Design Authority provides expertise and guidance on a specific area to ensure there is appropriate alignment and control when changes are being planned and implemented. At a programme level this role may advise or own the Business Blueprint management on behalf of the programme manager. At the enterprise level, this role may manage the Enterprise Architecture of the organization.

Dis-benefit

An outcome perceived as negative by one or more stakeholders. Dis-benefits are actual consequences of an activity, whereas a risk has some uncertainty about whether it will materialize.

End Project Report

A report given by the project manager to the Project Board that confirms the handover of all products and provides an updated Business Case and an assessment of how well the project has done against its Project Initiation Document.

Enterprise Project (or P3RM) Management (EPM)

A term usually referred to by software vendors in relation to software (i.e. EPM tools) that assists an organization manage across multiple projects and programme delivery using a common resource pool through to strategic analysis of investment through portfolio management. This term does not reflect the actual offerings of the tools in that they generally can support at portfolio, programme and project (P3RM) level.

Expert Reference Group

A team of subject matter experts that can be used in a P3RM organization to provide input, advice and challenge to the role accountable for an output or outcome to ensure that it reflects the wider experience rather than an individual's perspective only. It is important to note that the role accountable for the output or outcome maintains the final decision and should not treat an Expert Reference Group as a committee. An Expert Reference Group may be drawn together at points in time or may be fully allocated to a project or programme.

Full-time equivalent (FTE)

A technique used to measure human resource involvement in a project, programme or operational activities. It is required generally where human resources are allocated across multiple roles (e.g. 70% allocated to a project and 30% allocated to business operations). An FTE of 1 means that a person or the sum of all people's effort is 100% allocated to an activity, based on the number of working hours available, treatment of overtime and other parameters.

Gated Review

Structured reviews of a project, programme or portfolio as part of formal governance arrangements that are carried out at key decision points in the lifecycle to ensure that the decision to invest as per agreed Business Cases and plans remains valid.

Governance (business change)

Encompasses the structures, accountabilities and policies, standards and process for decision-making within an organization for business change to answer the key strategic questions of 'Are we doing the right things?', 'Are we doing them the right way?', 'Are we getting them done well?' and 'Are we getting the benefits?'

Health check

A health check is a quality tool that provides a snapshot of the status of a project, programme or the portfolio. The purpose of a health check is to gain an objective assessment of how well the project, programme or portfolio is performing relative to its objectives and any relevant processes or standards. A health check differs from a Gated Review in that it is a tool used for assurance purposes by the P3O to inform specific actions or capability maturity development plans, whereas a Gated Review is part of formal governance arrangements.

Hub and Spoke

A term to describe a system of organizational design for P3O where there is a centralized office (the hub) connected to a number of smaller decentralized offices (the spokes) each with a subset of the centralized office's business objectives, functions and services. All information and processes (connections) are arranged so that they move along spokes to the hub at the centre. A Hub and Spoke model provides the benefit of scalability for large organizations and supports business ownership by maintaining a level of decentralization.

Information Hub

The centralized element of the Hub and Spoke model for P3O in terms of information flows (see Hub and Spoke definition). It supports highlight and exception-based reporting for projects, programmes and/or portfolios by amalgamating information with the process and information owned by the central office as the Information Hub.

Information Technology Infrastructure Library (ITIL)

A set of guides on the management and provision of operational IT services.

Informed customer

An individual, team or group with functional responsibility within an organization for ensuring that spend on IS/IT or other procurement is directed to best effect, i.e. that the business is receiving value for money and continues to achieve the most beneficial outcome. The term is often used in relation to the outsourcing of IT/IS. Sometimes also called 'Intelligent customer'.

Key Performance Indicator (KPI)

Metric is (either financial or non-financial) that is used to set and measure progress towards strategic objectives for an organization.

Management Board

Generic term used to describe either project Management Boards, programme Management Boards or Portfolio management boards, or any combination based on the P3O context.

Management Dashboard

A technique to represent vast amounts of decision support information at an amalgamated level using tabular and graphic representation such as graphs and traffic lights.

Managing Successful Programmes (MSP)

An OGC publication/method representing proven programme management good practice in successfully delivering transformational change, drawn from the experiences of both public and private sector organizations.

Mandate

Information created externally to a project or programme that forms the terms of reference and is used to start up a PRINCE2 project or identify an MSP programme. A Mandate may be initiated through an unstructured approach, or it may be derived from strategic planning, business planning or portfolio management processes.

Matrix management

A type of organizational management in which human resources with similar skills are pooled together for the assignment of work to other parts of an organization. In this approach, there is a separation between line management and line of authority in that a person may report to several project, programme or business managers to undertake multiple work assignments at different times but have a line of authority to a different manager altogether.

Organization Portfolio Office

A type of P3O model that is designed to centrally manage the investment process, strategic alignment, prioritization and selection, progress tracking and monitoring, optimization and benefits achieved by an organization's projects and programmes on behalf of its senior management.

P3M3

OGC's Portfolio, Programme and Project Management Maturity Model.

P3O Sponsor

A senior manager with appropriate authority who champions the establishment and evolving operation of the P3O. They will ideally be a member of the main board.

P3RM

An acronym to describe portfolio, programme, project and risk management together.

Peer review

Specific review of a project or any of its products where personnel from within the organization and/or from other organizations carry out an independent assessment of the project. Peer reviews can be done at any point within a project but are often used at stage-end points.

PESTLE

Acronym for 'Political, Economic, Social, Technological, Legal and Environment' and is a technique used generally in organizational change management to undertake an environmental scan at a strategic level.

Pet project

A project that is championed by an executive in an organization that may be aligned to an individual goal or goal for a specific part of the business, but not aligned to the strategic imperatives of the organization as a whole.

Portfolio, Programme and Project Offices (P3O)

The decision enabling and support business model for all business change within an organization. This will include single or multiple physical or virtual structures, i.e. offices (permanent and/or temporary), providing a mix of central and localized functions and services, integration with governance arrangements and the wider business such as other corporate support functions.

PRINCE2

A method that supports some selected aspects of project management. The acronym stands for Projects IN Controlled Environments.

Programme Brief

A statement that describes the specific objectives, required benefits, potential risks, outline costs, timescales and potentially options for delivery for a programme.

Project Brief

A statement that describes the purpose, cost, time and performance requirements/constraints for a project.

Project Executive

The individual who is ultimately responsible for a project. Their role is to ensure that the project is focused throughout its lifecycle on achieving its objectives and delivering a product that will achieve the forecast benefits.

Project Initiation Document (PID)

A logical document that brings together the key information needed to start a project on a sound basis and to convey that information to all concerned with the project.

Resource

An organization's physical or virtual entities (human or other) that are of limited availability and can be used to undertake operations or business change.

Risk potential assessment (RPA)

A standard set of high-level criteria against which the intrinsic characteristics and degree of difficulty of a proposed project are assessed. Used in the UK public sector to assess the criticality of projects and so determine the level of OGC Gateway Review required.

Scale of risk

A standard technique for estimating the probability and impact of a risk across an organization, portfolio, programme or project. This may be provided as part of a risk management standard (external) or a Risk Management Strategy or Policy.

Senior Responsible Owner (SRO)

The single individual with overall responsibility for ensuring that a project or programme meets its objectives and delivers the projected benefits.

Swimlane

A method for documenting business process flows that separates each process step into a row (or lane) of accountability for individual roles or groups.

SWOT

Acronym for 'Strengths, Weaknesses, Opportunities and Threats'. An analysis technique to determine favourable and unfavourable factors in relation to business change or current state.

Taxonomy

A classification of things, or the principles underlying such a classification. The term may be applied to relationship schemes such as parent–child hierarchies and network structures. A taxonomy might also be a simple organization of kinds of things into groups, or even an alphabetical list.

Zero-based Cost Centre

Similar to a cost centre, except that the division, business unit or part of the organization cross-charges other parts of the organization for some or all of its services or activities to achieve a spend of zero when its costs and income from cross-charging are added up.

Index

Index

References to tables are in *italics*; references to figures are in **bold** type.